Syria from Reform to Revolt, VOLUME 2

Modern Intellectual and Political History of the Middle East
Fred H. Lawson, *Series Editor*

Syria from Reform to Revolt, VOLUME 2

Culture, Society, and Religion

Edited by
Christa Salamandra
and Leif Stenberg

 SYRACUSE UNIVERSITY PRESS

Copyright © 2015 by Syracuse University Press
Syracuse, New York 13244-5290

All Rights Reserved

First Edition 2015

15   16   17   18   19   20   6   5   4   3   2   1

∞ The paper used in this publication meets the minimum requirements
of the American National Standard for Information Sciences—Permanence
of Paper for Printed Library Materials, ANSI Z39.48-1992.

For a listing of books published and distributed by Syracuse University Press,
visit www.SyracuseUniversityPress.syr.edu.

ISBN: 978-0-8156-3425-6 (cloth)
978-0-8156-3415-7 (paperback)
978-0-8156-5351-6 (e-book)

Library of Congress Control Number: 2014953864

Manufactured in the United States of America

Contents

Acknowledgments

In October 2010 the Center for Middle Eastern Studies, Lund University, hosted "Syria under Bashar al-Asad," the first international, cross-disciplinary gathering of scholarly experts on contemporary Syria. The Swedish Tercentenary Foundation (Riksbankens Jubileumsfond) and the Center for Middle Eastern Studies, Lund University generously funded both the conference itself and subsequent publication of select contributions. The editors offer special thanks to Jaleh Taheri and Lars-Erik Olofsson for planning and organizing not one but two meetings; the Icelandic volcano eruption of 2010 truncated the initial conference into a workshop for participants able to reach Lund by train, and necessitated a rescheduling, and a repeat of the challenging logistics, of the larger conference. Our gratitude extends to Eric Hooglund, editor of *Middle East Critique*, for accepting—and Jaleh Taheri and Erin Frazer for fine tuning—a number of contributions for a special issue. Deanna McCay of Syracuse University Press eased the project through each stage with patience and tact. Martha Lincoln, who molded chapters from diverse scholarly traditions into a stylistically coherent volume, deserves particular recognition.

Syria from Reform to Revolt, VOLUME 2

1

Introduction

A Legacy of Raised Expectations

CHRISTA SALAMANDRA
AND LEIF STENBERG

The antiauthoritarian uprising that began in March 2011 and subsequently evolved into civil war has brought contemporary Syria to global consciousness. This conflict, and the often confusing, ill-informed news coverage of it, have exposed the dearth of expert writing on the country, rendering urgent the need for scholarly insight. The contributors to *Syria from Reform to Revolt, Volume 2: Culture, Society, and Religion* offer a unique body of research that delves beneath a perplexing surface. Some have studied Syria throughout their careers and write from decades of experience; others have recently completed doctoral dissertations, and bring to their chapters the rich intensity of recent fieldwork. All reveal how Bashar al-Asad's pivotal first decade of rule engendered changes in power relations and public discourse that fed the 2011 protest movement. They also explore the complex and intersecting social, political, and religious fault lines that have obstructed peaceful transformation.

Syria has been an infrequently chosen destination for researchers interested in the contemporary Arab world.[1] During the five decades of Ba'th Party rule that began in 1963, specialists in the region feared the regime's notorious security apparatus. The difficulty some researchers have had in obtaining official clearance may have led academics to avoid the risk of planning a project only to be denied the necessary residence papers. For American and British academics, brittle diplomatic relations with Syria meant receiving none of the practical support available to researchers working in countries such as Egypt, where the United States has maintained longstanding relationships with local academic and other institutions. There have been no American or British research institutes established in Syria, and in the case of the U.S. scholars, unreliable embassy support made obtaining residency permits a time-consuming challenge. As a result, Syrian specialists today form a small, marginalized subfield, working from disparate disciplinary backgrounds and academic traditions.[2] Many of us met for the first time when Lund University's Center for Middle Eastern Studies, with sponsorship from the Swedish Tercentenary Foundation (Riksbankens Jubileumsfond), brought us together in 2010 to assess Bashar al-Asad's first decade in power. *Syria from Reform to Revolt: Culture, Society, and Religion* offers a series of specialized analyses drawn from this conference. The following chapters demonstrate how Bashar al-Asad's rhetoric—and occasional implementation—of reform led social actors in various realms to believe the dismantling of dictatorship was at hand, and to work with and through institutions in the hope of rendering the regime more responsive.

Contributions to this volume demonstrate the paradoxical affects surrounding hope, anticipation, and betrayal that animated life in Syria during Bashar al-Asad's first decade. The "Damascus Spring"—the period of reformist discussion and debate during the new leader's first months in office—raised expectations of change among Syrians of all classes, regions, and religious and ethnic affiliations. This promise of greater expressive freedom and political participation—however unfulfilled—was never completely repressed or forgotten. It lingered through the decade, ultimately offering a language of critique and a precedent for activism that helped protestors transform shared grievances into collective action.

A Moving Wall of Fear

Throughout the 2000s, dissident activists, artists and intellectuals continued to press for realization of the Damascus Spring promise, using subtler, more ambiguous methods rather than overt demands. They experienced cycles of raised and dashed hopes, during which the occasional loosening of censorship restrictions was predictably reversed. Nevertheless, many believed that a more participatory polity could gradually emerge without a violent overthrow of the regime, and worked toward this outcome through the small margin for maneuver the leadership allowed. By sustaining expectations of transformation, offering a critical language that diverged from the regime's neoliberal rhetoric, and revealing the hollowness of official slogans, their efforts laid the groundwork for the uprising. While commentators celebrated the 2011 protestors' breaking of the so-called wall of fear, this process had been initiated long before by human rights activists, socially committed artists, and political critics chipping away at that wall, moving it incrementally to widen the range of public discourse. Continuity has been as significant as rupture.

Indeed, such efforts to effect gradual, nonviolent change continued through the first months of the protests. Though some Syrians viewed these attempts as reactionary and believed them more likely to bolster authoritarianism than to undermine it, individual cases proved more complex. After the screening of his documentary *The Road to Damascus* (2006) at Lund's Center for Middle Eastern Studies, eminent filmmaker Nabil Maleh described one such instance of reformist advocacy. Before the outbreak of violence, this "father of Syrian cinema," longtime dissident, and key Damascus Spring activist devised a plan he believed could spare Syria the ravages of violent conflict. Knowing the centrality of satellite television to Syrian social and political life, he proposed a new station, National Dialogue, to serve as the Ba'thist state's first open forum for discussion and debate. As he envisioned it, National Dialogue would nurture a nascent democratic atmosphere where opinions could be exchanged without fear of reprisal. No such arenas existed, as political gatherings were forbidden and media strictly controlled. Maleh hoped that dialogue would render the al-Asad regime more accountable, helping to avoid the bloodshed that appeared imminent. Believing the authoritarian status quo untenable, Maleh had worked toward a peaceful transition to participatory governance for a decade, and he saw this television forum as a last opportunity toward this end. In April 2011 he brought the idea to Bouthaina Shaaban, the president's spokesperson and a member of his inner circle, who encouraged him to proceed. Maleh quickly garnered support from opposition figures throughout the nation and submitted a written proposal to Shaaban, emphasizing a precondition: the station's "complete immunity from security and political interference." Receiving no reply, the director sent Shaaban a text message pleading for a green light to open the station because, as unrest mounted, "every day counts." He received no response. Maleh believes the regime found his demand for editorial freedom a step too far in the democratizing direction. Even more bitterly, Maleh realized his language had been coopted to pacify the opposition when four months later, with Syria's armed forces turning their weapons on peaceful protestors and with the death toll escalating, the regime invited opposition figures to a conference on "national dialogue." Most who were invited boycotted. Many dissident intellectuals, as well as ordinary citizens, began to leave the country in the spring of 2011, as the regime cracked down on nonviolent protest. Maleh did so just before security service cars pulled up to his Damascus apartment.[3]

The burial of Maleh's proposal for a television station featuring open political critique echoed official practices during Bashar al-Asad's first decade in power. Regime gestures toward greater participation amounted to mere "authoritarian upgrading," a restyling of repression in the latest global fashion, as the kleptocracy was dressed in neoliberal language and government-controlled NGOs created the façade of a civil society.[4] But this is not how it appeared in July 2000, when thirty-four-year-old Bashar inherited the Syrian regime. With an elegant financier wife burnishing his public image, the British-trained physician seemed poised to transform an antiquated polity.[5] Outwardly more president than dictator, the new leader discouraged the worshipful iconography that had marked the three decades of his father Hafiz al-Asad's rule, and he promised a range of political and economic reforms. He closed the notorious Mezze prison, releasing hundreds of political prisoners. As the tech-savvy head of the Syrian Computer Society, Bashar al-Asad began reversing Syria's previous telecommunications isolation, broadening Internet access and permitting the satellite dishes that had been in limbo under his father's regime: usually tolerated but never formally authorized. He accelerated the economic liberalization process initiated but only fitfully implemented by his father in the 1990s, a move that pleased urban merchants and industrialists and prompted the return of expatriate Syrian businessmen. Sunni business classes, long both intertwined with and resentful of the 'Alawi-dominated ruling elite, anticipated a dismantling of sectarian privilege that would advance their interests. It was not exactly Basharmania, but the new leader was received with a cautious optimism.

New prospects—which were, in hindsight, a mirage—temporarily revitalized Syrian activists, intellectuals, and entrepreneurs long inured to regime-engineered inertia. The technocratic language of modern institutions displaced Ba'th party slogans, with terms like "social market economy" and "pluralism" filtering through public discourse.[6] Relaxed controls on freedom of expression permitted a brief honeymoon for cultural producers and the rise of venues for political opinion. In December 2000, political cartoonist 'Ali Farzat launched *Al-Dumari* (*The Lamplighter*), the first independent publication of the Ba'thist era.[7] Emboldened activists, artists, and entrepreneurs seized the moment, and a long-suppressed civil society movement emerged. Independent gatherings called *muntadayat* (forums) sprang up, first in Damascus and then throughout the country. These gatherings began discussing arts and culture but quickly moved into the danger zones of politics, the role of religion, human rights, and the future of Syria. Prominent among these groups was the Committees for the Revival of Civil Society (*Lijan ihya' al-mujtama' al-madani*), which gathered in filmmaker Nabil Maleh's Damascus home. The group produced a document called "Statement of the 99," signed in September 2000 by leading intellectuals, academics, and artists. It called for practical steps toward democratization, including an end to the emergency law in place since the Ba'thist coup of 1963, a pardon of all political detainees, amnesty for exiled dissidents, and a loosening of restrictions on public life. In the subsequent "Statement of the Thousand," released in January 2001, a larger coalition of artists, academics, and intellectuals reiterated these demands, adding calls for multiparty democracy, an independent judiciary, and the abolition of laws discriminating against women.[8] The movement flourished into 2001, despite signs of an impending backlash.

By the end of 2001, much of the progress had been reversed: The regime closed all but one of the forums, silenced the oppositional press, and arrested or intimidated reform movement leaders.[9] The leadership also channeled development energy into GONGOs, government-operated nongovernmental organizations that mimicked civil society but remained firmly under regime control.[10] It blocked social media sites and email services. Many Syrians now interpret the brief period of relaxation as a cynical attempt to gauge the strength and sources of opposition, and to imprison some of them.

Yet for a broadening upper-middle class willing to enter into partnerships with the regime, business flourished.[11] Monied classes enjoyed a burgeoning leisure industry of restaurants, hotels, and cafés. Upscale boutiques offered Syrian clothing made under European license. Freed from socialist restrictions on ostentation that Ba'thist ideology had viewed as invidious, advertisers hawked new, expensive commodities in an expanding and privatizing media landscape. Billboards sprang up on once-barren desert highways. This apparent prosperity belied the resilience of older power structures and the growing class divide:[12] devastating droughts and the repeal of welfare subsidies rendered everyday life increasingly difficult for most Syrians.[13] An April 2011 decree formally ended the state of emergency, but this had little practical effect. Repressive measures intensified rather than lessened as the uprising unfolded.

The reformist language favored by the Bashar al-Asad regime has had contradictory effects. One has been to hijack pro-reform sentiment so successfully that those adopting it risked accusations of complicity.[14] Strict censorship of privately owned media may have merely outsourced propaganda to non-state producers. Indeed, the granting of media licenses primarily to those with personal or professional links to the regime attests to the survival of authoritarian strictures. Yet another more nebulous and politically significant outcome of the regime's uptake of reformist language was that its circulation in the public arena highlighted the absence of substantial change, a contradiction critiqued in popular culture and the arts, and ultimately one that engendered disillusionment, as several chapters in this volume illustrate.

Amid the fallen leaves of the Damascus autumn, a legacy of raised expectations among activists and reform-minded intellectuals persisted. Artistic expression continued to flourish in officially sanctioned commercial enterprises like television drama, in overtly dissident autonomous works like novels, and in seemingly apolitical cultural forms like dance. Oppositional voices continued to murmur, forums operated below the radar, and Syrians criticized the government in private conversation. Two English-language periodicals, *Syria Today* and *Forward Magazine*, gingerly broached sensitive issues. Religious leaders became more outspoken on issues of gender, justice, and human rights. These dynamics fed the 2011–12 uprising against four decades of Ba'thist dictatorship, a movement often misrecognized as an unprecedented, spontaneous, and youth-driven rebellion operating with entirely novel ideas.

It is this legacy of expectations raised during the Bashar al-Asad era that the contributors to this volume trace, writing from various disciplinary perspectives and addressing different arenas of Syrian society. As their chapters demonstrate, the anticipation of change encouraged actors in religious, cultural, and political life to work with and through the state in attempts to reform or undermine the regime. During this critical period, political novelists, television drama creators, experimental choreographers, and independent religious movements and organizations attempted to cooperate with, manipulate, undermine, or sidestep state control, frequently offering overt critique at the same time. Discourses of dissatisfaction formulated during the Damascus Spring were reworked within official strictures rather than abandoned, only to emerge more loudly in the 2011 protest movement.

Competing Narratives and Unexpected Convergences

The diverse contributions to this volume illustrate how, in various realms and through a process of economic liberation, social actors and groups built on a legacy of raised expectations in efforts to reform the regime through the state or state-controlled institutions. Key to an understanding of this prewar era is what Salamandra and Stenberg refer to as limited autonomy: a form of agency that Bashar al-Asad's mode of rule has engendered with its discourse of change. The margin of freedom afforded varying degrees of leverage and possibilities for evasion, but also facilitated cooptation and containment. Perhaps more significantly, it kept alive the hopes for greater freedom and participation that ultimately fueled the uprising. The following explorations of this legacy aim to render legible the uprisings of 2011–14.

Culture, as Max Weiss notes, has remained a site of dynamic contestation, despite—perhaps even spurred by—the regime's attempts to co-opt cultural producers and their work. Fictional literature, with its narrow audience and minimal production costs, is perhaps the art form most autonomous of state control. Weiss explores a new genre, the *mukhabarat* (intelligence services) novel, which has emerged from the relative relaxation of political expression in the 2000s. Published outside and banned within Syria, texts such as Fawwaz Haddad's *Solo Piano Music* ('*Azf munfarid 'ala al-biyanu*), a surrealist study in paranoia, and Nihad Sirees's *The Silence and the Roar* (*Al-Samt wa al-sakhab*), a satirical treatment of intellectual cooptation, nevertheless circulated widely through informal, officially tolerated channels. As Weiss argues, these works employ conventions of police and satirical novels to unveil practices of ideological policing in a culture of surveillance. Offering neither salvation nor resolution, these novels conclude with apathetic resignation. Innovative forms of literary irony broadened the range of critical reimagining and may ultimately constrain official co-optation of the cultural field by sidestepping editorial restrictions. Unlike most other cultural producers, novelists can publish abroad to reach a black-market readership in Syria and attain renown beyond its borders.

As a medium lacking literature's autonomy, realist and satirical television serials are subject to ideological strictures, equipment requirements, budgetary constraints, and market forces. Nevertheless, contemporary Syrian television shares somber sensibility and biting critique found in the *mukhabarat* genre. Syria has become a leading supplier of TV drama to pan-Arab satellite television stations located in the wealthy Gulf Cooperation Council states. Syrian drama creators have competed successfully with their more established Egyptian counterparts and introduced Syria's lilting dialect to new generations of viewers. What Christa Salamandra refers to as a "dark aesthetic" lends contemporary Syrian serials a style easily identifiable to pan-Arab satellite television audiences. These programs tend to convey the political resignation expressed by contemporary novelists—a quality of realist art generally, and one long criticized for failing to offer hope or alternatives.[15] Often ridiculed by Syrian intellectuals as part of the regime's "safety valve" strategy to control criticism, TV serials nevertheless reflect thematic and formal innovation that cannot be dismissed as mere sophisticated propaganda. Salamandra demonstrates how TV creators, working within the commercial and political restraints of state-controlled production, have used televisual language to convey oppositional messages. Social realist serials may reinforce the status quo by depicting "the way things are" rather than offering visions of "the way things could be." Yet Salamandra argues that they stand as an ongoing reminder of what should not remain: that which the regime promised to change, but still remains to be changed. For instance, realist drama and dark satire critique the system merely by evoking it. Syrian state television's existentialist satire *No Hope* (*Amal ma fi*) has found a revolutionary echo in the oppositional Orient TV channel's production *Freedom and Nothing But* (*Hurriya wa bas*). In the latter, a pair of young activist actors adopt *No Hope*'s mise-en-scène, but transform the program's tone of somber resignation into revolutionary fervor. Their debt to the state-sanctioned satire is unmistakable.

Bashar al-Asad's regime understands the transformative potential of television fiction and has sought to employ it by influencing its creators. Drama creators, in turn, must interact with various factions of the regime and its security apparatus to see their productions air. In contrast to Salamandra, Donatella Della Ratta sees a strong alliance between drama makers and the regime. She suggests that the leadership has enabled and manipulated private production, ultimately determining the contours of mass media expression by indicating issues it wants to see dramatized on television. Analyzing the production and consumption of Bashar-era series, she proposes that different camps within the ruling elite have used a "whisper strategy" to promote particular, often competing agendas. She illustrates this feedback mechanism in, among other works, *Above the Ceiling* (*Fawq al-saqf*), state television's failed response to the pro-democracy uprising. Through suggesting content and rewarding those cultural producers who take notice, the regime has shaped public debate. Television makers whisper also back to manipulate the censorship process and promote their own interests. A selective neoliberalization of the industry has brought wealth and prestige to the cultural producers who listen and respond to the regime most dutifully. The rewards have ensured a level of obedience, even gratitude, among a new generation of drama makers invested in the status quo.

Shayna Silverstein explores how professional dancers have negotiated shifting aspirations and tastes amid the social market reforms that widened class divisions during the 2000s. She situates these efforts within debates on cultural heritage to discuss how symbols of nationhood differ between dancers who have embraced populist expressions of *thaqafa wataniyya* (national culture) and those who have adopted cosmopolitan forms that draw on ballet and musical theater. Folk dance troupes appealed to artists who depended on state employment and welfare, while elites who benefited from the clientelist networks linked to the regime adopted the globalized aesthetics of contemporary dance. Yet contemporary dance also negotiates historical and contemporary understandings of the *shaʿbi* (folk), itself a multivalent signifier that denotes populist, traditional, folkloric, and everyday street practices evinced in the *dabke*. The debate over whether and how to adapt *dabke* in contemporary dance productions therefore illustrates how choreographers and audiences have negotiated shifting attitudes toward national identity and cultural heritage, while at the same time aspiring toward more global imaginaries. Elite uncertainty over how to represent *shaʿbi* identity reflects cultural producers' ambivalence over the spread of crony capitalism and growing class divisions.

The Function of Religion—Motivating Support or Justifying Opposition?

The state's control over disparate sectors such as the arts, public imagery, neoliberal economic policies, and religious practice has often converged during Bashar's presidency. Religious affiliations, like cultural production, have remained fields of contestation in which actors vie for power, prominence, and perhaps most important, protection. Since the new president took power, the number of religious organizations increased, and some have adopted a reformist language spurring them to work with rather than around state officials and institutions.

The Syrian religious landscape includes a number of religious and ethnic minority groups such as the Druze, Isma'ilis, 'Alawis, and numerous Christian denominations. Their respective numbers are difficult to ascertain; official government statistics do not reflect recent migration and are founded on state policies rather than actual numbers.[16] Ba'thist ideology had long disavowed social, regional, class and confessional divisions, while at the same time concentrating powerful positions in the security apparatus in 'Alawi hands. This has intensified during the current war, as most government institutions have cleansed non-'Alawis, especially Sunnis, from the civil servant ranks.[17] Given both these factors, religiosity remained politically sensitive, especially if the regime perceived it as a possible foundation for opposition.

When not suppressed—or merely tolerated—by the regime, religion has been operationalized through the building of institutions, organizations, movements, and networks. During Bashar al-Asad's presidency, religious leaders have participated openly in social and political activity. They took part in the "Damascus Spring" forums advocating reform, although most accounts of this movement in particular, and of the opposition in general, have focused on secular voices. Some religious officials have remained oppositional, some have remained silent, and others have publicly supported Bashar al-Asad's government. Yet the regime remained wary: religious figures' participation in media discussions, an increased presence of religion in the public sphere, and tensions between religious groups prompted a 2008 presidential decree regulating Muslim religious movements. Religious belonging has played a significant role in the creation of both support and opposition to the regime.

Syria's Christian denominations have received little scholarly attention; their study provides valuable insight into how religious minorities function in repressive states, and how they may serve to sustain authoritarian structures. Political life for Christians in Syria is complex, and they, like many groups documented in this volume, hoped the new leader would enact change during the first decade of the twenty-first century. Christians' prominence in Syria's religiously pluralistic society has long showcased Ba'thist state tolerance. Bashar al-Asad's regime permitted Christian denominations to run their own schools, to conduct religious rituals, and to practice a personal status law, especially in regard to marriage and divorce.

A private religious welfare sector has expanded in the wake of neoliberalism in Syria, representing one arena of reinvigorated religious participation. In Syria, as in many Middle Eastern countries, the past decade has witnessed a growth in non-state charity organizations that have provided social services to populations increasingly impoverished by the shrinking welfare state. Charities have become important benefactors for poorer segments of the society, and most have been linked to religious denominations and organizations.

While much academic research examines Muslim charities, Christian organizations have been less well studied, as Laura Ruiz de Elvira shows. She analyzes the activities of Christian charities as part of a wider shift in public authority giving non-state actors new roles in social and economic development: a nod in the direction of promised reform. Under Bashar al-Asad's regime, Christian associations have operated through church patronage; the associations were supported by religious leaders, and registered with the appropriate ministry. De Elvira finds that although Christian associations have been easier for the regime to control than their Muslim counterparts, they have also gained a relative degree of freedom. Because these organizations lacked significant political or social power, the regime did not regard them as a threat to its stability. As a pillar of the sociopolitical status quo they formed a centerpiece of the regime's professed secularism and protection of religious minorities. In what de Elvira refers to as a positive-sum relationship, Christian charities allied with the 'regime to maintain selective minority religious rights and oppose a common enemy—Sunni revivalism. She concludes that in return for their support of the regime, Christian associations have gained political advantage over their Muslim counterparts; an exceptional legal status and links to foreign actors have afforded them a greater degree of autonomy. Christian support for the regime through much of the uprising can be attributed to these longstanding practices of mutual benefit, but it has intensified with the perceived threat some Islamist opposition groups pose to non-Sunni Muslim minorities.

One of the key questions in Andreas Bandak's chapter concerns the position of Christians in Syria's broader polity. It is important, in Bandak's view, to comprehend the role Christian minorities have played in meaning-making during Bashar al-Asad's presidency. Through an account of a cultural event, Bandak analyzes the social and political situation of Christians in Syria and their perceptions of their position. Christians contributed to the construction of an official image and ethos of Syrian national unity on occasions such as the Christmas concert in the Damascus Opera House that Bandak describes. However, such displays were not mere expressions of their complicity or coercion. Bandak argues that Christians' participation on the national stage, while accommodating the regime's rhetoric of national unity, has led Christians to regard themselves as integral to the nation. Bandak concludes that with the concert at the opera house and similar expressions of Syrian Christianity, Christian identity became solidified on a national stage.

The connection between economic liberalization and Sunni Muslim 'ulama' (religious scholars) is an example of the significance of religion in Syrian society. Muslim scholars are, according to Thomas Pierret, not part of the official neoliberal ideological shift. Rather, they have upheld entrenched relationships with merchant networks, especially when economic changes have taken the form of Islamic finance. State neoliberalism coincided with but did not trigger this process. Pierret maintains that when leading Syrian religious scholars formulate economic ethics, social and economic conditions outweigh theological considerations. He explores the economic ethics that leading religious scholars espoused in the pre-2011 Syrian context, stating that the 'ulama' relied on resources from the private sector. Hence, the 'ulama' prioritized material conditions, embracing the bourgeois values of self-employment, hard work, and individual success and prosperity in lieu of socialism.

Questions concerning religion, politics, and the public sphere are central to Leif Stenberg's chapter on the role of the Ahmad Kuftaro Foundation, one of Syria's key Sunni Islamic institutions, during the 2000s. Stenberg examines the shifting doctrinal, administrative, and political position of this institution in Syria's religious landscape. Through a discussion of recent transformations in the organization's structure and ritual practice, Stenberg uncovers a complex relationship between the Kuftaro Foundation and the state. He analyses the Syrian government's ambivalence toward the foundation and events leading to the incarceration of its leader. In his conclusion Stenberg reflects on the possibilities of agency in a repressive state. Instead of a top-down relationship between the state and religious movements, Stenberg points to a multifaceted interaction between state and religious groups in which informal networks play an important role. He concludes that religious actors like the Kuftaro Foundation have carved out a space to operate, exercising a limited autonomy that the regime permitted but controlled. As long as the foundation maintained informal ties (such as state officials' relationship to the Sufi framework of the foundation), did not appear to oppose official policies, and abided by state-sanctioned interpretations and practices of Islam, it enjoyed freedom to maneuver.

With the State, Against the Regime

Syria from Reform to Revolt, Volume 2: Culture, Society, and Religion explores the space between public criticism and wholehearted support of the regime, which emerged powerfully during Bashar al-Asad's first decade in power, and which many Syrians hoped pointed in the direction of political liberalization. The works presented here offer a nuanced account of unstable position-taking meant to reform the regime short of what was then unthinkable: revolution. As Nabil Maleh's aborted National Dialogue television forum illustrates, efforts to push the leadership to make good on its reformist rhetoric continued until the outbreak of armed conflict. This volume demonstrates that many Syrians who were not public dissidents were nevertheless dissatisfied with the authoritarian status quo: they laid claims to greater control of their own domains, and to a stake in what they hoped was a transforming political system. Those working at the margins of the system, and those outside it, complicated the regime's harnessing of social and economic change. These chapters explore the various strategies adopted by differently placed social actors to operate under an oppressive regime that sometimes dangled the possibility of political participation. They show some Syrians siding with power; others trying to manipulate it to their own ends; and still others nudging the smallest openings to push open the door to political transformation. Some were subtly oppositional; others more overtly dissident. Such contestations and accommodations have historical precedent; they have characterized competing visions for modern Syria since independence. Oscillating degrees of opposition and compromise in the hope of better governance intensified, however, during the transformations of the 2000s. Religious leaders and secular artists worked with and through the state, although they may have been against the regime. This crucial distinction helps explain the multifarious and shifting alliances and allegiances that appear to support dictatorship in the face of an apparent revolution. The contributors to this volume bring critical and historically informed understandings of the conditions that led the once hopeful "Arab Spring" revolution to morph into a catastrophic civil war that has cost over 250,000 lives and indescribable misery for many more.

2

What Lies Beneath

Political Criticism in Recent Syrian Fiction

M A X   W E I S S

Mustafa Tlas (b. 1932), intimate confidant of Hafiz al-Asad (d. 2000), publishing mogul, and stalwart Syrian defense minister for more than three decades (1972–2004), compiled a collection of aphorisms uttered by the late president. One chapter in this admittedly hagiographical compendium concerns the media, among the only sections in which al-Asad remarks on anything even remotely cultural or intellectual in nature. "Our battle has many fields," al-Asad declares, "the military field is not the only one, and we must wage it in every field in absolute lockstep."[1] Although the original time and place of these pronouncements are not provided, the bombastic self-assuredness found in these public remarks cannot negate the fact that the cultural field in Ba'thist Syria never fully moved in absolute lockstep with the demands of a single individual or a specific ideology. Although attempts were made to monitor—if not ideologically straightjacket—Syrian cultural politics during this period, the cultural and intellectual field remained a site of contestation and dynamism. Be that as it may, there was certainly less ideological deviation or

Portions of this chapter also appear in "Who Laughs Last: Literary Transformations of Syrian Authoritarianism," in *Middle East Authoritarianisms: Governance, Contestation, and Regime Resilience in Syria and Iran*, edited by Steven Heydemann and Reinoud Leenders, 143–68 (Stanford, CA: Stanford Univ. Press, 2014). I thank the editors and the press for permission to reprint.

formal experimentation in Syrian letters during the final three decades of the twentieth century than there have been in the first decade of the twenty-first. Indeed, something very interesting has been happening in Syrian fiction writing over the past decade, which coincides with the first ten years since Bashar al-Asad acceded to power in the wake of his father's death in June 2000.

Syrian novels have become more and more explicitly engaged with the matter of politics, which is increasingly represented and understood in clear-eyed and highly realistic ways. Whereas the spectrum of political discourse was relatively narrow during the first three decades of Ba'th Party rule (1970–2000), obscured by the haze of Ba'thist propaganda (a persistent problem), the same period witnessed a similar sort of ideological conformity in the literary field, but this was by no means ever complete. At some point during the late 1990s and early 2000s, Syrian writers—without any apparent coordination, as they remained as individuated and atomized as the rest of Syrian society—began experimenting with new forms of novelistic expression that had overtly political plot structures and thematic concerns. It is worth noting, moreover, that this phenomenon predates the uprising that broke out in March 2011 to galvanize the attention of the region and the world. The courage required to continue interrogating the conditions of possibility for politics in contemporary Syria in the shadow of widespread and brutal techniques of repression and torture, which seem to grow worse by the day, suggests both admirable bravery and indomitable spirit.

The persistence of authoritarian rule in Syria had unanticipated consequences. Historians and literary critics will have to wait before identifying possible outcomes and implications of the current uprising in Syria, but what was already abundantly clear during the first decade of the twenty-first century is that literary culture and perhaps popular culture more generally had begun to probe the conditions of possibility for politics and the nature of political life more broadly. My aim in this chapter is not simply to point out that Syrian fiction has acquired new qualities of political didacticism. Indeed, numerous Syrian novels written over the past several decades could justifiably be classified as *romans à clef*; much of the ubiquitous socialist realism, "commitment" literature, and even the "prison novel" was rife with facile universalizing and moral didacticism. What matters more than the simple appearance of politics in fiction, I would argue, is the way in which the place of politics itself is in the process of being redefined through these new literary works, and, more subtly, the extent to which the form of politics is intellectually or aesthetically separated (and separable) from its content. Syrian writers are concerned with surfaces, but the recent outpouring of writing in Syria and by Syrian writers is far from superficial. This growing literary concern with the formal aspects of politics, as opposed to its content, may also have had some kind of an impact on political life in general. In this sense, the subtle insight expressed by Lisa Wedeen in her profound analysis of Syrian Ba'thist authoritarianism under Hafiz al-Asad that certain transgressive acts "are meaningful" even though "they may not be transformative" remains particularly resonant.[2]

Steven Heydemann argues that the successful production of compliance by the Ba'thist state under Hafiz al-Asad hinged upon the production and maintenance of corporatist "social pacts" between the regime and the people.[3] Meanwhile, a substantial and growing body of research offers fresh insights into ongoing developments in contemporary Syria—from the accelerated pace of economic liberalization (*infitah*) and its myriad consequences to infrastructural modernization projects and the grinding process of political "reform."[4] In her "political ethnography of power" in late-twentieth-century Syria, Wedeen convincingly demonstrates how Syrian citizens regularly engaged in a politics of "as if," simultaneously appearing to comply with ideological hegemony while also critically engaging with politically sensitive topics in both public and private settings. Her analysis of jokes and films, everyday life, and state spectacle underlines how the "cult" of Hafiz al-Asad was perpetually in flux and therefore subject to subversion, inversion, or, at least, informal critique.[5] In her own study of writing and the plastic arts, miriam cooke looks at the ways in which "official" state culture and "dissident" cultures coexisted and cross-pollinated in 1990s Syria, showing how the cultural field in contemporary Syria has been both regulated by and filtered through the hegemonic ideology of the state.[6]

There has been relatively less discussion of the continuing transformation of cultural life in early twenty-first-century Syria.[7] If the political, institutional, and military foundations of authoritarianism contribute to the production of certain cultural formations, it should be emphasized that those cultural worlds are produced, invented, sustained and nurtured under authoritarian conditions but also curtailed by processes of state control, surveillance, repression, coercion, and hegemony. Syrian Ba'thist authoritarianism succeeded, to a large extent, in managing, muffling, and ultimately absorbing political, social, and cultural challenges to regime legitimacy. More than ten years since the succession of Bashar al-Asad, and amid what is perhaps the greatest challenge to the post-revolutionary Syrian state, now is a particularly opportune moment to consider new perspectives on the ongoing transformation of Syrian society and culture, on Syrian history in the making. Integrating the methods and insights of both literary critics and social scientists may provide a more satisfying analysis of both literary and nonliterary responses to the highly differentiated ideological and political field of authoritarian rule in Syria.

What might be conceived of as relatively benign neglect on the part of the regime vis-à-vis novelists and other writers can be attributed, at least in part, to the minor and marginal role that literature plays in contemporary Syria. Space will not allow for a more detailed history of the production, circulation, and reception of literary works during the late twentieth and early twenty-first century. It is sufficient to briefly point out that Syrian novelists directly confront both endemic obstacles to their literary endeavors as well as estimable aesthetic challenges presented by the dogged persistence of a stultifying authoritarian political culture. The remainder of this chapter reflects upon the contemporary state of novel writing in Syria as it relates to the persistent problem of authoritarian government, focusing in particular on two novels—*Solo Piano Music*, by Fawwaz Haddad, and *The Silence and the Roar*, by Nihad Sirees—that raise critical questions and exemplify the limits of such critique for challenging the ideological and political techniques of rule in contemporary Syria. Before turning to those works, however, I will contextualize them by considering some recent literary historical background.

Novels and Novelists in Syria

From a certain viewpoint, the aesthetic and political challenges presently confronting Syrian intellectuals are not all that different from those faced by previous generations of writers. To be sure, the reading public in Syria is quite small; the country is also affected by global trends toward declining readerships more broadly. Mechanisms for censorship and repression remain well in place, and writing under such authoritarian conditions remains dangerous, to say the least. The General Union of Syrian Writers and other less public agencies, including the Regional Command of the Ba'th Party (*al-Qiyada al-qutriyya*) regulate the publication and sale of printed materials in Syria. Many Syrian writers—like other cultural producers, including visual artists and actors, filmmakers, and screenwriters—will sidestep local problems of literary production, circulation, and consumption by simply publishing their work abroad, typically in Beirut, and increasingly with one of two publishers—Dar al-Adab or Riyad el-Rayyes. Intriguingly, the Syrian regime does not seem inclined to retaliate against writers who publish highly critical or controversial works, but rather, permits them to proceed, even though their works may technically be banned inside the country. The regime tightens the screws on political dissidents and human rights activists rather than monitoring and prosecuting novelists.

Nearly a decade ago, at precisely the moment in which Syrian culture and society began grappling with the implications of Ba'thist regime change, novelist and literary critic Mohja Kahf argued that state crackdowns on the Muslim Brotherhood and its allies in Hama and elsewhere, in addition to the low-intensity warfare conducted by the Ba'thist regime against its own people throughout the 1970s and 1980s, constituted a blind spot in Syrian cultural memory.[8] Indeed, Kahf argues that the state massacre of tens of thousands of people in Hama in 1982 was among the greatest traumas suffered by the Syrian people in the twentieth century.[9] Over the ensuing ten years, there has indeed been a steady trickle, if not a veritable torrent, of controversial novels and other writings that deal directly with those themes, which has rendered Kahf's judgment both incredibly prescient and now more or less obsolete. Considering the substantial constraints weighing upon intellectual life in Syria under Hafiz al-Asad, and the attendant evisceration of society and culture during that period, it is remarkable to witness Syrian literary culture tentatively emerging from the shadows and hesitantly stepping into a global limelight.[10]

This is clear in the recent work of Mustafa Khalifa, *The Shell* (*Al-Qawqaʻa*) (2008). Khalifa was arrested upon returning home to Syria from his studies in France and imprisoned in the Tadmur military prison for nearly thirteen harrowing years, from 1982 until 1994, before being moved to several other facilities. The novel is a veritable carnival of horror in which Khalifa presents his tale of wrongful imprisonment, inhuman torture, suffering, and human camaraderie against all odds. In this fictionalized memoir billed as the "diaries of a voyeur" (*yawmiyyat mutalassis*), Khalifa documents the atrocities taking place around him in the spirit of testamentary witnessing. Although it could be argued that the novel has a happy ending, in the sense that Khalifa lived to tell the tale, there is nothing even remotely approximating redemption for Khalifa or his prison comrades, not all of whom are lucky enough to survive the horrifying ordeals of Syrian jailers and executioners, or the psychological and emotional damage that their survivors endured.[11]

Much has been written about "the prison novel" in Arabic letters, particularly as an instance of "resistance literature" or "commitment" literature more broadly speaking.[12] That prison literature remains a mainstay of contemporary Syrian writing is relatively unsurprising considering the abysmal human rights record of the regime.[13] But it must be recognized that prison literature is only one genre within a broader, richer, more diverse literary field. Indeed, a broader study of contemporary Syrian literature would have to take note of the fact that a wide range of writers are increasingly engaged with the *problématique* of politics from multiple perspectives. In addition to the two particular works I discuss below, a veritable spate of recent novels exemplifies the continued evolution of what has been called the *mukhabarat* novel.[14]

The Rise of the *Mukhabarat* Novel

Critics and readers should remain wary of the often (over)stated case that thought control and political repression approaches anywhere near absolute in Syria. As mentioned above, state cultural policy hardly resembles a coherent, systematically applied set of principles. Many intellectuals in Syria whom I interviewed between 2008 and 2011 pointed out how the organs of the cultural establishment employ no consistent or discernible strategy; they rue the loss of meaningful public culture in Syria, which they understand as one direct consequence of the demand for intellectual conformity in official cultural policy.[15] One aspect of this demanded intellectual conformity concerns a willful avoidance of political matters, whether of an everyday and local matter or pertaining to the behavior of the state and its affiliated individual actors and agencies. Indeed, if the political realm is governed by a logic of irrationality, the Syrian cultural field is similarly chaotic. In this context, the Syrian regime promotes and presents itself as both the leading force in politics and a cultural vanguard.

Contemporary novels confront the obfuscation, arbitrary rule, and the sheer violence of life in Syria through a range of literary devices, ranging from avoidance and detachment to plain talk, discursive intellectualizing, and irony and other forms of humor. Meanwhile, a number of recent Syrian novels contain plots that revolve around themes of conspiracy and state control, and they ultimately purport to pierce the veil of ideology and obscurity that surrounds the practice of politics, which in recent years has come to be described as the functioning of a "*mukhabarat* state*.*" The Lebanese poet and critic Abbas Beydoun identifies the emergence of a "*mukhabarat* novel" in Arabic literature, novels in which the state security apparatus (*al-mukhabarat*) or the individual security agent (*al-mukhabarati*) may play an integral part in the setting, plot, and characterization. In the Syrian case, according to Beydoun, this has turned many such a work into "a quasi-police novel but without the structure, techniques or formula of a police novel."[16]

Syrian writers have certainly taken risks before by critically engaging with themes or tropes of politics in fiction. But more recent writing extends that criticism of arbitrary arrest, detention, torture, and the general climate of fear in the country into new territory. The novels examined in this chapter—*The Silence and the Roar* by Nihad Sirees, and *The Treasonous Translator* and *Solo Piano Music* by Fawwaz Haddad—openly engage with the problem of authoritarianism in multiple, complicated ways. But can it be said that these novels open up a space for interrogating the place of politics, of repression and freedom in contemporary Syrian fiction? To be sure, such broader philosophical or political engagements with the concepts and practices of freedom remain more or less sequestered within the realms of prose, poetry, and human rights discourse, all of which are subject to the capricious regime of censorship that remains firmly in place. The greater irony, though, may reside in the fact that these novels tend to wind up at common existential conundrums: how one can or ought to exercise moral agency under political conditions in which the modern Syrian subject appears to have been eviscerated.

Pulling Back the Curtain: Fawwaz Haddad's *Solo Piano Music*

The early novels of Damascus-based writer Fawwaz Haddad evinced deep interest in historical fiction, evoking an exceptionally rich imagination of Damascene urban detail. His recent novels have taken a decidedly different turn, veering sharply toward hard-boiled realism. Solitary male figures in the main, Haddad's protagonists get swept up in unexpected tales of intrigue and deception. The plot is ultimately revealed at the end in order to convey some sort of moral or to call into question some piece of news or history. His later works, therefore, closely resemble the "quasi-police novel" suggested by Beydoun.

The protagonist in *The Treasonous Translator*, Hamid Salim, is an aspiring intellectual whom the reader first encounters just after he has published an Arabic translation of an African novel originally written in English. His translation ends with a slight twist; Hamid has modified the ending to suit his particular ideological taste.[17] When Sharif Husni, a towering local cultural figure, gets wind of this, he tries to expose Hamid and ruin his career before it can even start. Hamid is battered by the cultural establishment before realizing that his life is being threatened as well. As a result, Hamid retreats into a series of assumed identities—taking on no less than three different pseudonyms—in order to continue writing without being identified. Along the way, even as he dissolves himself (and his identity) into this string of pseudonyms and fake lives, Hamid finds his reputation increasingly impugned and his life at greater and greater risk.

Despite the relative freedom with which Haddad and his characters pontificate on matters of profound intellectual, philosophical, and cultural significance, the various settings for all of his novels are bathed in an icy solution of liquid fear. In the end, though—and in spite of an almost laughably formulaic moment of potential vengeance or revenge upon his previous tormentors—Hamid chooses the way of moderation, forgiveness, and, ultimately, social peace.

I prefer to conceive of this novel in terms of "treason" rather than "treachery" or "traitorousness," both for the term's connection with the ancient double entendre of *Traduttore, traditore* ("Translator, traitor"), but also for its semantic connections with notions of betrayal, and in particular, sedition or betrayal of country. The act of translation—simultaneously the professional identity of the novel's protagonist as well as Fawwaz Haddad's structural role within the global political economy of writing and publishing—is always already suspect in the eyes of the gatekeepers of the nation and their conception of national security, and is regularly subject and subjected to scrutiny and misunderstanding, if not outright affront.

In October 2009, during a conversation in which we discussed a wide range of literary, cultural, and political issues, Haddad claimed that he can talk about more or less anything he chooses, that he can write about anything he likes in his novels, and that the novel form is effectively an "open stage" (*masrah maftuh*), albeit one with a particular frame, which he can populate with whatever events, characters, and stories he chooses. Perhaps unsurprisingly, given the relatively limited range of personal freedoms in contemporary Syria, Haddad went so far as to claim that he is freer inside the novel than he is outside of it. Curiously, though, when I pressed him on whether he was any freer than other citizens because of this ability to imagine, invent, and inhabit stories, he demurred, saying that he considered himself less free for being confronted by certain boundaries as a writer and public intellectual. Be that as it may, he repeatedly indicated how his writing and his novels have allowed him (perhaps even obliged him) to exceed the limitations of the culture he lives within, to walk back and forth, as he put it, across a red line until it no longer appears to be red.[18]

These themes recur in Haddad's next novel, *Solo Piano Music* ('*Azf munfarid 'ala al-biyanu*), the tale of Fateh al-Qalaj, an unsuspecting secular intellectual who gets mugged inside the stairwell of his own apartment building by an unknown assailant in the opening scene.[19] Saleem, the street name of a young investigator from the so-called terrorism affairs bureau, begins to piece together the case, discovering along the way certain inconsistencies in Fateh's public secularist identity even as Fateh comes to believe that he is being targeted for his outspoken views on, among other things, religion and the separation of mosque and state. Saleem soon discovers that Fateh passed through a brief period in which he was a practicing believer, when his wife was suffering from a terminal illness. In the wake of her death, Fateh increasingly relied upon his wife's old friend, Haifa, whose character and personality remain relatively undeveloped, and who more or less functions as a source of comfort for Fateh.

Fateh and his controversial rhetoric eventually acquire greater public significance amid ongoing negotiations between the government and representatives of Islamist forces from both inside the country and abroad. After an inflammatory public lecture—provocatively entitled "A School without Religion, a School without Gender"—Fateh receives anonymous threats. He becomes disconcerted upon learning that there are now larger organizations involved in his situation, including an International Agency for Combating Terrorism, protection from which appears to be his only hope. His fear becomes irrational and overtakes him even as he accepts Saleem's offer for protection. Fateh explains some of his concerns to Haifa: "A man overtaken by the idea of killing me as a means of getting closer to God, who has no connection to any Islamist organization or movement, who doesn't have any need of funding or matériel, who needs nothing more than a simple metal implement, a kitchen knife for example. If one isn't available he'd tear me to shreds with his fingernails and his teeth" (199). After all, the narrator continues, "If the state itself isn't concerned with its own reputation, why would it be concerned with his?" (200). With these two statements, Fateh seeks to distance himself from both the regime and the Islamist opposition—a stance that is, in the end, the appropriate moral position according to the logic of the novel.

Meanwhile, Fateh is reacquainted with a childhood friend who appears to be mixed up with illegal Islamist politics. By the end of the novel, the pas de deux between "the investigator" and "the secularist"—as those two

characters are abbreviated—turns out to be mirrored by a similarly shadowy relationship between "the secularist" and "the fundamentalist." Fateh
confides in his old friend his incredulousness at the fact that he might be at
the center of such high-stakes political intrigue involving the regime, the
Islamists, and global counterterrorism agencies:

> "What have I got to do with what you're talking about?!"
> "It's the script you're living in."
> Noticing that he was serious, Fateh shouted back at him:
> "You must be joking."
> He wasn't joking.
> "Know then, that the international secret apparatus for combating
> terrorism is behind everything from beginning to end."
> Oh my God . . . if he knows about the international apparatus, he
> must know everything!! (253)

Haddad employs free indirect style here as in much of his writing, shifting
back and forth between third-person omniscient narration and internal
consciousness. This passage also indexes the recurring theme to which
Fateh repeatedly returns, namely, that he is locked into some movie-like
script that reinforces a certain sense of ineluctable fate but also activates
his feeling of paranoia. There is a hint of irony here that might be interpreted as poking fun at the extent to which conspiracy theory rules the
day in so much of Syria's political discourse, although Fateh's general state
of paranoia is more or less normalized if not explicitly confirmed over the
course of the novel.

   In a jarring and violent conclusion, the regime successfully stamps
out what it had labeled and perceived to be a terrorist threat, with Fateh
the secularist/ex-secularist figure literally caught in the crossfire; in the
end he is left speechless, absolutely dumbfounded. Moreover, Fateh is left
with a vague sense of shame and remorse for having been played, but he
resignedly accepts his difficult situation—unending conflict and contestation between the regime and its opponents. There is no clear or easily discernible moral message. Regardless of whether the international agency
for combating terrorism is to blame, whether the Islamists whom Fateh
knows personally or those whom he has never met deserve such a brutal

fate, whether Saleem even works for the Syrian government, or whether the two agencies are working hand-in-glove, Fateh can do no more than come to the cynically apathetic conclusion that there is little difference between truth and its lack, between good and evil. In this way he affirms that all conflicts are futile, and in the end one can but learn to rely upon oneself. In some ways, the total atomization of Syrian society is fully accomplished here, despite, or perhaps even as a result of, Fateh's unsuccessful attempts to claw his way to the truth.

The novel ends without passing unequivocal judgment on either the regime or the Islamists. In *Solo Piano Music*, the climax reveals something about one possibly essential attribute of the regime—veiled violence. But here the individual experience of authoritarianism does not only implicate the state. Impersonal forces not always traceable to particular individuals or institutions weigh heavily on the lives and fates of these characters; generalized fear is an everyday reality. Danger, violence, and repression might come from anywhere, from next door, from a casual acquaintance or an old friend. More often than not, they originate with individuals who have ties to the system or from unknown shadowy figures inhabiting the uncharted underworld of spies, secret agents, and international intrigue. Agents of the *mukhabarat* and the state end up looking like, at worst, nefarious manipulators, or, at best, bumbling yet well-intentioned functionaries caught up in an impersonal apparatus or regime. The characters in Haddad's novels are tragic and alienated, and they wield precious little power. Social relationships are confused, obscured behind a veil of uncertainty and relative anxiety. But unlike traditional police procedurals or crime novels, Haddad's more recent "hard-boiled" novels don't resolve in a cut-and-dried manner; they end with no small measure of apathy or despair, rather than a call to action or a clear didactic message. The curtain is pulled back but no wizard can be found.

Poking Fun at the Party: Nihad Sirees's *The Silence and the Roar*

The gradual transformation of Syrian authoritarian culture allowed for the emergence and coalescence of literary forms that took greater liberties in criticizing the regime. Recognizing this broad spectrum of literary conventions, including humor, might result in other ways of conceptualizing and analyzing contemporary and historical Syrian literary cultures and intellectual life. Literary critics and cultural historians would do well to analyze and critique the ways in which humor has been put to certain uses in the Syrian novel. Syrian writing has often been identified with socialist realism, ideological conformity, and stern seriousness. But the sense of humor expressed in one recent novel, *The Silence and the Roar*, produces an entirely different perspective on the early twenty-first-century Syrian regime than has been expressed.

The Silence and the Roar is the most politically charged novel to date by Nihad Sirees. Born in Aleppo in 1950, Sirees went abroad to study civil engineering, eventually earning a master's degree. Even as he maintains a private engineering firm, Sirees has also written successful television serials, plays, children's drama, and historical novels.[20] *Silence* confronts the problem of the individual in a society dominated and disciplined by a dictator, a repressive state apparatus, and "The Party."[21] The time frame of the novel is one twenty-four-hour period, in an unnamed Arab city that bears a striking resemblance to Aleppo, on a day in which yet another state-sponsored march is being held. The first-person narrative is told from the perspective of Fathi Sheen, an unemployed writer who is down on his luck after crossing the cultural establishment, and has consequently been consigned to oblivion and social death. Following a brief run-in at the march with security goons whom Fathi tried to pull off a young man they were arbitrarily roughing up, the agents confiscate his ID and tell him he must pay a visit to *mukhabarat* headquarters in order to pick it up.

Meanwhile, Fathi has been involved with a woman named Lama, whom he has failed to marry for both personal and financial reasons. Perhaps adding insult to injury, Fathi's widowed mother is romantically pursued by the nefarious party functionary Ha'el 'Ali Hassan, a man who owes his meteoric rise to a single stroke of dumb luck; at a public event in the small, remote town where he once lived, Ha'el instinctively reached out his hands in order to prevent "the Leader" from falling, earning a place as part of the intimate coterie of advisers surrounding the dictator. But Ha'el 'Ali Hassan has an ulterior motive for marrying Fathi's mother, which is to bring Fathi back inside the ideological fold and convince him to return to writing and do so in the service of the regime. Moreover, this metanarrative of intellectual cooptation by the regime—the literal union of the regime man with his mother—is reinforced further by the parallel story of Fathi seeking to reclaim his ID, his very physical identity, from the *mukhabarat*. Amid the clamorous noise all around him in the city on this demonstration day, and throughout the persistent uncertainty surrounding his life, Fathi must determine both the practical matter of how best to recover his ID—again, in perhaps a relatively simplistic reference to how personal identities are stolen by the regime—and the thornier existential matter of whether it would be better for him to collaborate or resist, compounded by the emotional strain of what to do about his mother's prospective relationship with Mr. Ha'el.

The silence and the roar named in the title index Fathi's extreme sensitivity to sound. The roar (*sakhab*) schematically stands in for the incoherent blathering of an authoritarian regime with little to no credibility in the eyes of its citizenry. Indeed, some of the novel's most beautiful passages relate how Fathi conceives of sound itself: both its deeply personal experience but also its potentially political nature. "I wished that all the man-made sounds would fall silent, leaving only the soft sounds of nature, like those made by the breeze when it blows through trees with hardy dusty leaves" (156). In the end, the dialectic between silence and roar comes to represent the binary logic through which the regime frames the world. Silence becomes a politicized habit, as Lama reminds Fathi in one of their discussions regarding the ethics of his option to write on behalf of the regime. Fathi manages to carve out the space to valorize silence as a virtue. Moreover, Fathi resents the fact that Ha'el 'Ali Hassan has forced him to choose between "the silence of prison" and the "roar of the regime"; in response he is admonished to be careful, lest he find himself confronted with "the silence of the grave." In the end, Fathi subverts this false choice between the silence and the roar by embracing (and perhaps unwittingly making a fetish out of) laughter.

Irony and other forms of humorous discourse are just some of the narrative techniques available to critics and opponents of autocratic regimes, and Fawwaz Haddad and Nihad Sirees use different kinds of humor in order to poke fun at "the Party." In *The Treasonous Translator*, Hamid

Saleem is convinced that the well-known writer Sharif Husni is plotting both real and rhetorical attacks against him. While trying to come up with a strategy in order to defend himself, Hamid runs into a journalist who writes about economics at the paper where Husni works; he tells him how Husni is responsible for having sent other people to jail and that the same fate could very well await him:

> "Is [Husni] the one who sent him there?"
> "Who else? He wrote a report to the *mukhabarat* in which he accused him of writing stories filled with anti-government and anti-Party references. Tell me, who would dare to ask about this, the Writer's Union, his friends, his family?!"
> "The Party wouldn't allow that to happen."
> "What do you know about what the Party would or wouldn't allow?"
> "Don't tell me Party members don't read."
> "The Party is mad about poetry, at certain times, on nationalist occasions. But they don't like literature, and if they read it, it's only in order to ban it." (41)

Beyond this jab at the arbitrariness of the Party and its censorship regime, this critique of the ideological uses of poetry strongly resonates with several moments in *Silence*. In one early instance of foreshadowing, Fathi muses about the relationship between poetry and prose:

> . . . [W]e are a people that loves poetry, to the point that we love anything that even resembles poetry. We might even be satisfied with some occasionally rhyming speech, regardless of its content. . . . Prose is oriented toward rational minds and individuals whereas poetry is directed at and directs the masses. . . . Poetry inspires zealotry and melts away individual personality whereas prose molds the rational mind and individuality and personality. . . . As for my works and prose writings, they are the imaginings of a traitor and a motherfucker, as the man in khaki was kind enough to remind me a little while ago (17).

Interestingly, these authors ascribe similar political and cultural valences to the distinction between prose and poetry, essentially valorizing the former over the latter as one means of underlining the intellectual and moral bankruptcy of the regime. Rather than portraying poetry as the cultural patrimony of the Syrian citizenry, the Arab nation or the Muslim *umma*, both Haddad and Sirees take an ironic stance toward its production and circulation.

This point about the mechanics of poetry turns farcical when an entire institutional apparatus is literally "discovered" beneath the party headquarters. In an industrious underground hive, cultural workers slave away at sloganeering for the commemoration and reinforcement of party authority, hegemony and legitimation. One of them expresses hope that Fathi will join them, but Fathi prefers to stay out of the limelight, observing the world around him and, in the process, opening a window onto some of the more absurd dimensions of these fictionalized Syrian landscapes. In their conversation, Fathi asks:

> "But, I mean, who comes up with the sayings and the slogans that you put on the posters?"
>
> Pointing toward another room, he said:
>
> "There's a special team whose members are specialists in psychology and education. Comrades, intellectuals and poets who work twelve hours a day coming up with slogans or writing poetry for the masses to recite at marches that are then printed on posters or published in the media and online."
>
> "That is very special work."
>
> "Indeed, it's tremendous educational and emotional labor as well, because the matter involves affection, that is, affection the masses have for the Leader. It's never easy work. . . . The best poems and slogans are those that somebody can remember after only hearing once."
>
> "It's an important consideration for choosing slogans." (148–49)

Fathi feigns indifference at the sight of this literalization of an entity he had actually theorized about earlier, and his deadpan response is one way in which political criticism can be staged through humor. Such representations of the banality of poetry may be read as critique of "traditional" forms of Arabic culture, but also of the cynical packaging and reinvention of the "traditional" by the progressive, secular Ba'thist regime.

Laughter is portrayed as an effective weapon of resistance. "We would take revenge on our situation through laughter," Fathi declares, before equivocating "[B]ut laughter is accursed chattering that only exposes us and gets us into uncomfortable situations" (78). After a party cadre asks for a moment of silence at a mourning session held in honor of a recently deceased intellectual who was a friend of Fathi and Lama, it soon emerges that this functionary has consecrated this moment to the recently deceased father of the leader. Lama is unable to prevent herself from exploding in laughter. Here Lama is clearly laughing at the absurdity of an out-of-touch regime. At another point, after Fathi is temporarily thrown into solitary confinement underneath the party headquarters for failing to accede to demands that he return to work for the regime, what might be described as "laughter out of place" apparently subverts the force of authoritarian repression.

> This was the first time I had even been imprisoned. I hadn't even been reprimanded once during my military service. I measured the length and width of the cell by my steps to calculate that it was three by six steps. Then I sat down against the wall, taking pleasure in the quiet and replacing the bandage around my wrist . . . I tried to figure out whether I was truly happy there or had deceived myself into believing I was. Coming to the conclusion that I was really quite comfortable, I laughed out loud, because the tranquility had calmed me and I didn't regret anything (168).

This is a far cry from the impassive or defiant prison literature so common in late twentieth-century Arabic prose writing. In a somewhat anticlimactic conclusion, Fathi recovers his ID card and unceremoniously leaves the building.

Silence concludes with Lama and Fathi falling asleep together at the end of his very long day. The final scene takes place in a dreamscape, where Lama and Fathi watch Mr. Ha'el and Fathi's mother locked in a violent struggle, but their only response to this brutality is to collapse on the bed laughing. More space would be necessary in order to adequately chart the ethical implications and political effects of making a joke of authoritarian rule and its attendant violence. Nevertheless, by transforming the juggernaut of Syrian authoritarianism into humorous spectacles, Sirees endows his characters with some measure of control over that infernal scenery. The strategic deployment of laughter subverts the false choice between silence and the roar. "To this day, whenever we're together," Fathi says of his relationship with Lama, "we still laugh whenever the Party is mentioned" (76).

The Content and the Form of Syrian Politics

"The freedom of writers of fiction in the Arab world to write and publish their creative output," the literary critic and translator Roger Allen noted, "is restricted in varying degrees and by a number of methods, both overt and covert."[22] Although he devotes only a small amount of attention to Syrian writers—most notably, Nabil Sulayman—in his essay on freedom and modern Arabic literature, Allen touches upon themes that suffuse their lives and work. "When one recalls that what may be termed the 'art' of contemporary politics increasingly involves the creation and manipulation of public perceptions through carefully crafted images and scenarios," Allen continues, "it follows that those societies which believe themselves empowered to co-opt fiction to the cause of fostering and reflecting such visions will clearly find attempts at undercutting their message to be a political threat."[23] The limits of the Syrian literary field continue to be bounded by certain ideological, stylistic, and formal criteria, the definition and determination of which remain at least partially beyond the control of novelists and other writers. Indeed, one may be witnessing a popularization of the political art of perception management, to follow Allen, in shaping the worldview and sentiments of an imagined Syrian readership. Well before the slow-motion collapse of the political order in Syria that began in 2011 (the country has now disintegrated into civil war and international proxy conflicts), as more and more writers took greater liberties in depicting moral and political issues in fiction, the prospects for state co-optation of the literary field grew increasingly dim.

As we have seen, however, an ironic perspective permits political and imaginative acrobatics that might seem implausible in realist fiction. Do these upended representations of authoritarianism in literature actually subvert the power of an autocratic regime in any way, though, or do they inevitably contribute to the reinforcement of state power and ideological consensus? Is there any chance that the truth of the regime, the wizard behind the curtain, might be exposed through such cultural production? By the same token, is it possible that the controlled exercise of the imagination in such bounded terms serves to further insulate the regime from legitimate political criticism in the real world?

In *The Silence and the Roar*, Fathi amasses a surfeit of eyewitness information that brings him to take the regime and its minions less and less seriously. By satirizing the ostensibly all-powerful regime, Sirees's characters acquire power that would be far more difficult to muster in reality. In *Solo Piano Music*, the reader is reminded that security "apparatuses" run the world and control the situation inside Syria. A paucity of reliable information sends Fateh further and further into paralyzing paranoia. One might argue that the plot reinforces Ba'thist rhetoric about how there are dangerous forces in the world—radical Islamists, international security networks, and powerful foreign governments—and that the regime is uniquely positioned and capable (and bold enough) to tackle those challenges. In this reading, it would seem that the regime lies beneath every narrative turn, and that, in the end, the powers that be shall have the last word.

The extent to which Syrian novels might help transcend the tensions between authoritarian culture and political authoritarianism, therefore, will depend upon the complex outcome of myriad and ongoing political, social, and cultural processes and struggles, which are growing increasingly dire and bloody day by day. By 2010, the gradual liberalization of politics and the economy in Syria was beginning to produce noticeable effects in the realm of culture. As opposed to what might be termed the speakeasy situation of late twentieth-century Syria, in which writers, intellectuals, and cultural producers were obliged to speak in code for fear of potentially swift and automatic censorship or more brutal tactics of repression, during the early 2000s "straight talk" gradually became the order of the day in the domain of literature. Widespread corruption at all levels of government, the ruthlessly repressive nature of rule under President Hafiz al-Asad, the ideological and practical bankruptcy of the regime—these were no longer taboo topics in everyday Syrian discourse, even if they remained subject to censorship and control in the approved public sphere.

The bureaucratic *mukhabarat* and the paramilitary *shabbiha* continued to play very real, very terrifying parts in the lives of the Syrian people during the first decade of Bashar al-Asad's presidency. Meanwhile, fictionalized renditions of the *mukhabarat*—both its characterization and caricature, as it were—create at least the potential conditions for critical distancing, objectification, and reimagining of the most ruthless and brutal arm of the state security apparatus. What seemed to persist, however, at least until March 15, 2011, was an almost universal awareness of the fact that direct criticism of President Bashar al-Asad and his family and coterie of advisers, as well as a handful of other issues, remained highly sensitive topics, if not off limits altogether. Nevertheless, one domain that had "become more pluralistic," as political scientist Volker Perthes put it, where Syrians were capable of "debating politics quite freely," was the novel.[24] Indeed, in the fall of 2011, after the "fear barrier" in Syria had fallen so dramatically, it appeared that no topic would remain taboo. Unfortunately, the Syrian people and their supporters have still not found a way to turn this relative freedom to voice their opinions about politics aloud into real and meaningful political gains on the ground.

3

Syria's Drama Outpouring

Between Complicity and Critique

C H R I S T A   S A L A M A N D R A

As antigovernment protests gripped Syria in 2011 and 2012, journalists celebrated a new generation of activist artists and their forms of
creative dissent. The wall of fear that had long curtailed artistic expression
had collapsed; youthful satirists, flooding the Internet with caustic carica-
tures and enlivening public demonstrations with imaginative tactics, were
said to have moved beyond the despair and complaisance of older cultural
producers. This notion of rupture, articulated in the international media
and echoed in scholarly discussions, attributed no role to Syria's artistic
establishment. Such celebrations assumed the "traditional opposition,"
which includes many media makers, had been marginal to the protest
movement. Through omission, media accounts of dissident youth implied
the older generation's impotence.[1]

The Syrian television drama industry, with its draconian state control and multifarious ties to the regime, appeared an unlikely source for
evidence complicating this narrative. While some members of the television industry have risked intimidation, violence, and arrest to join the

Earlier, shorter versions of this chapter appeared in "Prelude to an Uprising: Syrian Fictional Television and Socio-Political Critique," *Jadaliyya*, May 2012, http://www
.jadaliyya.com/pages/index/5578/prelude-to-an-uprising_syrian-fictional-television;
and in "Spotlight on the Bashar al-Asad Era: The Television Drama Outpouring," *Middle
East Critique* 20, no. 2 (2011): 157–67.

protests, many have remained silent. In fact, several high-profile drama figures—actors in particular—publically supported President Bashar al-Asad, lending credence to views of the industry as a veritable propaganda arm of the ruling elite. I argue that despite their limited autonomy, Syrian drama creators active during the young president's first decade in power developed a dark aesthetic that equipped antiregime activists with a visual language of critique.

Spotlights and Limelights

The fraught cultural politics of Syria's uprising offer media figures no neutral ground. Those who have supported, even faintly, the protestors' calls for reform have been harassed by al-Asad loyalists. Those demanding the regime's demise have faced stronger forms of intimidation, including assault and incarceration. Many have fled into exile. Those backing the regime encountered an Internet defamation campaign, ending up on a Facebook "Wall of Shame." It is unsurprising that television industry figures face pressure from all sides, given their growing prominence in Syria and beyond. Over the 2000s, serial dramas and comedies (*musalsalat*, sing. *musalsal*) produced in Syria have come to dominate Arabic language entertainment programming.[2] In many ways, the story of Syria's "*fawra dramiyya*," television drama outpouring, is the story of the Bashar al-Asad era, with all its complexities and contradictions.

Through dark comedy and social realism, television drama creators worked within state structures to push the boundaries of permissible expression. Their efforts paralleled those of intellectuals and others who rode the peaks and troughs of this hopeful decade. Like many in the state-tolerated opposition, television creators navigated a perilous ideological landscape, a cultural field mined with potential for castigation, co-optation, and complicity. One program serves as an apt bellwether for this late Ba'thist moment. *Spotlight* (*Buq'at daw'*), a satirical sketch series aired during Bashar al-Asad's first years, seemed to herald a new openness.[3] In 2001, SAPI (*Suriya al-duwaliyya*), a private production company owned by a member of parliament with strong links to the regime, commissioned two of Syria's leading young comics to come up with a new show.

Ayman Rida and Basim Yakhur enlisted newcomer Laith Hajjo to direct the series. The three held a brainstorming session at the newly opened Beit Jabri restaurant in Old Damascus. In Hajjo's account of the meeting, the producer gave the team a wide and vague brief: "I asked Ayman and Basim 'What are we doing?' and they said, Gosh [wallah] we don't know. So I said, 'What sort of thing have you gotten me into?'"[4] The format they ultimately devised differed from older comic Yasir al-'Azma's Maraya (Mirrors), a lighter-hearted, yet incisive, star-centered sketch program. Spotlight emerged as an ensemble work that daringly lampooned sectarianism, regionalism, Islamic revivalism, state corruption, and even the dreaded intelligence services (mukhabarat). Spotlight lent a fresh, satirical edge and technical sophistication to social and political critique. Drawing on critical cultural forms from the 1970s and 1980s—notably the work of Durayd Lahham and the Thorn Theater collective—Spotlight continued a tradition of comedic critique for a new generation of viewers and creators. The series' creators justified their risk-taking with the president's 2000 inaugural address, which called for a new era of transparency and a campaign against corruption. Hajjo notes, "The producer didn't really know what we were up to. We kept telling the censors that, look, the president said X, so we're following that policy."[5]

Reference to this first speech was no mere opportunistic strategy. Drama creators projected their hopes for change onto the persona of the new president. Like other reform-minded elites, they believed transformation would occur gradually (bi al-tadrij), and Bashar al-Asad appeared likely to implement it. With his Western education and British-born wife, the new leader seemed the consummate modernizer, poised to dismantle the militarized, kleptocratic police state that had grown over nearly four decades of Ba'th Party rule. He introduced a discourse of reform that industry people hoped would translate into practice. The president, in turn, took pride in the drama industry, purportedly boasting that foreign leaders commended him for airing the critical Maraya (Mirrors) on state television.[6] The warm relationship the new leader forged with actors and directors, and his willingness to overrule censorship committees on their behalf, convinced many of reform's imminence. Tales of the president's personal interventions abounded, particularly his reported intercessions on behalf of the groundbreaking *Spotlight*. Television creators distinguished between Bashar al-Asad the reformer and the ossified security apparatus standing in his way. For instance, Laith Hajjo sees the president as the champion of *Spotlight* in the face of criticism that had presumably issued from conservative elements of the regime:

> . . . In my meeting with the president, I discovered that really, he had a lot of problems. The president said, "I get telephone calls about what you all are doing." The decision to allow us to speak came directly from him. There were a lot of complaints, and really if the president himself had not made the decision that we should be free, we wouldn't have been able to continue.[7]

To drama creators, Bashar al-Asad appeared a natural ally in battles against interference from the security apparatus. Many industry people dismissed the regime's 2001 suppression of the Damascus Spring, the brief flowering reformist discussion that marked al-Asad's first months in office, as a temporary revisitation of the old system. They remained optimistic that the young president would eventually launch the transformation he had promised. Some retained that hope even when the country's armed forces turned their weapons on peacefully protesting citizens. But others grew disillusioned with the continued restrictions on freedom of expression and the persistence of corruption. A number of television creators, including the *Spotlight* team, began to criticize the economic liberalization process, one that Hafiz al-Asad initiated and Bashar al-Asad accelerated, which transformed their industry and rendered life miserable for millions of Syrian workers.

As the decade unfolded, *Spotlight* peaked and fizzled, much like the reform project it sprang from and satirized. Artistic infighting among the production team, accusations of co-optation within and outside the industry, and mushrooming competition from newer comedy series pushed the *Spotlight* from center stage in Syrian public culture. Some drama makers and critics claimed it had lost its critical edge, particularly after the conflict began and the regime struggled to control the uprising's narrative.[8]

Yet *Spotlight* and programs like it undoubtedly helped to broaden public debate and blur the boundaries of taboo. Critical remarks that would once have been unlikely to occur either in public forums or private conversations began proliferating in discussions of television programs. "Just like on *Spotlight*" became a catchphrase denoting the everyday absurd, and references to the series appeared in the uprising's creative dissidence. Worsening economic conditions and enduring authoritarianism had thrown into relief the emptiness of the regime's reformist rhetoric and the persistence of a police state, providing fodder for biting satire. Other episodes lampooned state officials and security agents. Some mocked the growth of Islamism despite the state's avowed secularism. Many pointed to the contradiction of broadening class divisions in a nominally socialist system, pushing the parameters of the possible. Ultimately, by challenging the limits of expression, the series revealed the deceitfulness of state rhetoric. As Laith Hajjo puts it: "The director of [state] television himself was changed, because he agreed to air *Spotlight*. That was a real action, because it confirmed that in the end, censors are unable to be open or free. When a director is fired because he agrees to air certain sketches, this shows that we've hit our boundaries. We've discovered that this freedom they're talking about doesn't exist."[9]

From Employees to Stars

With innovative works like *Spotlight* in their growing repertoire, Syrian drama creators find themselves at the forefront of a pan-Arab satellite industry with a global reach. Variety channels such as the Saudi-owned and Dubai-based MBC (Middle East Broadcast Center) and Dubai TV and Abu Dhabi's Infinity offer Arab viewers a wide range of entertainment formats, from game shows and situation comedies to reality programs and music videos, but the *musalsal* stands out among them. Across the Arab world and beyond, millions of viewers follow Syrian series as they had once tuned into Egyptian productions.[10] The industry has survived wartime conditions: since the beginning of the uprising, production continued at roughly half the preconflict average of forty-five dramas per Ramadan broadcast season. Through coproductions with Lebanon, Egypt, and the Emirates, drama circumvented both the Gulf station boycotts and economic sanctions placed on key producers. Many creators also escaped the war itself: since 2012, most series have been filmed outside Syria.

The industry's endurance amid the conflict reflects its broad market base. The creators of *Spotlight* and other new programs have benefitted from an expanded, well-financed media landscape that imposes new conditions and constraints. Television creators' recent fortunes, both economic and symbolic, reflect economic liberalization policies. These reforms, initiated by Hafiz al-Asad in the early 1990s and accelerated by his son Bashar in the 2000s, facilitated private production. They also entailed the regionalization of Arabic-language media, as a rising number of Gulf Cooperation Council–owned, pan-Arab entertainment channels—including several specializing in drama—purchased Syrian series. Since the early 2000s, increased demand and foreign financing have thus transformed the television production sector from a handful of socially marginal and financially modest state-owned interests staffed by professionals to an industry of private production companies hiring contract labor.

While ensemble casts have remained the norm in Syrian series, distinctions between creative and technical workers have widened. A transnational industry of fan literature, in print and on the Internet, has also enhanced the fame and social legitimacy of those at the top.[11] Leading Syrian actors have become regional celebrities, fêted in Arab capitals and mobbed by fans. Several have worked in Egyptian productions, one playing the lead in a King Faruq biopic. They commonly refer to themselves as *nujum* (stars). Those employed behind the scenes—writers, directors, and visual artists—earn a living that is sufficient to finance their more "serious" creative endeavors. Benefiting from sluggish book, film, art, and theater markets, the industry has harnessed the country's finest creative talent.

For those lower down in the production hierarchy, the benefits of the drama outpouring have been uneven. Flexible labor conditions have rendered struggling actors, technicians, and other "below the line" workers especially vulnerable.[12] Hours are unregulated, insurance is nonexistent, and contracts can be cancelled on a whim.[13] Despite its regional prominence, the Syrian industry has developed little infrastructure. Some television creators see the term "industry" (*sina'a*) as a misnomer; drama production, they argue, is a mere "activity" (*nashat*) that could vanish in the wake of the slightest economic downturn. Screenwriter Najib Nusair invokes the black garbage bags Syrian producers use to distribute funding as a symbol of this precariousness:

> They take a garbage bag, put money in it, and distribute it to the scenarist, the actors, equipment rental, and that's it; nothing else. Practically all Syrian drama now is financed from the Gulf, and it is rudimentary, it's not like there are big, complex companies with capital and stocks. Bank notes come in a black bag and get distributed. And this is related to infrastructure. The infrastructure we have amounts to a camera and editing machine. This is all we have. And you have seen, you went to the filming locations, and these are real sites they rent from the black bag, natural places: cafes, houses, hospitals . . . it's built on relations not of industry, but of simple commerce. There are no advertising companies interfering, it's a sector on its own, separate. The production companies are just investments: you buy *musalsalat* the same way you buy Nescafe . . . this year there were thirty-eight Syrian series; next year there might be zero. So there is nothing you could call an infrastructure, nothing. There's the garbage bag, what we call the black bag, what they put money in, and make drama.[14]

Yet this apparent instability has also facilitated mobility, and may, along with the move toward coproduction, have enabled drama production's survival during the conflict. While Syrian state censorship persists, public-sector involvement in production has shrunk, despite a recent restructuring effort aimed at harnessing private-sector involvement.[15] Gulf Cooperation Council (GCC) satellite networks now finance or purchase most dramas and receive exclusive Ramadan broadcast rights in return.[16] In this competitive environment, Syrian drama creators lack their rivals' advantages. Egypt's state protectionism spares its TV makers the vagaries of the pan-Arab market by limiting the number of non-Egyptian *musalsalat* government-owned stations that may air. Egyptian producers also market packages of Egyptian series to GCC networks. The Syrian industry has enjoyed few such favors, despite annual, highly publicized meetings between President Bashar al-Asad and key drama creators as well as periodic assurances of his personal support. Yet its need for commercial protection is greater. With only a single recently launched private satellite station, Syria has no national drama market comparable to Egypt's array of channels. Syrian producers argue that this lack of state involvement exposes them to the notorious caprice of Gulf business practice.[17]

Drama creators take pride in what they achieve with so few resources and with the additional burdens of ideological, financial, and now wartime constraints. Many express a passion for the *musalsal* and its potential. Those in creative positions see themselves as artists first but remain committed to a left-leaning notion of progress. They foreground issues difficult to broach in nonfiction media, hoping to spark discussion and, ultimately, social and political transformation. But as they are keenly aware, they operate in commercial conditions not of their own choosing. The spread of satellite access has generated vast audiences and increased financing. Yet the burgeoning regional market threatens to co-opt social critique and derail reformist impulses as socially committed works make up an increasingly smaller percentage of an ever-broadening program flow.

The Syrian regime maintains control over content. Drama makers' perceptions of censorship interference fluctuate from year to year and project to project. The script of every series filmed in Syria must be approved; those aired on Syrian stations must also subject their finished production to additional censorship, a stage that those broadcast only on pan-Arab networks avoid. Wartime strategies of filming outside the country evade regime control entirely. Yet many industry figures point to a social censorship all productions face, a growing religiously based conservatism, which endures as GCC networks—largely Saudi and Emirati—now dominate pan-Arab television.[18] Discernible thematic shifts have emerged, notably a subtle religiosity at odds with the largely secular and socially progressive orientation of many Syrian media makers. Some Syrian television drama creators have responded to the Islamizing current by inflecting their works with religion, a move others in the industry deride as pandering to "prevailing values in the societies of the oil states."[19] Thrillers depicting militant Islam, historical epics of Islamic Empire, and folkloric evocations of Old Damascus attract large-scale funding and international media attention. These programs rarely challenge political or religious authority directly.

Yet embedded progressive messages, and potential alternative readings, sometimes complicate their conservative nostalgia.[20] They provoke lively public discussion over historical issues and events that are never relegated to the past. Representations of history, and debates about them, become critiques of the present.

Enduring Commitment

Syrian drama has oscillated between accommodating and challenging persistent authoritarianism, the Islamic tendency, and the neoliberal moment.[21] In addition to sensational thrillers and costume dramas, Syrians continue to produce works that harken back to an earlier era of Arab cultural production. Realist dramas join sociopolitical satires in critiquing social and economic conditions, with an underlying ideology of enlightenment (*tanwir*). They reflect an enduring secular, socialist tradition that lives on in Syrian cultural production despite the current regime's abandonment of these values, and within market preferences for big-budget historical blockbusters.

Much of Syrian social drama is best described as social realism, although it also incorporates melodramatic elements. Broadly, realism involves a commitment to representing everyday life as it is. Melodrama also depicts the real but moves beyond it to evoke a moral universe: as Peter Brooks has famously argued, melodrama is an imaginative mode originating in nineteenth-century Europe, involving a "polarization and hyper-dramatization of forces in conflict," that makes legible a shared moral code for a secular era.[22] Lila Abu-Lughod has discussed Egyptian *musalsalat* of the presatellite era as melodramas,[23] and my reading of Syrian social dramas as realist highlights the differences between the two national styles. This is not an absolute dichotomy. Realism and melodrama are more closely related than is often acknowledged, particularly by those maintaining an elitist view of melodrama as vulgar sentimentality. Peter Brooks has demonstrated their potential synthesis by exposing the melodramatic threads of elite nineteenth-century realist literature. Conversely, Christine Gledhill emphasizes the realist underpinnings of the television soap opera, a genre typically associated with melodrama.[24]

Syrian social dramas uphold key tenets of Ba'thist ideology; they also subvert it by depicting the failure of state practice. In her study of dissident high culture in Syria, miriam cooke argues that oppositional artists use state pronouncements as critique.[25] They play on the distance between rhetoric and reality, illustrating the hollowness of regime slogans. However prosaic they may be, television dramas do this as well, even while operating within official structures. Television creators remind us of Syria's role as the birthplace and "beating heart of Arab nationalism" (*qalb al-'uruba al-nabid*), and many cling to Arab socialist ideals. The senior generation, including esteemed directors Haytham Haqqi, 'Ala al-Din Kawkash, and Ghassan Jabri, studied in the former Soviet Union or Eastern Bloc nations and passed on a social realist aesthetic to their young apprentices, who have transformed it with fast-paced, slick camera work and higher production values. The form is considerably updated; the social concern remains central.

Conditions of production also promote the persistence of the real. Standard realist techniques, such as on-location filming, are adopted by default in the absence of studios. Cinematic techniques, such as the use of a single camera, afford greater depth of image. Recognizable places, with passersby as extras, lend a gritty texture that distinguishes Syrian works from their studio-based Egyptian counterparts. These elements of form are matched by content. In place of melodrama's Manichean ethical universe, Syrian social drama offers deep moral ambiguity. It reflects the dilemmas facing those who live amid authoritarian repression, rigid class hierarchy, and entrenched patriarchy. Similarly, thematic choices echo longstanding concerns of visual realism. A range of social problems are regularly treated, including gender inequality, generational conflict, class struggle, regional tensions, emigration, mental illness, child abuse, and domestic violence. With their distinctive dark aesthetic, Syrian dramas typically end unhappily and lack resolution. Realism has long been criticized for the ultimate conservatism of its vision.[26] Syrian drama articulates a degraded present but offers no redemptive future.

Syrian social drama shares sociopolitical satire's dark sensibility. The work of *Spotlight* director Laith Hajjo, former apprentice to the Soviet-trained Haytham Haqqi, exemplifies this link. Hajjo's hard-hitting drama debut *Behind Bars* (*Khalf al-qudban*) traced in parallel storylines the misfortunes of characters sharing a prison cell. Aired on the Emirati channel Infinity during Ramadan 2005, the work featured negative depictions of Islamic piety and scenes of prostitution, rape, and masturbation.[27] *Behind Bars'* reformist impulse was legible in depictions of official abuse, including the imprisonment of rape victims to prevent so-called honor killings.

Hajjo's deft hand with social issues reemerged the following year with the series *Waiting* (*al-Intizar*). A story of ordinary people struggling to escape urban poverty, *Waiting* was filmed in Dwaila'a, an impoverished neighborhood of the outskirts of Damascus. The use of informal settlements like Dwaila'a to evoke marginality—real and metaphoric—is a longstanding visual realist convention.[28] Long before they erupted in antiregime sentiment, these nether regions, which slipped so easily from middle-class consciousness given the veneer of neoliberal prosperity, were featured in drama series. While Syrian cities' poorest neighborhoods never match the destitution of Cairo, Rio de Janeiro, or Mumbai, urban blight has prevailed. The United Nations estimated that 40 percent of prewar Damascus dwellers, and over one-third of the total urban population in the Arab world—57 million people—live in informal settlements, or "haphazard neighborhoods" (*al-harat al-'ashwa'iyya*) as they are referenced in Arabic.[29] *Waiting* was among the first drama series set primarily within such a region.[30]

The writers of *Waiting*, journalist Najib Nusair and novelist Hassan Sami Yusuf, are Syria's highest-paid screenwriters; they have earned a reputation for artistic depth, and they share a fascination with Damascus's informal neighborhoods. Their screenplay traces the life paths of characters who come to Dwaila'a through various misfortunes. Noble thief 'Abbud and struggling journalist Wa'il are both born to the *hara*, the neighborhood, and inured to its ills. Characters are locked into a frustrating limbo, dire circumstances consigning them to—in Wa'il's words—an endless waiting list. For most *ahl al-hara* (neighborhood folk), especially those worst off at the start of the series, *Waiting* ends in everyday tragedy: jobs are lost, engagements fall apart, and a recovering addict relapses.

Those from outside, like Wa'il's schoolteacher wife, Samira, seethe with desperation. Wa'il waxes romantic about the neighborhood's goodness and humanity; Samira rails against its dirt and danger, a position the series producers underscore in the series' dramatic turning point. While playing soccer in the neighborhood's only available clearing—a rubble-strewn lot at the edge of a busy highway—the couple's youngest son is struck by a minivan and blinded.

Since *Waiting*'s broadcast "'*ashwa'i*" (haphazard neighborhood) series have become an established subgenre. Numerous evocations of urban blight, set in areas now stricken with antiregime ferment and regime repression, followed on its heels, notably Marwan Barakat's *Summer Cloud* (*Sahabat saif*, 2009), which dealt with the plight of Iraqi and Palestinian refugees, child sexual abuse, and cybercrime; Samir Hussain's *City Dregs* (*Qaʻ al-madina*, 2009), which begins and ends with floods devastating already desperate lives; Samer Barqawi's *After the Fall* (*Baʻd al-suqut*, 2010), depicting efforts to rescue tenants caught in the rubble of a collapsed building; Muthanna Subh's *Medium Sugar* (*Sukkur wasat*) of 2013 and set in 2010, which posits the haphazard neighborhood and its pathologies as precursors to the uprising; and *Tomorrow We'll Meet* (*Ghadan naltaqi*, 2015), in which the settlement becomes a refugee neighborhood in Beirut.

Filling in the Blanks

Waiting's somber mood and dark critique recalls Hajjo's earlier works, principally *Spotlight* and the series of brief vignettes entitled *No Hope* (*Amal ma fi*). Aired on Syria's state-owned satellite television station in 2004, *No Hope* presents a Beckettian dialogue between two armchair intellectuals played by eminent actors Fayiz Qazaq and Bassam Kusa. Shabbily dressed, sipping tea across a rickety tray in a dimly lit shack, the two expound on a different topic each episode in a tone of existentialist gloom. Opening graphics begin tracing the word "hope," then add its negation as the theme song croons, "It won't work out for you, no one listens to you, perhaps there's no hope." In one memorable episode, "Democracy," Kusa's character pontificates on respecting others' opinions, but doesn't allow Qazaq to complete a sentence. In another, "The Revolution," when Qazaq asks what distracts him, Kusa responds "the revolution that hasn't happened yet," and the problem of who will lead it. "Maybe he's among us in some unknown corner, or a child in school," Kusa ponders. "Maybe he hasn't even been born yet." "That's it!" Qazaq exclaims, "that's the most likely scenario." In "Applause," Kusa tells Qazaq he has been busy clapping, by himself and for no reason, just for practice. Qazaq tells him people have no reason or desire to clap, but Kusa begs to differ: "You say this now, but when push comes to shove, everyone will clap." He begins clapping loudly, and is soon joined by a chorus of applause timed to the martial strains of Strauss's Radetzky March. Syrians in earshot join in a surge of praise for an unseen regime spectacle; failure to do so carries consequences.

Syrian intellectuals, especially those involved in "higher," more autonomous fields of artistic endeavor, often dismiss the type of critique conveyed in *Spotlight*, *Waiting*, and *No Hope* as a safety valve mechanism, offering repressed subjects an opportunity to vent (*tanfis*). In their functionalist reading, seemingly transgressive programs like *Spotlight* work to perpetuate the status quo by siphoning off and defusing dissent, and lend the regime an appearance of openness that foreign dignitaries applaud. They also convey an impression that the leadership is aware of social and political problems and engaged in addressing them, so no real change need follow. Scholars have analyzed versions of the *tanfis* argument. Lisa Wedeen points to both conservative and transgressive potential television comedy that she sees as open to multiple readings.[31] She concludes that the ambiguous works that some dismiss as regime manipulation are the result not simply of state policy, but of artistic struggle over political messages conveyed in popular culture.[32] Rebecca Joubin emphasizes the transgressive qualities of drama, arguing that creators regularly employ domestic relations as allegories of the nation, which serve as subtle yet powerful political critique.[33]

Other scholarly interpretations slightly echo the *tanfis* theory, placing the regime in near complete control of meaning-making. For example, miriam cooke argues that the Syrian state pressures the nation's leading artists to censure the system in what she refers to as "commissioned criticism." Ambiguous censorship ensures that artists—and their audiences—never know if they are truly dissenting or doing the regime's bidding.[34] Donatella Della Ratta (chapter 4 in this volume) stresses the convergence of interests and personal relationships among television creators and the regime. Through a "whisper strategy," factions of the leadership and security apparatus vie to convey messages in a tightly controlled national media landscape through subtle interactions with drama makers who are themselves invested in the status quo. Negotiations among drama creators and regime representatives ensure ideological alignment rather than subversive critique.

These studies focus on the persistence of authoritarianism through state control of cultural production. If these scholarly versions of the *tanfis* theory accurately represent regime intent, the safety valve strategy has backfired. Now firmly entrenched in the state-sanctioned artistic establishment, few of the *Spotlight* team have joined the protest movement, and one has openly supported the regime. Yet the uprising's explosion of satirical dissidence draws, sometimes vaguely, often explicitly, on the innovative works aired during the 2000s on Syrian state television. Send-ups posted on the Internet, such as the puppet show *Top-Goon: Diaries of a Little Dictator*, target the president and his inner circle, stomping over a red line that established cultural producers never dared approach. Such works reinvigorate a comedic form bearing a long history of struggle. Their creators move well beyond the boundaries their predecessors fought to extend.

One *Spotlight* character particularly resonates: Homsi comedian Ahmad al-Ahmad's "Spray Can Man" (*al-Rajul al-bakhakh*). The opening graphic features a ticking bomb. In the first scene, the camera pans a dilapidated hovel adorned with photographs and medals commemorating the character's athletic glory days. The hero opens his front door to find bags of trash left by a neighbor from the surrounding—and much nicer—apartment buildings. Unable to identify the culprit, he buys a can of black spray paint and writes "don't throw trash here" on his outside wall. Inspired, he carries the can with him, and, upon finding a nearby trash bin overflowing, sprays "cleanliness is civilization," reworking a regime slogan. He returns to buy another can, finds the price has risen suspiciously, and leaves "this grocer is a cheat" outside the shop. On a roll, he masks his face with a *kufiyya*, and against a *Star Wars* musical backdrop, vents his frustrations on high-rises and government buildings. He twists the proverb "patience is the key to remedy" into "patience is the key to poverty." Spray Can Man becomes a folk hero and heartthrob who taunts the bumbling security agents assigned to capture him. Newspaper headlines pronounce: "The Spray Can Man and the Contemporary Condition." When the hero plasters "get off our backs" (*hillu 'anna*) on what looks like an intelligence services headquarters, an exasperated official tries a new tactic: a television appeal addressing the graffitist as a citizen who has merely expressed a shared angst but cannot change the country with a spray can. He invites Spray Can Man in for a "civilized, democratic dialogue." The hero turns himself in, but instead of a platform to address the nation, he is given a whitewashed prison cell and dozens of spray paint cans. While Spray Can Man languishes in jail, another gadfly writes "to be continued" (*lissa*) in the sky with a jet pack.

The sketch plays on the regime's manipulation of reformist language, exposing it as doublespeak. It invokes the system's co-optation of dissent through the pretense of cooperation and the control of cultural production. Like other promised reforms, the lifting or easing of censorship never materialized. Artists of the Bashar al-Asad era have expressed themselves from behind metaphoric bars.

Protestors modeling themselves on Spray Can Man emerged in numerous Syrian cities during the uprising.[35] The Dubai-based oppositional Orient TV aired a news story on the phenomenon, interspersing Ahmed al-Ahmad's *Spotlight* antics with footage of real-life graffitists. One such agitator was killed after "causing *shabbiha* (regime thugs) and security men in Homs a headache for weeks" by writing antiregime sentiments on "sensitive" buildings. Another spray can graffitist disappeared in Damascus "under mysterious circumstances."[36] Even for the established artists of state-controlled media, metaphoric bars may become real: Spray Can Man's creator, actor and screenwriter 'Adnan Zira'i, was arrested outside his Damascus home in late February 2012. In April 2013, his wife was taken into custody apparently after enquiring about her husband's fate. Officials purportedly argued that Zira'i's *Spotlight* sketches incited rebellion.[37] Reports of his incarceration, and Facebook calls for his release, celebrated the influence of his famous character on activists of the uprising.[38] If antiregime messages conveyed in state-controlled works like *Spotlight* and *No Hope* were strategically ambiguous, autonomous dissidents now render them explicit. The day after Bashar al-Asad's March 2011 speech to parliament, anonymous activists operating as *Shamrevolution* posted on YouTube a remix of *No Hope*'s clapping episode. The new version interspersed the Qazaq-Kusa dialogue with scenes of cheering crowds and parliamentarians' obsequious applause, replaying the ominous line "When push comes to shove everyone will clap."

The youth collective "With You" (Ma'kum) has produced a send-up of and homage to *No Hope* entitled *Freedom and Nothing But* (*Hurriya wa bas*), featuring Nasser Habbal and Saleem al-Homsi. Aired on two oppositional stations, Orient TV in Ramadan 2011 and al Aan TV in 2012, these vignettes have a strong YouTube and Facebook presence. The series title reworks the regime mantra "God, Syria, Bashar and Nothing But" (*Allah, Suriya, Bashar wa bas*). The opening graphics of *Freedom* begin with the word "freedom," (*hurriya*) then add "and nothing but" (*wa bas*). Young activist actors adopt *No Hope*'s scruffy mise-en-scène, transforming somber resignation into revolutionary fervor. Two disheveled youths replace the older actors' curmudgeons, and the table moves outdoors to a junkyard.[39] Episode seven, "Puppet Theater" (Masrah al-'ara'is), evokes both the *No Hope* clapping sketch and the president's address. One character, holding a newspaper, reels off a list of disasters: an earthquake in Japan, a hurricane in Mexico, and a friend's death, as his companion punctuates each item with applause. Exasperated, the reader cries, "What's wrong with you, have you no feelings, no conscience?" "No, it's not that," the clapper replies, "I'm thinking of running for parliament."

While embracing the format of *No Hope*, the *With You* team's expatriate activists distance themselves from its makers. The Hajjo work, they argue, "only skimmed the surface of Syrian issues."[40] Episode one of the new work begins with a declaration: "Freedom is coming, despite some artists' hesitation."[41] The members of *With You* were pointing to the bitter irony that those who ridiculed the establishment now upheld it: a number of prominent television creators either failed to join the protest or, in the case of actors—the industry's public face—overtly backed the regime. At the "Spring of Arab Cinema" festival held in Paris in September 2011, a *With You* spokesperson remarked that the team sought to "awaken professional artists in Syria, and tell them if they don't wake up, there are young people to take your place." Veteran drama director Haytham Haqqi took issue, reminding the audience that drama creators were among the first to call for "a democratic, pluralist state with an equal citizenry under a just law."[42]

Conclusion

Among Syria's drama producers, a legacy of social and political concern endures. The modes of televisual critique honed during the Bashar al-Asad era inform and inspire antiregime protesters to new heights of artistic dissent. The debt that programs like *Freedom and Nothing But* owe to the televisual innovations of the 2000s is easy to miss amid celebrations of the uprising's creativity and condemnations of the pro-establishment stance of some high-profile drama makers. Moments of rupture obscure lengthy processes and incremental shifts in critical public and private discourse. Critics have long bemoaned the limitations of Syrian drama, as television treatments of corruption never attacked the upper ranks of the political elite and intransigent authoritarianism suggested the impotence, indeed the regime's manipulation, of critique. Yet as the works of *Shamrevolution* and the *With You* team illustrate, programs of the Bashar al-Asad era succeeded through implication. Avid viewers, some now turned activist cultural producers, filled in the blanks.

Employing a distinctive dark aesthetic, Syrian drama creators have pushed the limits of expression, and they have done so through the very institutions and structures they seek to reform. Despite stringent censorship constraints and despite inhospitable market conditions, programs like *Spotlight*, *Waiting*, and *No Hope* brought critical reflection to the center of Syrian—and Arab—public life. Scholarship on Arab broadcast media often limits its focus to journalism, where the margin for maneuver is considerably narrower and the privileging of event over process obscures a complex history of meaning-making and remaking found in television drama. The Syrian drama industry's legacy of social realism and political satire percolates through the current protests, reflecting the *longue durée* of creative struggle.

4

The "Whisper Strategy"

How Syrian Drama Makers Shape Television Fiction
in the Context of Authoritarianism and Commodification

DONATELLA DELLA RATTA

Introduction

This chapter focuses on the relation that binds some components of the Syrian powers (*sultat*, sing. *sulta*)—namely, the president and his reform-minded collaborators at the Palace (*al-Qasr*)—with television drama makers; it explores the nature of this connection and the strategic needs as they are expressed by both sides.

I argue that these parties engage in an ongoing dialogue aimed at staying connected through feedback loops. I use the metaphor of the "whisper strategy" to hint at the communication mechanism through which the president and Syrian TV drama makers discuss and agree upon issues deemed worthy and suitable to disseminate through media outlets, particularly television serials (*musalsalat*, sing. *musalsal*). My analysis of this communication mechanism and its recurrent features explains how elite political communication and cultural production work in a market-oriented autocracy.[1] It can also help explain how, after several years of a bloody conflict that started with a violent crackdown on protests, Bashar al-Asad has managed to persuade some factions in international diplomacy that a political solution to the crisis could still be brokered, provided that he stays in power.

In the context of the relation between the reform-minded *sultat* and the drama makers, the "whisper" metaphor indicates a noncoercive

53

conversation where priorities are negotiated and common interests established. This metaphor seems particularly appropriate to describe the communication between Syrian drama makers and the Palace. As this chapter will show, media content, particularly *musalsalat*, results from a circulation of suggestions and advices between the abovementioned parties about issues deemed worthy of being discussed in public.

By describing the whisper as a strategy that involves both Syrian drama makers and the Palace but does not identify those who conceived it, I am borrowing Foucault's idea of a "strategy without a subject."[2] The French philosopher speaks of "strategic necessities"[3] that converge to form the objective of the strategy. However, while the latter's objective can be identified, the "subject"[4] cannot, as the real nature of power lies in the relations between heterogeneous elements and in their continuous "interplay of shifts of positions and modifications of functions."[5]

Similarly, in the context of the "whisper," none of those parties who are actively involved in shaping it as strategy can claim ownership of it. Yet their strategic necessities can be clearly identified. On the one hand, there is a need for the Palace to preserve a reformist façade before the Syrian public and other components of the *sultat*. When Bashar al-Asad seized power he declared that reforms and modernization were his "highest priorities."[6] Although the new president's vow to reform clearly proved to be a way to secure loyalty and expand his power base rather than a real commitment, his reformist credentials needed to be safeguarded in public. Seemingly progressive media content resulting from the "whispers" helps reiterate the idea of a young, educated, up-to-date, knowledgeable leader as the only guarantee that the reformist tendency will not disappear from within the Syrian regime's power structure and will always have a chance of being implemented, on condition that the leadership remains unchanged.

On the other hand, Syrian drama makers have to regain centrality in the cultural production process which has, since the early 1990s, shifted in favor of a new class of private producers.[7] This class is mostly made up of entrepreneurs connected to different *sultat* by family, marriage, or kinship ties, or via business affiliations. These producers are businessmen involved in enterprises from real estate to import-export; they seek to maximize their profits both domestically and in the pan-Arab market.[8] They see television production as yet another business investment, one providing the influence and prestige needed to strengthen political connections and pave the way to new and profitable ventures.

On the contrary, Syrian drama makers see their TV work as committed to a project of *tanwir*,[9] that is, an effort to guide Syrian society toward progress through a gradual process engineered and managed by cultural elites. This *tanwiri* commitment is aligned with Bashar al-Asad's vision of political reforms, "settled on a somewhat elitist approach . . . : democracy is premature as long as people are poor or lack education."[10] Such a vision is evident throughout the 2000s in *tanwir*-inspired Syrian *musalsalat*, which had pointed at social evils like corruption, sectarianism, religious intolerance, and extremism as the main justifications for an enlightened minority to rule over an allegedly backward society, to help the latter overcome its own "backwardness";[11] and eventually to achieve political reforms.

Thus, the needs of both president Bashar al-Asad and Syrian drama makers have converged in the whisper strategy. The "discourse" of *tanwir*, the idea of enlightening the society, served to support the vision over reformism—both at a media level and at a political one—jointly backed by drama makers and by Bashar al-Asad's reformist circle at the Palace.[12] *Tanwir* functions as a strategy for maintaining the prestige, prominence, and power of both sides. Yet none of those involved in the strategy can claim ownership or control over it; there is no clear distinction between those who have produced the strategy and those who are reproducing it. Relations between power holders are in fact fluid,[13] and either side can initiate the "whisper."

However, the Syrian regime is not a single homogeneous entity embodied by the president, but an assemblage of different *sultat*—the state and its government apparatus, the different branches of the secret police or *mukhabarat* and religious authorities—that comprises the complex infrastructure of power created by the ruling family in an effort to manage the country in all its aspects. These *sultat* are loosely interconnected, and are also capable of miscommunication or failures to communicate. They might also ignore or refuse communications. The various opportunities for communication and miscommunication suggest that alliances between one *sulta* and another in Syria's power structure are not stable and can shift and recombine.

The "open, more or less coordinated cluster of relations"[14] that describes the nature of power in Foucauldian terms can determine the failure of objectives and priorities set by the whisper strategy. As this chapter will underline by examining different media content, the "whisper" only engages two sides of the Syrian regime: the president and his entourage at the Palace composed of those officially committed to implementing reforms—such as Bouthaina Shaaban, Bashar al-Asad's media and political aide—along with cultural producers; that is, the *tanwiri*-inspired drama makers.[15] Their sotto voce negotiation of priorities in the content of cultural production can accomplish its objectives; yet it can also be hindered or blocked by other components of the Syrian *sultat*.

By analyzing different *musalsalat* produced during the first decade of Bashar al-Asad's rule[16]—from the first season of *Buq'at daw'* (*Spotlight*, 2001) through *Ma malakat aymanukum* (*Those Whom Your Right Hand Possesses*, 2010) to *Chiffon* (2011) and *Fawq al-saqf* (*Above the Ceiling*, 2011)—this chapter will spell out the main features of the communication mechanism of the whisper and reflect on its implications at a political level. I will discuss how this strategy might fail as a result of other powers within the regime interfering in the communication loop between the drama makers and the Palace. However, as I will underscore using the example of *Fawq al-saqf*, a *musalsal* produced during the unfolding of the Syrian uprising, a "whisper" can be also sabotaged by those very subjects, such as the Palace, who have initiated it, in light of their shifting political priorities and security concerns.

I propose the whisper strategy as a useful metaphor to read into the Syrian regime's complex strategy for making and maintaining power by playing with its several components. The "whisper" can help shed light on the complex nexus of *sultat* that make up the Syrian regime and express its ever changing aspirations and priorities. As the chapter will underscore, the president's personal interventions in favor of *tanwiri* drama help distinguish a seemingly enlightened leadership from the rest of the regime, and ideally connect it to a reform-minded tendency as opposed to more security-minded priorities of other *sultat*. The analysis of the selected *musalsalat* will show how, even after the Syrian uprising broke out, this strategy has been employed to emphasize and reiterate the rhetoric connecting Bashar al-Asad's personal leadership to the promise of implementing reforms in the future, provided that Syria's power structure remains unaltered.

The Whisper Strategy and a New Generation of Syrian Drama Makers

This paragraph identifies and reflects upon the main characteristics of the whisper strategy as a communication mechanism binding political and cultural elites, and on its implications in the making of cultural production in contemporary Syria. I argue that the "whisper" happens in public or quasi-public venues; that it reflects an oral dynamic engaging the *sultat* and the cultural producers; that it is multilateral, meaning that it can be initiated and circulated by any side, and not necessarily by the political powers.

The "whisper" is public as it often takes place during public hearings officially organized by the Palace, where Bashar al-Asad reaffirms his commitment to pushing a reformist agenda through the media. Since his rise to power in 2000, the Syrian president has regularly hosted debates with drama makers to discuss the future of the country's cultural production; sometimes in the form of private informal meetings, but mostly in the format of public hearings. Underscoring the president's identification of TV drama as a strategic sector for communicating with domestic audiences and marketing a new image of Syria to the outside world, these meetings have institutionalized the status of Syrian *musalsalat* as a national industry and discussed how to improve its assets.[17] They have also served to reiterate the commitment to a shared *tanwiri* project that should inspire TV drama and make it instrumental in healing "the backwardness of society," as Bashar al-Asad reportedly affirmed during one of these meetings in 2004.[18]

Public hearings with TV drama makers that Bashar al-Asad hosted during his presidency—and even in 2011 after the unrest exploded[19]— have been widely documented by Syrian media. Publicity serves to convey the idea that the country's political leadership and cultural elites are in tune with each other, sharing the same progressive vision in the name of national interest.[20] In fact, these hearings are quasi-public venues where "whispers" are exchanged concerning which politics and policies should find their way into *musalsalat* and be reinjected into the public sphere in the form of narrative fiction.

At times messages that have already been spread by other media outlets are reiterated in different formats, such as *musalsalat*.[21] As Taysir Khalat, an expert in Syrian TV drama and a former journalist at the Sham Press group, has pointed out: "By looking at the written press one can guess what the power (*sulta*) thinks of a certain issue and what it wants to be done. There is no need to give orders, everything happens through a circulation of ideas."[22]

In this way, political messages and slogans such as *mukafahat al-fasad* (the fight against corruption)[23] become stories and characters in Syrian *musalsalat* like *Ghizlan fi ghabat al-dhi'ab* (*Gazelles in a Forest of Wolves*, 2006) or the satirical sketches from the multiseason series *Buq'at daw'* (*Spotlight*, 2001–12).[24]

TV dramas critically dealing with corruption had existed in Syria since Hafiz al-Asad. But never was this topic so emphasized as during Bashar al-Asad's decade, when the president used socially and politically engaged Syrian *musalsalat* as evidence of his openness, transparency, and willingness to reform.[25] Corrupt characters like that portrayed in *Ghizlan*, who bears more than a passing resemblance to Mahmoud al-Zoubi, a former Syrian prime minister accused of corruption; or like the protagonist of *La'nat al-thin* (*The Curse of the Mud*, 2010), who seems to hint at former vice president 'Abdul Halim Khaddam, a "hawk" from Hafiz al-Asad's old guard, are probably the best case studies to illustrate how the *mukafahat al-fasad* campaigns travelled from Bashar al-Asad's public speeches— which always stressed the idea that the leader was personally committed to the issue—to news items, and then reached the narrative universe of the *musalsalat*.[26]

Ghizlan, in particular, deals with corruption at the highest level, featuring a prime minister's delinquent son who eventually succeeds in evading justice and punishment. The inner message of the *musalsal* is only apparently at odds with the regime's rhetoric of fighting corruption: it shows that corruption is naturally intertwined with any form of political system even at a high level; yet never at the highest, as it does not reach the leader, whose role is to embody the fight against the system's malfunctions.[27]

Sophisticatedly elaborated by the Syrian scholar Imad Fawzi Shoaibi in his theory of "the necessity of corruption,"[28] this vision suggests that corruption is a natural—and necessary—component of the political system; and that it should never be eradicated completely, as its very existence contributes to the making of the leader's moral authority, as he is the only one entitled to fight it.

Following the same logic of looking at corruption as a natural evil of the system which only the leader is entitled to contrast, "Hawamish" ("Margins," 2003), a satirical sketch from the *Buq'at daw'* series, features an enlightened top official encouraging his staff to make an effort toward criticizing authority and express their thoughts freely.[29] However, the sketch points out, these efforts fail, as low-ranking elements of the system are unable to keep up with changes promoted by an enlightened and open-minded leadership.

There is no evidence that either *Ghizlan* or *Buq'at daw'*, the TV series that represented the quintessence of the Damascus Spring's reformist spirit,[30] were ordered or commissioned by the Palace or by the president. And, in fact, they probably were not. As one of *Buq'at daw'*'s creators, director Laith Hajjo, remarked: "People thought the show had a green light [from the authorities] because of the producer. . . .[31] In fact, the producer didn't really know what we were up to. We kept telling the censors that, look, the president said X, so we're following that policy."[32]

The whisper strategy guarantees that issues and concerns are disseminated and shared in a feedback loop. Things do not need to be directly commissioned or imposed by the *sultat*; they are rather circulated.

The whisper strategy is an oral dynamic, where nothing happens in a formal, written, obligatory way: everything works informally, phrased as subtle hints. As to suggest the importance of oral communication in the making of cultural production, TV drama writer Najib Nusair once stated: "Syria is the country of phone calls."[33] This image well resonates with the oral, informal, unofficial character of the "whispers."[34]

Following the metaphor of the circulation of ideas and thoughts in the feedback loops involving Syrian *sultat* and TV drama makers, sometimes the latter use the expression "public mood" (*al-jaw al-ʿam*) to describe the atmosphere that inspires them to pick up topics and issues and turn them into TV fiction. Hani al-ʿAshi, the owner of Aj production company, has pointed to a sort of "harmony" (*insijam*) with this "public mood"[35] when asked why he chose the topic of a woman pregnant with a handicapped child for his Ramadan 2010 drama *Wara' al-shams* (*Behind the Sun*, 2010).

Going back to analyze the public debate over handicapped people and their acceptance in Syrian society, it is not difficult to discover that the first lady Asma al-Asad had organized outreach campaigns and mobilized public opinion on this issue since 2005.[36] Her public awareness efforts culminated in the September 2010 Special Olympic Games that Syria hosted[37] a few weeks after the broadcast of *Wara' al-shams*. During this sporting event, Asma al-Asad was frequently photographed with ʿAlaa, the disabled boy who plays the leading role in the *musalsal*.[38] ʿAlaa became a public icon who traveled across the wider media spectrum, turning from a Ramadan *musalsal* character into an engaged athlete joining the First Lady's awareness efforts, and ending up on the red carpet of the Addounia prize ceremony, the annual "Oscars" of Syrian drama.[39]

The *Wara' al-shams* example illustrates how the whisper guarantees that issues relevant to some *sultat* are injected into the public space of the media and absorbed by TV drama. *Musalsalat* reproduce these issues in the public arena by stimulating a debate differently than the news. Moreover, they are able to prompt emotional discussion driven by affection for the drama's characters and storylines.[40]

The "ongoing dialogue"[41] between TV drama producers and political leaders also affects the official censorship mechanism, which very rarely has to prevent a topic from being addressed.[42] Drama writer Adnan Aouda confirms that this is the case, stressing that "it is very rare to see our works censored, usually we just have to change small details. . . . We writers know what and how to talk about something, because we are *awlad al-balad* (children of the country)."[43]

In public, many drama makers like to stress the magnanimity of the official censorship, and the possibility for self-expression granted even when dealing with highly sensitive topics. As Muthanna al-Subh, director of the TV drama *Laysa saraban* (*It's Not a Mirage*, 2008), which treats relations between Christians and Muslims in contemporary Syria, emphasized: "Honestly, we did not face any problem. That was both surprising and pleasing to me. I actually respect the fact that they allowed us to deal with such sensitive issues."[44]

Yet it is unlikely that a work like *Laysa saraban* would be censored or rejected, as it perfectly matches Bashar al-Asad's official rhetoric concerning the issue of religious minorities. The *musalsal* seems to suggest that Syria's religious and ethnic groups, especially Muslims and Christians, can live together but are not ready to merge in a multicultural society. The gloomy ending, in which the two lovers—a Christian woman and a Muslim man—split and the man dies, suggests that Syrian society is not ready for interreligious relationships, as it is still trapped in the backwardness of honor killing, sectarian revenge, arranged marriages, etc. This message is not at odds with what the official rhetoric of Bashar al-Asad's leadership has always suggested: that an enlightened minority should rule to protect minorities in the country and make sure the state remains superficially secular and the population stays as controlled as possible, in order to avoid chaos, social disorder, and religious extremism.

By dealing with the sensitive issue of honor killing (*jarimat al-sharaf*), *Laysa saraban* provides yet another example of how the whisper strategy helps feed the public with issues that both the *sulta* and the *tanwiri* drama makers deem worthy of public discussion. The *musalsal* also features a (Muslim) male character who kills his sister because he suspects she is having an affair.

The public debate on such a sensitive topic for Syrian society had not yet been initiated at the time *Laysa saraban* was broadcast. A BBC report filed in October 2007 had documented that more than two hundred women were murdered every year by their brothers, fathers, or cousins. "The Syrian authorities are trying to crack down on the practice of 'honour killing,' and they have widespread support," the BBC noted at the time. The report included a quotation from the highest authority of (regime-backed) Islam, Grand Mufti Shaykh Hassun: "It is difficult to change laws that people are used to it and considered it as *Shari'a*. In many cases, it is traditions rather than laws. . . . . What we need is to educate people and spread awareness among the society."[45]

A year later and only a few months after the broadcast of *Laysa saraban*, the Syrian council for family affairs hosted the largest meeting in Syria's history to discuss the phenomenon of honor killing. In July 2009, Bashar al-Asad abolished Article 548 of the penal code, which waived punishment for a man who had murdered a female family member involved in "illegitimate sex acts" or in an extramarital affair.[46] Although the new article continued to permit limited punishment in cases of honor killing, the sentence for perpetrators was increased from one year to at least two. The president's intervention in the penal code came a year after *Laysa saraban* and provoked a public debate.[47]

Here I do not want to imply that the *musalsal*'s media message and the regime's political message were aligned as a result of a conscious plot that was elaborated, structured, and then communicated from the top down. As already underscored, the circulation of messages between the *sultat* and TV drama makers happens as a result of the "capillarity"[48] which characterizes a power system that enables both sides to circulate suggestions and advice about topics strategically deemed worthy of becoming public issues. The circulation of messages in the feedback loop suggests a two-way communication mechanism where the whisper can be initiated indifferently by the *sultat* or by drama makers.[49]

This is why, I argue, the "whisper" is a multilateral strategy that implies an engagement from both sides. It does not take human agency away from the TV drama makers, regarding them as disempowered subjects who are passively submitted to the *sultat*'s will.

Moreover, some Syrian private production companies[50] are themselves a business *sulta* very closely intertwined with other *sultat* within the regime structure.[51] Through their business, institutional, family, and kinship ties to the regime, these companies enjoy influence and leverage and can easily initiate a whisper to the Palace and the president.

However, even cultural producers who are less close to the *sultat* can enter the feedback mechanism and make their whisper heard. As writer Adnan Aouda explains: "Things that are not allowed to be said in one way can be said in another. My belief is that you can always negotiate on controversial topics if you know how to deliver the message to the right people."[52] Aouda's take suggests that a multilateral, always-on communication channel connects cultural producers and regime components in conversation on public issues; it also hints at the active engagement of intelligence and military *sultat* in *musalsalat* production,[53] and at the possibility for them to interfere in the whisper strategy and sabotage it.

These characteristics of the whisper strategy—a public, oral and multilateral dynamic—suggest a new relationship binding the *sultat* and cultural producers. This new type of relation is built upon compliance, consent, and mutual benefit rather than dissent or struggle. One reason behind this is, as noted, that many drama makers are intertwined with the *sultat* through personal relations that have turned them into a *sulta* in its own right.

But, besides those who enjoy family or business ties with the *sultat*, there is something very peculiar that binds together the *tanwiri* drama makers and the president: a sort of "elective affinity,"[54] a shared feeling of being an enlightened minority charged with setting society on the path to progress.

These cultural producers are different from the previous generation of intellectuals living under Hafiz al-Asad described by miriam cooke.[55] They were involved in a struggle between the desire to criticize the regime and the obligation to compromise with it, negotiating what later became forms of "commissioned criticism."[56] The intellectuals cooke describes— writers like Sa'adallah Wannus, Muhammad Maghut, Mamduh 'Adwan— saw themselves engaged in an effort of criticizing the regime and trying to improve freedom of expression.

On the contrary, the cultural producers involved in the whisper strategy are committed to a dialogue with the *sultat*[57] and tend to deny the existence of censorship, preferring to justify the supervision of their works as if it were a mere "artistic evaluation" (*taqim fanni*): something they see as a necessity related to the essence of culture itself.[58]

Unlike cooke's intellectuals, these drama makers do not hide their relations with the *sultat*; rather, they show them off. They do not oppose the regime's cultural project, which aims at improving what they describe as a backward society; they want to heal the diseases of political and social corruption, gender inequalities, honor killing, religious extremism, and illiteracy[59] with their television products.[60] They endorse this project by giving it the noble attribute of *tanwiri*,[61] and they happily abide by the slogans and the awareness campaigns that the *sultat* have previously fabricated and thrown in the public space of media; they anticipate or relaunch these issues, helped by the mechanism of the whisper.

These drama makers are more than just "complicit":[62] they are comfortable with the powers that be. A new bond is forged between this new generation of cultural producers and the *sultat*. Pleasure and comfort derived from social status and financial privileges characterize this novel relation, as much as the condition of unbelief described by Wedeen[63] bound together Syrian citizens and the regime during Hafiz al-Asad's rule. To borrow from a market-oriented language that better describes the atmosphere of a "neoliberal autocracy"[64] under Bashar al-Asad, the *sultat* and cultural producers are both stakeholders and coinvestors in a political project where they concur in defining what is good and advisable for Syrian society.[65]

Fawq al-saqf: The Syrian Uprising Turns into a Television Drama[66]

As I have noted, Foucault's definition of power as a "more or less coordinated" and sometimes "ill coordinated"[67] cluster of relations well matches the loose functioning of Syria's *sultat*. The *sultat*'s capability and willingness to communicate or not to communicate can determine the success or the failure of objectives set through the whisper strategy. The *musalsalat* produced under Bashar al-Asad provide excellent examples: first, in the case where the alliance between the Palace and the drama makers has succeeded in injecting *tanwiri* messages into the public space through television drama; and second, in the case where other components within the regime's power structure, moved by different priorities and agendas, have managed to block such messages.

In particular, by discussing *Fawq al-saqf* (*Above the Ceiling*), a Ramadan series dealing with the Syrian uprising of March 2011, I will show how different *sultat* push forward clashing messages in the public space of TV drama. Yet they are also capable of supporting more than one political project at the time, sometimes openly contradicting one another. Because it can be revealing of the loose and ambivalent articulation of power in Syria, *Fawq al-saqf* provides a quintessential case study in the interaction between the *sultat* and cultural producers.

Despite its exceptional context—the Syrian uprising—the production history of the series points to a dynamic in the Syrian *musalsalat* industry that is routine rather than exceptional; that is, a network of loosely connected components of the regime, the Palace, the secret services, state media, religious authorities, and the president all interfere in TV drama making, each side pushing forward its own set of agendas, while being in loose communication or wanting to reject communication with the other. Hence, *Fawq al-saqf* offers a pattern that explains "how the system works"[68] in TV drama production; this very pattern could be applied to the functioning of the Syrian regime at large, providing an insight on how power is created, reshaped, preserved, negotiated, and shifted among the different *sultat*.

During Ramadan (August) 2011, Syrian Television aired a very peculiar, although fictional, scene in between the crowded schedule filled with *musalsalat*. A man who looked like a government official was standing by a crowd of people who chanted "*hurriyya, hurriyya*" (freedom, freedom), a familiar rallying cry of the various Arab uprisings and the slogan used when protests hit the streets of Damascus on March 15, 2011.[69] But it was odd, to say the least, to hear the phrase in a Syrian government-sponsored broadcast. Until that moment, state TV had not screened, not even in TV fiction, any such evidence of peaceful demonstrations in Syria nor of the violent crackdown by the regime.

In fact, the *musalsal* episode went on to show the same official ordering policemen to shoot at the protesters. Immediately afterwards, the character seemed to regret his order and muttered: "Maybe I should have . . . but precaution cannot stave off destiny." In parallel, an old man was featured in different situations where he seemed to be the only one untouched by bad events related to the uprising (robbery, arrest, crackdown). Like a mantra, he repeated the words: "Thank God, around us and not on top of us." The episode's grand finale featured these two characters—the official and the old man—gazing over a desolate landscape where only destruction and death were to be seen. The official spoke first, commenting on the scene: "What happened to this country?! I am responsible for this, I knew this was going to happen . . . but, in the end, precaution does not prevent destiny." The old man did not answer this comment directly, but obsessively kept repeating his mantra, pretending not to see that everything around him had already been destroyed.

This is just one of the several sketches of fifteen to twenty minutes each that compose *Fawq al-saqf*. The *musalsal* was commissioned by the Radio and TV Production Organization (*Mu'assasat al-intaj al-idha' wa al-tilifiziun*), a government-sponsored unit launched in 2010 after Syrian Television had been restructured with the mission of producing drama by acting within a "private company mindset."[70] The institution was intended to represent the new face of government involvement in Syrian drama, enjoying financial autonomy and the possibility of forming partnership deals with the private sector. *Fawq al-saqf* was produced by this government-backed agency and aired on Syrian Television. All the episodes were written by selected authors from *Buq'at daw'*, the *musalsal* that symbolized the new openness brought by the Damascus Spring in 2001. In addition to this, *Fawq al-saqf* director Samer Barqawi was deemed a talented and independent member of the younger generation of Syrian drama makers, and someone not directly aligned with the regime's positions.

Hence, the *musalsal* had all the elements of what many Syrians would describe as *tanfis* (letting off steam), a safety valve allowing people "to vent frustrations and displace or relieve tensions that otherwise might find expression in political action."[71] It could also have been seen as "commissioned criticism,"[72] "an official and paradoxical project to create a democratic façade"[73] that actually engineered a certain degree of political dissent and featured it on official media as proof of openness and an inclination toward reform.

In analyzing the production history of *Fawq al-saqf*, however, these arguments are not persuasive. Had it served the purpose of *tanfis* or commissioned criticism, the *musalsal* would at least have been promoted and advertised over the Syrian official media network to attract the public's attention. By contrast, the official Syrian TV daily show *Drama 2011*—which helped viewers navigate the crowded Ramadan drama schedule—did not even mention it. No promotions for the *musalsal* were aired on state-owned TV channels and, unlike other *musalsalat*, the serial was never re-scheduled after its first broadcast. Very few, even among prominent drama makers, were aware of it being produced.[74] The only station to mention the *musalsal* was Al-Arabia, which featured it once on its daily *Drama Ramadan* program. In addition to the lack of domestic promotion, advertising, and public awareness, the *musalsal* was halted without any official reason before the end of Ramadan 2011, when its fifteenth episode was broadcast. It disappeared from TV screens without leaving a trace.

From a strictly business perspective, too, *Fawq al-saqf* appeared unprofessional to say the least, since it was financed and produced but then not advertised, rebroadcast, or sold to any other TV station. Nevertheless, it is precisely for its failure as a *tanfis*, commissioned criticism, or business project that *Fawq al-saqf* is worth exploring to shed light on the reasons behind its production and its failure.

According to Maher Azzam,[75] the head of censorship at the *Mu'assasa* that produced the *musalsal, Fawq al-saqf* grew out of a proposal that was put on the table by Sami Moubayed during a meeting with the Palace in spring 2011. At the time, Moubayed occupied a prominent position among the reform-minded cultural elite: he taught political science at the private Kalamoon University in Damascus and was editor-in-chief of *Forward Magazine*, a monthly publication from the powerful media group Haykal,[76] which promoted a progressive, liberal Syria under the al-Asad family's leadership.[77] He was also in the personal circle of Bouthaina Shaaban, Bashar al-Asad's media advisor, who delivered the first official speech in Syria after the beginning of the uprising, seemingly advocating for dialogue and national reconciliation.

In the complex articulation of *sultat* that makes up the power structure of the Syrian regime, both Shaaban and Moubayed embody the apparently reformist agenda of the presidential palace and its diplomatic public face. Moubayed's articles on the Syrian uprising—some in American outlets such as the *Huffington Post*—display his skill in eschewing the rhetoric of the regime while embracing some of al-Asad's claims to legitimacy; for example, the fight against Islamism and religious extremism.[78] Moubayed was probably guided by his deep knowledge of Syrian media and the regime's strategy when he first conceived of a progressive TV series that would deal with the Syrian uprising and be produced by a government-controlled media organization, but at the same time would not have to appear as simply reflecting the government's official position.

In interviews, Maher Azzam has referred to an initial conversation that he witnessed at the Palace in spring 2011, when Moubayed first pitched the idea of a TV series that would depict "what is happening in the streets in an artistic way."[79] Moubayed labelled his project as a "third view which does not embrace the view of the regime or the street. Something that the regime would not feel was a provocation, nor the street would be angered at or encouraged to demonstrate after its broadcast."[80] In the spring of 2011, during the first months of the uprising when a political solution based on dialogue and gradual reform appeared to be a feasible response to the unrest, the Palace seemed to like the idea, as orders were given to the *Mu'assasa* to take responsibility for the project and start producing it. Hence, in this case a member of the cultural producers' elite (Moubayed) had "whispered" to the Palace, making the other side aware of a *tanwiri* message that should reach the public in the interest of a reformist project that both sides—Syrian cultural producers like himself, and President al-Asad with his reform-minded circle—could endorse and support.

From a media perspective, *Fawq al-saqf* endorses the same spirit of openness and national dialogue that, at a political level, has been promoted by the president and his reformist advisor Bouthaina Shaaban as a solution to the Syrian crisis. This dialogue, however, is to be conducted solely under the regime's auspices, driven by political and cultural elites; its margins are to be fixed strictly from the top down. The idea is transposed to the title of the *musalsal—Above the Ceiling—*which sets the standards of the dialogue at the highest level possible,[81] reproducing a metaphor often repeated in Bashar al-Asad's public speeches to suggest the great degree of freedom that Syrian media allegedly enjoys.[82] The metaphor is ambiguous, as it specifies neither who is entitled to set the standards of freedom nor where their margins lie. Yet it is precisely because of this ambiguity that it perfectly matches the *tanwiri* project endorsed by cultural elites, where access is restricted to only a few components of society, that is, those who are qualified to enlighten the rest of the population.[83]

This alliance between enlightened drama makers and the seemingly progressive components of the Syrian regime, however, may be hampered by other *sultat* pushing forward different agendas; it may also be that the reform-minded parties are actually promoting more than one project at a time, therefore these projects of different natures may collide with each other. The production history of *Fawq al-saqf* makes these fights and clashes apparent by showing how the *sultat*'s different views over the unrest (and over possible solutions to the crisis, whether dialogue-oriented or security-oriented) have resulted in a very troubled production process involving battles over every single detail of the *musalsal*.[84]

As an example, the original title of the series—*Al-Sha'b yurid . . .* (*The People Want . . .*)—was probably deemed too close to the antiregime slogan chanted by protesters all across the Arab world in 2011; therefore, it was changed to something more ambiguous and not directly related to the uprising.[85] Although the idea of the *musalsal* had been directly endorsed by the Palace, each edited episode had to receive approval from a viewing committee (*lajnat al-mushahada*), which actually rejected many of the episodes. Finally, the series was allowed on air only because the Palace itself was reported to have intervened to authorize its broadcast. But even during the broadcast, protests and complaints from "different parties" (*mukhtalif al-atraf*) were reported, and personal phone calls were made from "other official sides" (*jihat rasmiyya ukhra*), meaning secret services, to pressure state television to cancel the series.[86] Finally, *Fawq al-saqf* became a headache for Syrian Television, which eventually ceased promoting the series. Suddenly, a decision was made to halt its broadcast and rerun it after Ramadan, but it was clear that postponing would mean canceling it altogether.[87]

In fact, the *musalsal* was never re-aired or sold to any other station.[88] The silence of the Palace suggested that it endorsed the decision, abandoning its initial message based on dialogue; it might have been unable— or unwilling—to fight against more urgent, security-focused priorities, pushed by other *sultat* in the regime power structure in a time of unrest.

Fawq al-saqf's production history sheds light on a system where multiple *sultat* are operating with different agendas; it reveals how the power balance within the Syrian regime fluctuates in particular periods and can be completely reconfigured during a crisis. It is very likely that, once the unrest started in 2011, the *tanwiri* project, jointly backed by the Palace and by the elite of drama makers, had to succumb to the security plan pushed by the intelligence and the more hawkish sides of the Syrian regime. It might also have been, however, that the Palace itself decided to put the *tanwiri* project on hold in order to help the other *sultat* implement the security plan, judged as a priority in a time of unrest.

Whispering Media Messages: Reconfiguring Power Dynamics before and during the Syrian Uprising

Clashes between different *sultat* like those described in the case of *Fawq al-saqf* are not new in the production history of Syrian TV drama, and have occurred since Bashar al-Asad seized power. Interestingly enough, it was precisely *Buq'at daw'*, the *musalsal* that carried the reformist promise of the new president's inaugural address and transposed it into an edgy piece of television, which first turned into a media battleground for the *sultat* advocating different political priorities and agendas.[89]

Dealing with sensitive issues, such as political corruption and abuses by the secret services, the series initially enjoyed the open support of the president. Produced by Mohamed Hamsho's company SAPI—a fact that signaled the support of the new class of entrepreneurs, another powerful *sulta* within the regime structure, for the president's reformist project—*Buq'at daw'* was censored by Syrian TV before being broadcast. It was only thanks to the direct intervention of the Palace that the *musalsal* passed through Syrian TV censorship and finally aired.[90]

Yet during the broadcast the *sultat* continued to clash; former vice prime minister 'Abdul Halim Khaddam[91] was reportedly livid after the airing of a sketch satirizing daily life in Syria and discouraging foreign investment.[92] But neither he nor any other institutional or security element within Syria's power structure was able to stop the *musalsal*. Most likely, at the time a seemingly reformist façade was needed to show elite groups that the crackdown of the Damascus Spring would not mean bringing reform to a complete halt.

Direct presidential intervention in favor of *tanwiri musalsalat* is a recurrent pattern in the history of Syrian TV drama under Bashar al-Asad, and it can provide a useful insight into the way power is understood and communicated in contemporary Syria. The fact that, throughout the years, direct presidential interventions were the main way to get controversial *tanwiri* serials broadcast has helped shape the impression that reformism coincides with Bashar al-Asad's personal political project.

These public interventions in favor of progressive TV drama—together with the fact that the whispers involving the drama makers happen in quasi-public venues, such as hearings or receptions hosted by the president—reinforce the public image of a committed leader in tune with the country's cultural elites and ready to discuss the policies and politics of cultural production in an open and transparent way. When the media content agreed upon through the whisper clashes with different messages put forward by other *sultat*, the president's direct intervention becomes a strategy to reaffirm his very personal commitment to the reformist project at a media level, and hence at a political one. Yet this seems just a more sophisticated way for Bashar al-Asad to earn reformist credentials without being obliged to hand over responsibility to institutions that would have to find structural, rather than personal, ways to implement reforms.

In the spring of 2011 he had probably tried to implement the same strategy; that is, using media projects backed by *tanwiri* cultural producers to construct a reformist façade for his regime to survive the crisis. The very different fate of two *tanwiri musalsalat*, both of them directed by Najdat Anzour,[93] sheds light on the president's strategy vis-à-vis the other *sultat* within the regime and before the Syrian public. I will examine these cases, and will discuss how and why support for reformism in media (and in politics) in Syria is continuously being re-tuned and renegotiated between the *sultat*.

The first *musalsal*, *Ma malakat aymanukum* (*Those Whom Your Right Hand Possesses*, 2010), was aired during Ramadan 2010 after a very complicated production process and several hot controversies. *Ma malakat aymanukum* deals with the issue of Islam in contemporary Syria, condemning all forms of religiously justified extremism, such as suicide terror operations and violence against women; it exalts the freedom, tolerance, and self-determination to be found in religious piety instead.

This approach is in tune with the regime's strategy of advocating secularism to protect the various religious minorities in Syria, while at the same time proving itself religiously pious enough not to offend the country's conservative Sunni majority. The ultimate message is a warning to political Islam. The interests of cultural elites and those of the reform-minded circle within the regime—both keen on preserving the country's secular façade and their stakes in holding, respectively, the cultural and political leadership of the reformist process—thus converged in *Ma malakat aymanukum*.[94] This convergence of interests helped the script of the *musalsal* gain the approval of Syrian state television's *Lajnat al-qira'a* (reading committee), which is tasked with supervising and approving every TV series before it is produced.

However, as previously noted, the *sultat* are multiple and promote different agendas: state media are often caught in the middle and do not have a clear vision of which *sulta* they should endorse and why. Therefore, after being screened by the *Lajnat al-mushahada* (viewing committee) prior to broadcast, the *musalsal* was sent to the Ministry of Information for further examination. The most controversial point was its title, taken from a Qur'anic verse from the *Sura al-nisa'* (*Women*) conveying a feeling of ownership toward women.[95] Given the delicacy of the topic and its religious implications, the Ministry of Information, which should have had the final word, decided to send it to the Minister of Religious Endowments for advice. At this point, the negative reaction toward the *musalsal* from prominent scholar Muhammad Sa'id al-Buti (who was an authority on Sunni Islam in Syria)[96] forced Syrian TV to pull it from the Ramadan schedule just one day before its scheduled broadcast. Disappointed at "a decision that was made for the wrong reasons,"[97] director Najdat Anzour "made the president aware of the issue."[98] Former Minister of Culture Riad Nasaan Agha also lobbied to put the *musalsal* on air. He reported that "the president himself intervened in favour of it."[99]

While one or more *sulta* (the Palace, some government ministries, etc.) pushed for the *musalsal* to go on air, other *sultat* (other government ministries and religious scholars) demanded that it be banned. One *sulta* who was reported to have been very annoyed by the series was business-man Mohamed Hamsho, who is also behind the private Syrian satellite channel Addounia TV and the production company SAPI. *Ma malakat aymanukum*, in fact, features a corrupt entrepreneur whose profile is very similar to Hamsho's; the character founds a TV production company in order to gain prestige and leverage to run for public office, not hesitating to enter a business agreement with Islamic extremists to win elections.

Anzour has never officially confirmed Hamsho's direct intervention against his series;[100] however, when discussing the reasons behind the last-minute embargo, he spoke of "people with interests" and "people who have been bothered by the *musalsal*." "But for anybody who is important in the country, there is always somebody more important," Anzour argued, emphasizing the direct role played by president Bashar al-Asad in resolv-ing the *Ma malakat aymanukum* case. "When I attended the meeting with artists and producers, he mentioned the *musalsal* three times and said, 'Had I not personally intervened, the *musalsal* would have gone.' He used exactly this expression: 'Had I not personally intervened . . . '"[101] The presi-dent's intervention in favor of Anzour and the broadcast of his Ramadan TV drama may have made the director feel indebted; he paid back this debt zealously at the beginning of the 2011 uprising by producing written statements and public endorsements supporting Bashar al-Asad.[102]

The personal support expressed by the president in the *Ma malakat aymanukum* case probably encouraged Anzour to follow the same pat-tern[103] and produce something even "more daring."[104] *Chiffon*, the *musal-sal* Anzour was shooting when the Syrian uprising started in March 2011, portrays a number of teenage Syrian girls and boys dealing with taboo issues such as sex, drugs, and prostitution. It even features a scene where a female teenager who dresses like a man and lives among men walks pro-vocatively toward the conservative Sunni mosque of Abu Nur, surrounded by completely veiled women, which illustrates the director's idea of free-dom as opposed to religious obscurantism.

Chiffon would probably have enjoyed the same fate as *Ma malakat aymanukum* had the unrest not begun in March 2011. Yet in the tense atmosphere following the first protests for freedom and civil liberties, the priorities within the regime had likely shifted. The need for *tanwiri* products promoting progressive values was to be put on hold. Other, more urgent necessities took priority, and different alliances, rather than those with secular cultural producers, were being sought and secured.

Al-Buti, the cleric who just one year earlier had been forced to accept the broadcast of *Ma malakat aymanukum*, reiterated his opposition regarding the values promoted by the series in a speech broadcast by Syrian TV in April 2011. In his remarks, he held Anzour's *musalsal* responsible for the unrest. Shortly afterwards, and in response to a press release issued by some Syrian actors and directors calling for humanitarian aid for the besieged city of Daraa, Anzour was at the forefront of an alliance of producers signing a counter-petition to boycott those artists and prevent them from working in TV drama.[105]

Yet despite Anzour's zealous and open support for al-Asad, the president failed—or perhaps did not wish—to intervene in favor of *Chiffon* in 2011, as he had in 2010 for *Ma malakat aymanukum*. In fact, *Chiffon* was never broadcast during Ramadan 2011. Anzour justified the move as a matter of "national interest,"[106] it being not the right moment to broadcast such a controversial *musalsal* in times of unrest. However, at the same time al-Buti received the authorization to launch an Islamic religious channel, Nur, under al-Asad's auspices. In the social unrest generated by the uprising, the president most likely needed the support of the prominent Sunni scholar al-Buti much more than any alliance with secular cultural elites.

The different fate of the two *musalsalat* authored by the same director brings into stark relief not only how different *sultat* (business, government, intelligence agencies, and religious authorities) interfere in shaping media content and filling it with contradictory messages and agendas, but also how the fortunes of television serials are intimately tied to changing political exigencies.

The alliances between one *sulta* and another are continuously fluctuating, as they are based on temporary, fragile convergences of interests. In 2010, before the unrest started, the Syrian president used his personal intervention in favor of *Ma malakat aymanukum* in order to emphasize, in a public way, his alliance with secular cultural elites and a joint commitment to the *tanwiri*, reformist project. However, this strategy did not hold up in the case of *Chiffon*. In 2011 in fact, security concerns were more urgent than reform or dialogue in media and politics, despite the president's public statements in support of a political solution (*hall siyasi*) to the crisis.

The power struggle involving Syrian *sultat* had very different outcomes in pre-uprising *musalsalat*, such as *Buq'at daw'* and *Ma malakat aymanukum*, and in those produced after 2011, such as *Chiffon* and *Fawq al-saqf*. This difference clearly hints at an increasing weakness of the reformist project pushed forward by the Palace, and suggests that the project's influence is declining within the regime's power structure. Yet at the same time this apparent weakness might be read as a sign that reform-minded members are torn between one side of their political sensibilities—their reformist inclinations—and a more security-oriented project, especially at a time when their political survival is at stake.

Conclusions

This chapter has reflected on the mechanism by which a specific form of cultural production, television drama, in tune with the agenda of reform-minded political elites, elaborated and projected disciplinary and pedagogical messages for the Syrian public. I have used the metaphor of the "whisper" to describe the communication strategy through which cultural producers and seemingly reformist political powers debate, agree on, and shape ideas and messages that should be put out for public discussion using progressive media content, such as how to think about tolerance, piety, gender, religion, and freedom.

In Bashar al-Asad's Syria, local politics has employed more sophisticated, market-oriented forms to discipline and induce compliance by suggesting how to look at citizenship-related issues, and by offering new social and market freedoms in place of political freedom. Television drama has turned into yet another device for promoting this vision of social reform. Yet this chapter has put into stark relief how Syrian TV drama makers are not just executives in a project that has been designed and elaborated elsewhere; they are bound together with the president and his reform-minded circle by their "elective affinities," shared beliefs, mutual interests, and a sort of reciprocal fascination with each other.

Deeply tied to local politics, at the same time these drama makers are also active players in the regional and international markets,[107] without which their TV products would not be sustainable as financial projects. Indeed, they are entrenched in the complex nexus of places, situations and, above all, connections and networks that describes our neoliberal times. Reading this complex picture either in light of a resistance-to-power narrative, or within an authoritarian framework where Syrian drama makers are just passive executors of the *sultat*'s will, would mean ignoring how deeply they are enmeshed in a broader industrial process that continuously forges and reshapes cultural production as a commodified good on a global market.

As I have shown elsewhere,[108] the affinities between political and cultural elites in Syria expressed by the whisper strategy have also met the commercial needs of the pan-Arab market. The media messages elaborated through the "whisper" for the Syrian public seem, in fact, not to be at odds with the exigencies of the Gulf-backed pan-Arab market, where Syrian drama is interpreted as a commodity for regional consumption.[109] This dynamic still functions at a pan-Arab level, yet the March 2011 uprising has dramatically reconfigured the relationship between cultural and political elites within Syria. If, in fact, the golden days of Syrian TV drama coincided with Bashar al-Asad's first decade as a leader, marked by an excitement for the promise of free markets, an appetite for new social freedoms, and expectations of political reforms, then the uprising has called into question this cultural and media project, along with the political project—and their shared *tanwiri* vision for Syrian society and its future.

Through the analysis of seminal TV works produced during the first decade of Bashar al-Asad's rule and in the years following the March 2011 uprising, this chapter has shed light on how elite political communication and cultural production work in a market-oriented autocracy. It has proposed the whisper strategy as a useful metaphor to read into the mechanism of producing and maintaining power in contemporary Syria. It has linked media and cultural reformism to a project of political reforms, underlining the limits of *tanwir* as an elite-produced fantasy of a Syrian society that has dramatically changed over the course of a decade.

5

Cultural Liberalization or Marginalization?

The Cultural Politics of Syrian Folk Dance during Social Market Reform

SHAYNA SILVERSTEIN

A young female ballerina performs a grand jeté across the stage of Dar al-Asad, the world-class opera house in central Damascus. Adorned with a smooth bun and classical tutu, her trained body and fluid movements grace the stage. She turns toward the camera and smiles at her audience, millions of Syrians watching state television in 2008. During a pivotal year for cultural production in urban Syria, this break frequently aired between television programs on the state-sponsored channel. Young female dancers have stood for Syrian modernity since the emergence of the nation-state in the 1950s. However, earlier representations of Syrian cultural heritage drew primarily on folk dance, particularly the popular tradition of *dabke*, rather than on Western cultural forms such as ballet.[1] As popular dance (*raqs sha'bi*) became folklorized in the 1960s, femininity became equated with a sense of homeland (*watan*). On postcards, woodblocks, and other nationalistic paraphernalia that circulated in the early Ba'thist years, a young dancer in a traditional embroidered gown posed against a pastoral landscape. She signified authenticity in secular discourses on nationhood, cultural heritage, and modernity. These discourses continued to be articulated through *raqs sha'bi* until this television break in 2008, in which ballet redressed visions of Syrian cultural modernity.

77

Her embodiment of national imaginaries is indicative of the broader politics of culture during the liberalization of the state economy in the 2000s. The Syrian political and cultural elite aspired to update their national image with sophisticated and cosmopolitan forms of cultural expression that projected the image of a country opening up to increased flow of capital in a reformed market economy. Yet these elitist visions often masked unresolved tensions and issues that affected the masses, many of which surfaced during the subsequent revolts. The field of dance is particularly compelling for understanding class-based distinctions between cultural elites and ordinary Syrians. In 2005, *New York Times* journalist James Bennet interviewed First Lady Asma al-Asad about a dance theater (*raqs masrah*) production presented at Dar al-Asad: "When I asked Asma al-Asad what she thought of the dance, she winced. 'I think there was a lot of talent,' she said carefully. But, she added, 'I don't think it portrayed what Syria is, in any era.'"[2] Her hesitation to mark the Syrian experience through dance conveys the ambivalence held among the political and cultural elite over how to uphold symbols of cultural heritage while also conceiving new national imaginaries.

Symbols of nationhood were under intense debate in the 2000s as the Syrian regime attempted to formalize its development strategies into a "social market economy." This term referred to economic governance policies under President Bashar al-Asad that aimed to "preserve [the regime's] commitment to the populist and redistributive social policies that defined state-society relations under the Ba'th and retain the public institutions that such policies required but would complement these elements with newer, market-oriented policies and regulatory frameworks that would overcome the dysfunctions and inefficiencies associated with the public sector and give Syria the foundations for improved economic performance."[3] These policies benefited not only the business and political elite but also those on the margins of clientelist networks. Entrepreneurs thrived in this speculative economy that expanded opportunities to the upper-middle class, Syrian bourgeoisie, and those in the Gulf diaspora. These policies have been critiqued, however, as a reconfiguration of existing patronage networks that "renewed" rather than reformed the authoritarian framework of repression and co-optation.[4] Through tactics of "resilience,"[5] the regime deployed a "strategy that conveys the impression of openness but in reality penalizes reformist aspirations that are viewed as a threat by the ruling coalition."[6]

The affectations of social market reform extended to the cultural sector.[7] Social market reform was intended to steer Syria out of socialist economic frameworks and toward more privatized options. Relatedly, official state culture could no longer ascribe to the populist aesthetics of socialist realism that it had sustained since before former president Hafiz al-Asad came to power. In its stead, the regime chose to reinvent its popular (sha'bi) identity through the production of nostalgia, such as the reconstruction of Old Damascus or the endorsement of Bab al-hara, a television drama staged in a quasi-Ottoman era, that situated sha'bi identity in the past rather than reimagining it within the present.[8] Likewise, the regime supported artists who helped to convey a positive image of Syria, particularly original art that corresponded to Western norms.[9] Accordingly, the state took an active role in sponsoring the Damascus Arab Capital Culture Festival (DACC) in 2008 by investing major capital and administrative support in the yearlong initiative.[10] DACC 2008 brought together renowned artists who enjoyed a degree of autonomy with respect to regime and offered relatively open space for their creativity, something that neither traditional nor more autonomous structures of cultural labor could provide.

However, the regime's involvement in cultural affairs also served to perpetuate traditions of cultural elitism among the Sunni bourgeoisie.[11] Cultural entrepreneurs established arts organizations and initiatives that politically profited the regime. Echo-Sada was a music association that worked collaboratively with conservatory-based pedagogues to offer funding and support for young music graduates and to raise awareness for Syrian-based music projects. It was led by Talh Khair, wife of Manaf Tlass, who was central to facilitating Bashar al-Asad's connections to the Sunni merchant class until his defection from the regime in 2012. In addition to these patronage networks, cultural expression continued to be constrained by state censorship. Censorship was monitored through somewhat ambiguous and inconsistent practices. Though there was modest tolerance of sociopolitical critique, artists struggled to navigate the enigmatic red lines of censorship. Thus, while the country seemed to be experiencing a cultural renaissance, this surge in creative output arguably retained cronyism and, like other sectors of social market reform, helped to make authoritarianism resilient to change.

This chapter traces the effects of social market reform on the dance sector by illustrating how key figures in the dance world negotiated the shift from socialist to neoliberal forms of public culture. I will show how this shift arguably reinforced social distinctions between those who maintained the populist aesthetics of socialist realism and those who turned to contemporary and Westernized cultural forms as markers of a more globalized and open era. This period did not benefit dancers equally but rather hardened socioeconomic differences among dance theater, folk dance, and contemporary dance companies. The politics of contemporary dance within broader discourses of official state culture in the 2000s thus indicate how dance is a site for the control of cultural and political resources.

In particular, I will examine these cultural politics by exploring how contemporary dance negotiates historical and contemporary understandings of the *sha'bi*, itself a multivalent signifier that denotes populist, traditional, folkloric, and everyday street practices, through the representation of *dabke*. This popular dance has long been iconicized as the national dance of Syria that integrates disparate social groups across ethnic and sectarian divisions.[12] The debate over whether and how to adapt *dabke* in contemporary dance productions therefore suggests how choreographers and their audiences negotiated shifting attitudes toward national identity and cultural heritage at the same time that they aspired toward more global imaginaries. While heritage was a paramount concern for some, others focused on producing cosmopolitan works that privileged Western dance forms, from ballet to musical theater. Insofar as symbolic forms of capital tend to reinforce relations of state and power, elitists' ambivalence over how to represent *sha'bi* identity is ultimately reflective of how social market reform led to a disconnect between the authoritarian state and the underprivileged classes.

Dancing Modernities

Contemporary modern dance in Syria reached its zenith in the years immediately prior to the 2011 revolts. From experimental dance to dance theater, dance companies were launched by a young generation of emerging choreographers who came of artistic age during the period of social market reform. Trained primarily in Europe and Russia, these visionaries built a world of dance that inspired artists and entertained audiences. This dance world, like other fields of cultural production, was a complex set of overlapping projects and conflicting visions generally organized by three distinct scenes: dance theater (*raqs masrah*), folk dance (*raqs sha'bi*), and contemporary dance (*raqs mu'asar*). Dance theater companies typically entertained restaurant and theater audiences with carnivalesque pageantry that romanticized epic folklore from the Arab world. Popular dance troupes represented regional and national performance traditions at folk festivals and other state-sponsored events through dance techniques derived from Soviet-era folk art. In contrast to the popular appeal and public accessibility of dance theater and popular dance troupes, contemporary modern dance ensembles tended to perform for more elite audiences in venues for the high arts such as the Dar al-Asad Opera House.

Endorsed by the state along with private sponsors, the contemporary modern dance scene thrived as dancers pursued newfound opportunities for personal expression through movement. World-class artists such as Akram Khan offered workshops and exposure to international dance networks. The promises of economic liberalization were particularly visible through the efforts of several young choreographers working in this field. Trained in classical ballet, dance theater, modern, jazz, and tango, among other contemporary styles, choreographers Alaa Kreimid, Eyas Al-Moqdad, and Lawand Hajo founded their own dance companies and toured their productions regionally and internationally. They represented the first generation of graduates who studied with Motaz Malatialy, director of dance at the Higher Institute of Music and Drama in Damascus. After training at Czechoslovakia's National Conservatory in the 1980s, Malatialy returned to Syria to establish a dance department and launch a program in modern dance at the Higher Institute. The scene expanded further when artistic director Mey Sefan launched the Damascus Contemporary Dance Platform in 2009. This festival cultivated emerging local talent while strengthening regional connections with artists working in Lebanon, Jordan, Palestine, and North Africa. By jumping onto the world's stage and suggesting a veneer of cosmopolitanism in the creative economy, contemporary dance reinforced the neoliberal imaginaries of Bashar al-Asad's economic reform.

This outward display of sophistication arguably displaced, or attempted to displace, the production of national culture (*thaqafa wataniyya*) as the dominant mode of state-sponsored cultural production. As Cécile Boëx relates in her study of cultural commodification during this period, *thaqafa wataniyya* incorporated an "educational function" that encouraged the public to act "as social and moral agents rather than as mere consumers."[13] Artists were encouraged to "deal with 'serious' [*jaddiyya*] issues within the nationalist ideological framework . . . and consider themselves a distinct group endowed with the particular task of enhancing a moral conception of aesthetic value."[14] *Dabke* was particularly central to these ideological commitments. Since the establishment of the Syrian Arab Republic in 1963, *dabke* had been elevated to the status of a national performance tradition through state-sponsored dance festivals and folk dance companies that mediated the symbolic production of the state. Prominent among these was the Omayad Dance Troupe, which represented the Syrian nation for domestic and international audiences. Taking up the folk dance model of Soviet choreographer Igor Moiseyev, Omayad combined theatricality with folklorization. Nationalistic ideals of collective identity were grounded in programs that celebrated pastoral life and consolidated distinct local *dabke* practices into a unified national dance. Along with *sama'*, *raqs 'arabi*, and other folkloric dances, *dabke* articulated both the diversity of Syrian cultural heritage and the pluralist ideals of the Ba'thist state. By deeming *dabke* central to *thaqafa wataniyya*, Syrian nationalists deployed it as a cultural expedient that reinforced the central tenets of Ba'thist identity—secularism, egalitarianism, and pluralism.

Though *thaqafa wataniyya* no longer occupied center stage at Dar al-Asad, the regime's showcase venue for the high arts, it retained legitimacy among the popular classes. In the case of folk dance, state-sponsored and private dance troupes maintained active recruitment programs and toured regularly in the Gulf and former Soviet bloc countries. Participants tended to be recruited from the lower and middle classes, and they benefited from membership in the National Syndicate for Artists, a union that provided additional welfare, job security, and professional networking. In other words, folk dance troupes appealed to those who depended on state institutions for employment and welfare rather than those of the more privileged classes, who benefited from the clientelist networks behind the regime. The public sector thus maintained the core values of *thaqafa wataniyya* while the private sector, particularly contemporary modern dance, gained support tied to political and business elite networks.[15]

Both literally and figuratively, the collective Syrian was displaced from the national stage in favor of a more individualized form of cultural expression. Yet these choreographers and dancers also struggled to find a national identity that was commensurate with their understandings of historicity and contemporaneity. Their ambivalence resonates with what literary critic and poet Adonis has termed "double dependency," or the problem of "how to engage European culture successfully while presenting a link to the Arab past."[16] He contends that dependency on European aesthetics problematically positions Syrian culture as a sign of non-Western difference and privileges European models of political, economic, and social modernization.[17] At the same time, Adonis argues that nothing would remain if contemporary Arab societies were "to be cleared of Western influences."[18] Dance is implicated in these postcolonial debates on Syrian culture in several ways. First, directors working in *thaqafa wataniyya* nationalized performance traditions through a Moiseyev-based model of national dance that positioned Syrian dance on the internationalist stage. Syrian folk dance became a signifier of national difference in an otherwise standardized model of collective group choreography. Second, modern dance choreographers tended to erase local expressions and traditions in favor of Western dance styles that positioned contemporary dance on the Syrian stage. Finally, revolutionaries danced *dabke* in public squares during nonviolent protests to resist state domination.[19] For them, *dabke* articulated historical ties to a pre-Ba'thist past and mediated claims to new political identities. Whether oriented to nationalistic ideologies, Western cultural norms, or political uprising, the aesthetic politics of dance is deeply imbricated in the complexities and contradictions of Syrian modernity.

Resignifying Collective Identity

The 2008 DACC festival was a yearlong, multimillion-dollar initiative for interdisciplinary arts and culture that explored Damascene history and the city's future as a cosmopolitan center of the Arab world. Led by executive director Dr. Hanan Kassab Hassan, a leading figure in the theatrical arts, the initiative offered investment opportunities for an emerging generation of artists and arts administrators, increased resources and capacity-building for established arts centers and institutions, and invited a roster of high-profile international artists to Damascus to work with emerging artists. Curators commissioned a wide range of projects from Syrian artists and presented innovative festivals throughout the year. Some projects marked the modern history of central Damascus by nostalgically linking the past to the present, such as the screening of a 1932 silent film, *Taht samawat Dimashq* (*Under Damascus Skies*), directed by Ismail Anzour, with live musical accompaniment by a youth ensemble in the newly refurbished Dummar Cultural Center. Other events conveyed the diversity of Damascene cultural heritage by emphasizing historical and regional connections between ethnic and religious minorities, such as a series of concerts in May 2008 that showcased prominent women singers and highlighted North African, Andalusian, Iraqi, Kurdish, and Arab influences on Damascene culture.

The DACC brand logo, a multicolored rosette, symbolized such historical and cultural relations. The DACC initiative adapted the rosette from an older symbol of national unity, the mosaic, which stood for the multisectarian tenets of Ba'thist nationalism. A common decorative motif in Syria, the rosette evoked the commemorative rituals of ancient Mesopotamia and was frequently adopted to symbolize a connection between historical and contemporary forms of urbanity in Syria. The rosette logo was prominently displayed at all event banners and posters as well as on billboards throughout Damascus and in television promotions that broad-casted the festival's message of tolerance and cultural openness. Its urban cosmopolitan aesthetic evoked religious and cultural pluralism in ways that registered with other forms of Syrian national identity.

It could be argued that, like the rosette and mosaic, folk dance troupes stood for the integration of Syria's disparate social groups. By performing dance traditions from each region, dance troupes amalgamated provin-cial identities into a national performance tradition that they exported to international folk festivals in the Gulf and former Soviet Union. Despite the central role of *dabke* within discourses of Syrian cultural national-ism, however, it was not included in the DACC initiative. According to Dr. Kassab Hassan, *dabke* was in a "crisis" that forced her to omit it from her otherwise ambitious efforts to integrate Syrian cultural heritage into music, literature, film, and drama.[20]

For Kassab Hassan, the crisis referred to complications in the curatorial process. Though her program staff solicited numerous commissions from emerging artists across disciplines, they were not able to identify a chore-ographer interested in reimagining *dabke* for the DACC program roster. The internationally recognized dance theater company Enana declined their request to develop choreography that aimed for an ethnographic representation of Syrian heritage, notwithstanding Enana director Jihad Mufleh's role as the main producer for DACC's spectacular opening gala. Nor was Kassab Hassan keen to present folk dance troupes (despite the fact that her father had founded the Omayad Dance Troupe) that retained the socialist realist aesthetics of *thaqafa wataniyya*. In the absence of art-ists willing to envision Syrian dance heritage within the aesthetic model promulgated by DACC, the national tradition of *dabke* was excluded from the yearlong program that celebrated Syrian arts and culture.

Like Enana, directors of contemporary modern dance ensembles also maintained that *dabke* was a form of *thaqafa wataniyya* and refused to engage artistically with this dance tradition. When I spoke with Damas-cus-based modern dance choreographers about whether and how they drew on folk dance for artistic material, they explained that they were more interested in art for art's sake and turned to modern dance, jazz, and ballet styles. They were careful to differentiate their work from the state-sponsored folk dance ensembles that produce *thaqafa wataniyya* and measured this difference through *dabke*. Similarly, Lawand Hajo, director of the independent contemporary dance company Ramad Dance, stated that he was not interested in exploring *dabke* in his work. Though his controversial work tended to critique everyday Syrian life, such as the veiling of women and gender relations in the home, he did not find *dabke* to be a compelling subject for critical exploration, perhaps because of its associations with *thaqafa wataniyya*. In contrast, Motaz Malatialy, director of dance at the Higher Institute for Music and the Arts, explained to me that his choreographies for large-scale mass assembly events, such as a drill team performance at a stadium in Oman, were designed through computer software applications.[21] Though folk dance has been integral to these events for decades, he sought to make improvements through the use of computer technology. This, he emphasized, was an innovative method that distinguished his group choreography from those of state-sponsored folk dance ensembles. More broadly, it seemed that modern dance choreographers perceived *dabke* as coterminous with *thaqafa wataniyya* and were therefore ambivalent about linking their work to *thaqafa wataniyya* and its symbolic ties to the socialist state.

Noura Murad, the artistic director of Leish Troupe, broke this pattern in 2009 with her production of *Alf mabruk!* (2009). In this groundbreaking work that explores the psychology of marriage through movement theater, she adapted *dabke* as a symbol of social integration. Her reinterpretation of *dabke* as a set of kinesthetic idioms was a significant departure from the ethnonational rubric of *thaqafa wataniyya*. This paradigm shift toward kinesthetics was one of the main artistic aims for her movement theater ensemble. Over a span of ten years, Murad sought to cultivate a new language of Arab movement through social sciences research, extensive artistic training, and workshops.[22] Leish Troupe aimed to explore the body as a means for critical social engagement, or as Murad stated, "to deconstruct and reconfigure movement in the Arab world."[23] In 2006, Leish premiered the Identity series, a three-part production exploring identity relations through movement theater. In the first installment, *Once They Die, They Realize* (2006), Murad explored ritual mourning and its transformation from the pre-Islamic era to today. The second installment, *Alf mabruk!*

(2009), critiqued marriage as a social institution. The third piece, entitled *It's a Girl . . . !*, narrated the story of a woman who questions femininity in terms of societal expectations and experiences with men through pregnancy and childbirth rituals drawn from Islamic, Christian, and Jewish traditions. The final piece is still in development as Leish Troupe attempts to make a comeback after setbacks related to the ongoing war. The series critiqued gender norms and gendered segregation in Syrian society and provoked controversy. In a move that challenged audiences to respond to double standards in Syrian society, Murad segregated audience members and performers by gender. She was surprised by the response from some audience members: "Why do people accept that there is a row for men and one for women in the post office, but become angry when I ask my audiences to segregate into separate sections for the performance?"[24]

Titled after the colloquial expression for "congratulations," *Alf mabruk!* simulated the ritual events leading to marriage. The four movements of *Alf mabruk!* narrated the development of the self in marriage—from fear and self-directed violence to resignation and collective effervescence. The choreography simulated a wedding ceremony through four movements with a cast of four dancers. Each movement was staged in an unconventional space in the venue, such as a corridor or unused room. The stage design was specific to the architectural layout of each venue, with the exception of the original setting in the Citadel, a former prison that was converted into a venue for the arts.

The metaphor of the prison was central to Murad's production. She drew on a history of theatrical productions that liken marriage to a prison. In Rebecca Joubin's study of Syrian television drama,[25] she argues that marriage is symbolic of political and economic oppression. Male characters in certain television dramas are subjugated by their spouses and by governmental authority such that "the traditional position of the male provider directly links males' economic disempowerment to the fear of female domination."[26] However, Murad approached these issues from an egalitarian perspective rather than from the male perspective, as is commonly held up in television drama. For instance, the second movement consisted of the separation of the bride and groom into their alter egos. A strip of sheer gauze separated the stage into two arenas such that male dancers were hidden from female audiences, as were female dancers from male audiences. Dramatic conflict erupted between the dancers: when one shrunk in anxiety, fright, and anticipation, her alter ego emerged as defiant, angry, and reluctant. The pas de deux between each set of dancers embodied the internal conflict of a split self by means of movements that were cornered, violent, and desperate. A decorative satin sash became an instrument of bondage and restraint as each performer encircled and ensnared the other with the prop.

Resolution of this split self occurred through the adaptation of *dabke* in the final movement. A *haflat al-ʿurs*, or wedding dance party typical of Syrian wedding customs, was staged such that the four dancers formed a closed circle that framed the audience and dismantled the fourth wall between audiences and performers. Uniformity of movement dominated as the dancers performed a sequence of repeating figures loosely based on *dabke*. Steps, kicks, hops, and knee bends accelerated with increased intensity, resembling the kinesthetics of wedding festivities.[27]

The adaptation generated a variety of critical responses. A review published in *Discover Syria* described the last scene, entitled "Dabke," as a simple expression of joy following the arduous efforts of ritual preparation.[28] One audience member situated the performance of *dabke* within debates on cultural heritage and social progress. He commented: "Of the many Oriental customs presented in this production and located within the marriage ritual, the most important is that of the circle of dabke. The circle embodies a truism in which the beginning is the end; likewise, if the concept of marriage itself turns in a circle, we intellectuals are taken back to our primordialisms (*al-ʿaqliyya al-qadima al-taqlidiyya*) through this institution."[29] The commentary continued to praise this work for constructing a sense of authenticity (*asala*) that the commentator felt was lost in contemporary society. He highlighted specific cultural tropes that included the ironic play of a colloquial expression (Congratulations!) as the production's title, the ways that a stomp indicates a deep engagement or sense of belonging (*intima'*), and the unified movements of boys and girls that resemble the practice of *dabke*. He upheld *Alf mabruk!* as an aesthetic intervention against the diminishing value of cultural heritage and the corruption of Syrian youth.

Murad also attempted to collapse social barriers to contemporary art in several ways. First, she toured the production to local audiences in smaller cities beyond Damascus, including Homs, Aleppo, and Lattakia, who tended to receive less exposure to emergent and experimental work. She also presented *Alf mabruk!* outside of Syria at the Julidans Dance Festival in Amsterdam in 2010. Second, she cast actors rather than trained dancers for the roles and worked collaboratively with them to choreograph movements that best resonated with their personal experiences and modes of expression.

In addition to working through social barriers, *Alf mabruk!* challenged aesthetic and philosophical boundaries. Murad successfully adapted the stylistic idioms of *dabke* within a contemporary work that critiqued the process and rituals of marriage in Syrian society. In doing so, Murad arguably shifted staged *dabke* away from its associations with *thaqafa wataniyya* and folk dance aesthetics and toward experimental forms of movement. She deconstructed the social dance and reconfigured it in ways that resonated with contemporary experiences of Syrian life cycle events rather than provincial forms of identity. Moreover, Murad conceived of Syrian dance in ways that resisted hegemonic cultures of dance. *Alf mabruk!* did not depend on Soviet models of folk dance nor Western forms of classical and modern dance but rather resignified Syrian *dabke* within its own social grammar.

Conclusion

After the formalization of social market reform in 2005, it appeared as if Syria was opening up its cultural and economic borders in unprecedented ways. From café culture to shopping malls, a consumer culture emerged among the upper-middle classes who appreciated the commodities and services associated with a globalized lifestyle. Rapid shifts in the dance sector supported this veneer of cosmopolitanism and sophistication through the emergence of a scene for contemporary modern dance that encompassed young choreographers, talented dancers, and internationally renowned guest artists. It is clear, however, that cultural liberalization benefited some artists and marginalized others. Opportunities to participate in global arts networks were not extended to members of state-sponsored folk ensembles and professional artist associations, institutional relics of Syria's quasi-socialist past. These dancers were denied access to the new opportunities and forms of cultural production that constituted social market reform. Like the widening gap between elite and non-elite during this period, a polarization emerged between dance as high art in the contemporary modern dance scene and dance as populist art in the world of *thaqafa wataniyya*. In other words, those in the dance sector who benefited most from the expansion of resources under social market reform effectively marginalized those who benefited least. By increasing opportunities for conservatory graduates and prioritizing neoliberal forms of culture, Asad's liberalization policies exacerbated social divisions within the performing arts. The redistribution of cultural resources thus reproduced social and economic divisions that, as scholars in anthropology, economics, and political science have noted, also occurred in other sectors of Syrian society during liberalization.

This chapter has addressed how specific figures among the cultural elite, namely choreographers and directors, negotiated the perceived waning of socialism, failure of nationalism, and promises of liberalization. While it is beyond the scope of this chapter to fully address the experiences of those working within the state-sponsored dance troupes, they generally tended to uphold *thaqafa wataniyya* and continued to present folk dance through the aesthetic ideology of socialist realism. Comparatively, the cultural elite of the dance world lacked a cohesive vision as to how contemporary dance might best represent a national community and who might be represented by contemporary Syrian dance. Some choreographers chose not to pursue the question of national identity, others recognized that national identity was shifting but failed to envision how that shift might take place in terms of dance. One choreographer, Noura Murad, tackled the question of identity by pivoting from a nationalistic framework for *dabke* to an anthropological framework that critiqued social rituals through *dabke*. These divergent approaches to the representation of collective identity through Syrian dance traditions reveal the centrality of *thaqafa wataniyya* to the dance world despite a general ambivalence toward its relevancy in the era of social market reform.

The ambiguous relations of collective identity and dance quickly faded with the first protests in March 2011. Nonviolent creative revolutionaries reclaimed *dabke* as a symbol of popular power rather than state power.[30] Protestors staged *dabke* as part of Friday demonstrations organized across the country and uploaded video clips of these performances to social media platforms to mobilize revolutionary sentiment. Among the most cherished of media for the creative revolution, popular dance subverted the staid, deeply ideological official culture that had afflicted Syria for decades. Again the province of the non-elite, the collective movement of dancers in a *dabke* circle helped to sustain resistance to the state and to mourn the victims of its violence.

6

Christian Charities and the Ba'thist Regime in Bashar al-Asad's Syria

A Comparative Analysis

LAURA RUIZ DE ELVIRA

Introduction

Until the mid-2000s, as Benoît Challand notes,[1] scholars paid scant attention to local charities (*jam'iyyat khayriyya*) in the Arab world. The literature focused instead on "new generation" NGOs, both development and advocacy,[2] which were advantaged by being more accessible and visible to foreign donors and researchers, endorsing the international community's *doxa* about civil society promotion, good governance, and democracy. These NGOs also tended to promulgate a critical discourse toward the Arab authoritarian political regimes, a factor that contributed to drawing the attention of outside observers. Yet in recent years interest in these traditional associative structures has increased,[3] partly because of their revival but also because of their significant contribution to social welfare in Arab countries. In Saudi Arabia, for instance, the number of charities increased rapidly after the year 2002. This development took place within the framework of the "National Strategy for Remedying Poverty," which,

I would like to thank Myriam Catusse and Geraldine Chatelard (coordinators of the ANR program "Tanmia. Le développement: Fabrique de l'action publique dans le monde arabe") for the support given to this research, as well as Elizabeth Picard for her comments on earlier drafts of this paper.

instead of creating new state aid programs, led to the establishment of charitable foundations financed mainly by members of the royal family.[4] In Palestine, too, there was an increase in the number of charitable organizations.[5] As Jonathan Benthall has remarked, in the Arab region as in the rest of the world even the most ardent defenders of state intervention in society's activities have seemed more inclined in the last decades to recognize the legitimacy and necessity of the complementary role played by private charity.[6]

In Syria from 2000 to 2010, too, the growing number of charities[7] and organizations providing social services to the increasingly impoverished population was reported in the national newspapers and could be easily noticed in the streets, where the signs of the newly established charities flourished. According to official figures, charities represented more than 60 percent of the entire associative sector in 2008.[8] This percentage would be even higher if it included unregistered—that is, nonauthorized[9]—associations. Of the latter category, most—but not all—were Christian, as we will see.

In such a context, the study of charities had a twofold interest. First, research on Syrian charities offered an empirical approach to analyze the transformations occurring in the Syrian associative field itself, in terms of the renewal of actors, new balances of power, revision of strategies and approaches both by the state and the civil society actors, and the introduction of new methods and new rhetoric by the latter. Second, it represented a useful method for exploring the impact of the transition from a centralized economy to a "social market" model in which the past socialist polity of the Ba'thist regime had been reconfigured by the Syrian authorities.[10] Although the Syrian state had long served as the dominant agent of redistribution and the main provider of social welfare,[11] non-state actors— that is, the private sector and the associative sector—became increasingly important in ensuring economic growth and social welfare provision. Consequently, during Bashar al-Asad's first decade in power, Syria experienced a period of rising "participation." Public authorities urged non-state actors to play a new role and to contribute to the national development process. The purpose of this, according to the government, was to "encourage civil society organizations' contribution to local development efforts, and provide incentives to the development processes based upon collective efforts, and offer them financial, technical and human resources."[12] As a result, the number of associations registered with the Ministry of Social Affairs and Labor (MoSAL) almost tripled in less than ten years.[13] Likewise, the volume of associations' services significantly increased. For instance, the Sunduq al-'afiya (Health Fund), a charitable project of the Union of Damascus Charities,[14] experienced a spectacular evolution: the number of beneficiaries increased from 536 in 1997 to 4,455 in 2006. Over the course of ten years, 29,823 patients had their medical care paid for (including some 60,000 surgeries) at a total cost of 953 million Syrian pounds.[15] However, this development of the civic sector was not accompanied by a softening of state control and disciplinary mechanisms, but rather by their reinforcement and upgrading (registration of previous nonregistered charities, the creation of government-operated nongovernmental organizations, dissolution of boards of directors, etc.).[16]

Some recent research has contextualized Syrian civil society organizations in the abovementioned economic, political, and social transformation.[17] Yet these studies are either overly general[18] or are focused on Sunni-based initiatives,[19] which dominated the Syrian associative sector during the years 2000–2010. Therefore, little attention has been paid to the Christian associative structures in Syria, which remain relatively unknown, even though they were, before 2011, extremely active in the capital and Aleppo and more visible in Western circles than their Muslim counterparts. Their importance needs to be underscored in terms of the political economy they illuminate. Their study brings to light the relationship between the Christian communities, the Eastern Churches, and the Ba'thist regime.[20] Moreover, a close examination of these associations reveals the compromises made between a "minority-led" regime and a Christian minority afraid of losing its autonomy. Likewise, these associations generate and highlight interesting social solidarities (and rivalries) among the Syrian Christian communities that justify additional scholarly attention.

This chapter will seek to address this gap in the literature by providing a better understanding of Christian charities from a comparative perspective. I will first highlight several particularities of Syria's Christian communities, focusing on their overrepresentation in the Syrian associative sector, their cautious approach regarding religious and communitarian issues, their specialization in providing care for disabled people and, finally, their lack of gender segregation. I will then turn to the privileges Christian associations enjoyed during 2000–2010 related to their strong interaction with foreign actors and their legal status.[21] In doing so, I will demonstrate that Christian associations benefited from a greater autonomy than their Muslim counterparts within Syria's very restrictive political system, in which the most repressive measures were aimed at Sunni-based autonomous initiatives. Finally, I will offer some hypotheses to explain why the regime implemented what I call a laissez-faire policy toward Christian associations. I suggest that the Christian associations' privileged status constituted one element, among others, of a tacit accord between the Syrian regime, the Eastern Christian Churches, and the Christian communities more generally. Likewise, it symbolized the positive-sum relationship existing between the regime and Christian civil society actors. Besides shedding light on the functioning of the Christian associations, this chapter will provide a key to better understand the nexus between the Christian communities and the regime in Bashar al-Asad's Syria, which has become ever more evident since the uprising that began in March 2011, with demonstrations of public support of the Syrian Christian clergy and communities for the Ba'thist regime.[22]

The data analyzed here are based on two years of qualitative fieldwork undertaken mainly in Damascus and Aleppo between November 2007 and January 2010. This included over one hundred semistructured interviews and participant observation sessions, visits to more than thirty charities, and one year of ethnographic work with the *Bayt al-salam* (House of Peace) association, a Christian charity based in Damascus serving handicapped people. Therefore, my observations only address years prior to 2011, and no analysis is made of the uprising period that has deeply and durably transformed the third sector. This chapter is part of a larger research project examining the role of charities during Syria's reconfiguration of social policies in the 2000–2010 period. This research followed an interdisciplinary approach, drawing on political science, the sociology of associations, and the anthropology of charitable practices.

Christian Associations' Characteristics

In Syria, charities have traditionally been the backbone of associations. Rooted in a long tradition that is both Muslim and Christian, they have represented the manifestation of a fragile civil society shaped by a fraught relationship with public institutions and the Ba'thist regime. Charities have responded to a real need on the part of the population; unlike other types of organizations—such as "new generation" NGOs in Palestine, Morocco, or Yemen, intended mainly to collect funds from international sponsors or the state—few were inactive shells.[23] Several distinguishing features characterized the Syrian Christian charitable associations during the 2000s—both those that were registered with the Ministry of Social Affairs and Labor and those that were church-affiliated (and not registered with MoSAL)—and differentiated them from other charities working in Syria.[24]

The first feature I will discuss is the overrepresentation of the Christian associations in the Syrian associative sector prior to the 2011 uprising.[25] According to Soukaina Boukhaima, in 2002 Christian associations represented approximately 20 percent of the Syrian denominational charitable associations,[26] when the Christian communities did not represent more than 10 percent of the Syrian population. By 2010 this figure had undoubtedly decreased, given the associative boom of 2005–6 and the ensuing registration of hundreds of Muslim charities at the Ministry of Social Affairs and Labor. Still, Christian associations remained numerous and very active, especially in the capital and in Aleppo, where, in addition to Syrian beneficiaries, many Iraqi refugees received assistance following their arrival in the country starting in 2003.

Boukhaima ascribes this dynamism to a wider strategy of the Christian communities to obtain more autonomy within a Muslim majority,[27] but I suggest that the remarkable development of the Christian associative sector during the twentieth century is the product of two different factors. First, I argue it is the partial result of rivalry between different Christian religious communities and various Eastern Churches, with all of them wanting their own charitable or social associations.[28] Therefore, the overrepresentation itself symbolized the fragmentation of the Christian minority into different groups. Charitable work provides communities with visibility and prestige, and it helps to unite community members; in addition, charitable associations offer associative leaders a certain social capital and clientele. Finally, fostering charitable activities strengthens the position of the clergy as social mediators both between the charity and the community and between the state and the community. As a result, religious leaders, associative entrepreneurs, and communities themselves were interested in promoting these associations.

Yet competition alone cannot explain the historical overrepresentation of Christian charities in the Syrian nonprofit sector. This leads us to the second factor, which is the impact of political history in Syria's associative sphere. Most of the Christian associations operating from 2000 to 2010 had been created before Bashar al-Asad's 2000 ascension to the presidency; some were founded in the first half of the twentieth century (such as the Charitable Association of Saint Gregorius, al-Mustawsaf al-khayri, and the Charitable Association of Saint Laundius), others started working in the 1980s and 1990s (for example, al-Mahabba, Iman wa nur [Faith and Light], Bayt al-salam, al-Ard [The Earth], al-Safina, and Mashgal al-manara). Unlike Muslim charities, which experienced an important growth during the 2000s, few new Christian associations were founded during the same period. This observation leads to the following conclusion: while for decades the Ba'thist regime prevented the Muslim community from satisfying the demand for private welfare by creating autonomous charities—and even punished it after the Hama revolt—the Christian associative sector continued to expand without restraint, either under the patronage of the religious institutions or via the legal path (by registering with MoSAL). Therefore, rather than stressing the overrepresentation of the Christian structures, one might emphasize the underrepresentation of the Muslim associations, especially in the 1980s, after the Muslim Brotherhood revolt, and the 1990s.

The second feature I stress is the attitude of Christian associations toward religious and communitarian issues. Like most Syrian charities and similar organizations around the world, Christian charitable associations are generally based on what Elizabeth Picard calls "primary or primordial affiliations"; that is, on religious, ethnic, or regionally based cleavages.[29] Some visible examples include the al-Salib association for

Armenians in Syria, the Catholic charitable association of Aleppo, and charities sponsored by different religious institutions. Yet, my fieldwork has shown that unlike most Muslim associations, Christian charities in Syria, in general, prefer to define themselves as nonreligious and inter-communitarian. Usrat al-ikha', for example, although founded more than forty years ago by a Lazarist priest and composed mainly of Christians, insists in its leaflet: "In a country where one's religion is taken into consideration before all else, Terre des Hommes Syrie, after 25 years of efforts, is now recognised as a 'Non Governmental Organization' which is OPEN TO ANY PERSON in distress." In similar fashion, the Saint Vincent de Paul charitable association, affiliated with the international Saint Vincent de Paul religious organization, is described by its members as a secular ('ilmaniyya) and noncommunitarian (la-ta'ifiyya) charity.[30]

This tendency to present Christian charities as noncommunitarian organizations is linked to the missionary heritage that has historically characterized Christian charitable initiatives all over the world.[31] In fact, most of the Syrian Christian social and charitable associations that I visited between 2007 and 2010 had a percentage of Muslim beneficiaries and Muslim employees.[32] At Terre des Hommes Syrie, for example, 95 percent of the aid recipients in 2008 were Muslims.[33] Some associations even had Muslim members on the board. Bayt al-salam, a nonregistered association under the patronage of the Syriac Catholic Church, reported that seven of the thirty-three service recipients in 2009 and one of the members of the board of directors (Majlis idara) were Muslim. According to the director of this charity, this strategy sought to brush aside accusations of sectarianism from the Muslim majority. Still, this approach posed challenges, since Christian associations could face accusations of proselytizing.[34] Maintaining a nonsectarian image while avoiding the appearance of proselytizing was quite complicated, as is evident in the case of the Saint Vincent de Paul association. Their strategy consisted of accepting a small percentage of Muslims as temporary beneficiaries (the status of permanent beneficiary being reserved exclusively for Christians), provided that they had previously addressed their demands to a Muslim charity and been refused.[35] By providing assistance in this way, one of its members said, they could not be accused either of sectarianism, since some beneficiaries were Muslims, or of proselytizing, since they only helped those "abandoned" by Muslim charities.

The third particularity I wish to mention here is the specialization of the Christian associative sector in the provision of aid and services for the disabled, largely in line with Western conceptions of disability centering on tropes of "social integration," "capacity building," and "empowerment." The reasons for this specialization are not easy to state because of the lack of literature on the subject. However, two hypotheses, impossible to verify at the present moment, could explain this phenomenon: first, the strong relations between the Middle Eastern Christian communities and Western countries, where public interest in serving disabled people emerged in the second half of the twentieth century; and second, the need for specialized services for the Christian handicapped due to the high prevalence of disability ensuing from consanguinity in the Syrian Christian minority.

Dozens of new Church-linked associations serving mentally and physically handicapped people were created during the 1980s and 1990s, in addition to previously existing traditional charities providing welfare to the poor, the elderly, and orphans. Some of them were directly inspired by foreign models (al-Safina and Iman wa nur, for example), which revealed the deep ties between Middle Eastern Christian communities and the West (see next section).[36] According to a 2008 interview with Bayt al-salam's president, "at that period, little or no aid was provided by the state to the families and very few associations—public or private—were interested in offering specialized care to the disabled. . . . [H]andicapped people were thus confined to their homes without any aid." The foundational aim of Bayt al-salam was first "getting these people out of their houses" and then "teaching them something and making them feel useful and valuable."[37] A number of previously established associations, like Terre des Hommes Syrie, also provided services in this sector. According to that organization's brochure printed during the 2000s, the association aimed at "help[ing] the handicapped who need medical care, then help[ing] them accept their disability, help[ing] them regain their dignity, and help[ing] them reintegrate into society."

With time, service provision to disabled people has developed significantly in Syria and, by 2011, was no longer entirely in the hands of

Christian associations. Moreover, the First Lady's interest in disabled people turned the sector into a fashionable "business" in which many wished to participate.[38] Within the period 2000–2010, dozens of associations were created, mainly by secular or Muslim groups. A new office was established by MoSAL, the High Institution for the Integration of Handicapped People in Syria. This institution's goal was to oversee and manage all the NGOs working in this burgeoning sector. However, before the uprising, Christian associations remained pioneers in this area.

The fourth and final particularity I discuss regarding the Christian third sector prior to 2011 is its lack of gender segregation. The Syrian charitable sphere during 2000–2010 was otherwise generally characterized by a strongly enforced separation between men and women. Muslim charities were usually directed, managed, and run by men; very few were controlled and administered exclusively by women.[39] Sex segregation was even more visible in the case of the charities in which both men and women were involved but did not physically work together. This was often a result of the formation, inside a men's organization, of a women's committee (*Lajna nisa'iyya*). The committees were generally equipped with their own headquarters where only women worked; they undertook their own activities and programs, which usually targeted female beneficiaries. This was the case, for example, of the Jam'iyyat al-ihsan al-islamiyya (Association of the Islamic Charity), an old Shi'ite charity in the Old City of Damascus. The women's committee of this association ran its own professional training institute for women and girls and organized trips exclusively for the female members. For the latter, investing time in the charity provided not only moral and religious satisfaction but also social and cultural gratification. The example of the al-Ansar Charitable Association (from the Abu Nur religious complex) similarly shows how sex segregation was concretely applied on the ground. Here, segregation was not institutionalized by the creation of a special committee for women, but there was a very real de facto separation of gender roles. Women were responsible for the Dar al-rahma li-l-yatimat orphanage (House of Mercy for Female Orphans), created several years earlier for female orphans; the rest of the programs and activities were managed and directed by men.

Contrary to their Muslim counterparts, the Christian associations I visited during fieldwork usually mixed women and men at all levels—in management and in everyday work positions, on the one hand, and at the beneficiary level, on the other hand. At Bayt al-salam, for example, the president of the board was a man and the director was an Armenian woman. Moreover, among a dozen employees, only three were men. Likewise, at al-Mahabba and al-Safina the boards were composed both of men and women. In the everyday operations of these associations, female and male beneficiaries participated in the same activities and shared spaces and facilities.

This particularity must be partly understood as the reflection of the Christian communities themselves, which are less sex-segregated than the Muslim majority. The difference between the two models of gender relations in associative work is caused by a different conception of sociability that applies not only to the public sphere but also to the family. In addition, those involved in Sunni-based charities are generally religiously conservative in their daily life, which reinforces gender segregation in the spaces where they operate.

Although gender segregation (or its absence) in these associations did not necessarily have a concrete impact in terms of types and styles of action, discourses and justifications, and ways of thinking about charitable work, it did have effects on the social relations among the community (or group) involved in the organization (including both the recipients of aid and the members and the employees) as well as on the transmission of moral values and on the reproduction of the social model. In other words, while the Syrian associative sector was shaped by the gender norms upheld and reproduced by the different religious communities, it also contributed to reproducing and reinforcing these norms by applying them in the daily life of these communities.

Privileged Status of Christian Associations

In this section I argue that Christian charities enjoyed, under Bashar al-Asad's Syria, a de facto privileged status that ultimately symbolized the friendly relations between the Christian communities, the Eastern Churches, and the regime. Christian charities benefited from greater autonomy and wider freedom of action than the Sunni-based associations, which represented the large majority of the nonprofit sector. Within a very restrictive authoritarian political system, where civil society actors were first efficiently selected throughout different procedures and mechanisms, then actively controlled and, finally, from time to time, repressed, Christian charities were more or less allowed to do what they wanted, provided they did not overstep certain limits. The government maintained an older laissez-faire policy toward Christian associations, even regarding the most sensitive aspects of their activities, such as interaction with foreign actors or the securing of legal status. The state rarely used coercive powers against them. The next two points illustrate the implications of this privileged status.

First, in a political context where any contact between local and foreign actors was perceived as suspicious and was actively controlled by the regime, the Christian associations enjoyed—in Bashar's Syria, as in the past—privileged access to external actors. Ties between Middle Eastern Christian communities and the West, often but not exclusively established through the churches, are historical and cultural products dating to the nineteenth century;[40] even though the first missionaries in the Middle East date back to the thirteenth century, when the mendicant orders took the road toward the East.[41] Therefore, ties at the civil society level during the 2000s were only the continuation of older and broader linkages developed over centuries.

Examples of Syrian Christian associations affiliated with international and Western organizations are abundant, such as the Syrian Saint Vincent de Paul charitable organization (created in 1863), which is one of the oldest charities in the country. Other examples include the charitable association Usrat al-ikha' (created in Damascus in 1977), a member of the international network Terre des Hommes, and the Damascene association for the handicapped, al-Safina, which is the Syrian version of the international network L'Arche. By contrast, among Sunni-based charities, affiliation with Western, international, or even regional networks was rather unusual before 2011. The Islamic Relief international network, which has established over one hundred branches worldwide and more particularly in the Middle East (in Egypt, Lebanon, Iraq, Jordan, Palestine, or Yemen), did not officially work in Syria, for instance.

Both the regime's laissez-faire policy toward the Christian associations and the latter's tight cooperation with foreign organizations are evident in patterns of aid provision to Iraqi refugees between 2003 and 2011. In 2008, six of the seven local organizations providing aid to the Iraqi community in Damascus were either Christian charities (for example, Saint Vincent de Paul or Usrat al-ikha') or Christian initiatives undertaken by the church (such as the Ibrahim al-Khalil convent or the Sisters of the Good Shepherd).[42] These local actors all received economic, human, and material support from foreign actors. An important part of this support came from international intergovernmental agencies, such as UNICEF and the UN Refugee Agency (UNHCR). Another portion was supplied by some of the fourteen international NGOs that had been approved by the Syrian Ministry of Foreign Affairs to work in the country under the supervision of the Syrian Arabic Red Crescent Society (SARC). A third part of this support was directly provided by nonapproved international organizations such as the ICMC, Catholic Relief Services, or Terre des Hommes Lausanne. In other words, in 2008 several Christian associations had established partnerships with international organizations outside the legal framework dictated by the Syrian government. Furthermore, this exceptional situation was maintained with the tacit approval of the security apparatus until the beginning of 2010, when the regime showed its determination to put an end to the circumvention of its authority by expelling some of these foreign organizations.

Christian associations' privileged access to foreign actors can also be illustrated through the case of the International Charity Bazaar that took place annually in Damascus. Numerous embassies participated by selling national products of the countries that they represented. A limited percentage of the funds collected were designated for "the Syrian charities."[43] In 2007 only a handful of local associations were allowed to take part in the event. Among them, the GONGOs[44] of the First Lady (FIRDOS and MAWRED[45]) and the Christian associations (Bayt al-salam, al-Safina, al-Ard and the Small Roses organization) were best represented. Moreover, the following year, when local associations were no longer officially welcomed, the GONGOs of the First Lady and three Christian associations were again included among the participants. Al-Safina, for example, participated under the patronage of the Canadian embassy, given the Canadian nationality of Jean Vanier, founder of the L'Arche community. Similarly, Bayt al-salam participated in the bazaar under the patronage of the Belgian Embassy, where one of its board members was an employee.

Finally, other forms of collaboration between Christian associations and foreign NGOs became more common from the year 2000 onward. Sometimes they took the form of legal partnerships approved directly by MoSAL. For example, in 2010 at least four of the seven partnership agreements that had been signed by the IECD (Institut Européen de Coopération et de Développement) with local independent non-state actors were established with Christian institutions—specifically with the al-Ard center, the Friends of Maaloula association, the Small Roses organization, and the Custodie Franciscaine de Terre Sainte. This kind of partnership was still quite rare and strongly controlled by MoSAL. Consequently, by 2011 very few local associations had benefited from collaboration with external actors, and I found a significant number of Christian associations in the small set of lucky ones.

As I have shown, the examples that illustrate the strong alliance between Syria's Christian associations and foreign actors are quite extensive. Yet my aim is not to develop a complete account of this cooperation but to show the exceptional character of this collaboration, given the authoritarian nature of the Syrian Ba'thist regime, the limited external interference that it has historically allowed, and the consequent isolation of Syrian civil society. As these examples have suggested, while the Muslim charities generally had a very restricted and controlled access to foreign actors, Christian associations enjoyed a privileged status that enabled them to preserve and develop their long-established ties with the West.

Second, the relative freedom that Christian associations enjoyed during 2000–2010 is also particularly salient considering their occasional lack of formal legal status. Many Christian associations were not formally registered with the Ministry of Social Affairs and Labor. The state did not, therefore, consider them entirely legal, but in many cases they still operated as if they were.

According to the law governing the Syrian associative sector prior to the 2011 uprising—1958's law No. 93[46]—no association had the right to exist and work in Syria unless it had been authorized by MoSAL.[47] Yet because of the long-established difficulty of registering new associations, informal structures[48] had become quite widespread during the last decades of the twentieth century. In addition, a policy of de facto coercion and neglect of the "official" associative sector, which had been ongoing since the 1960s, plunged the sector into a state of inactivity and weakness that lasted until the 1990s. The number of legally registered associations consequently decreased from 596 in the year 1962 to 513 in the year 2000.[49] Thus, the blossoming of informal networks took place alongside the enervation of the formal associative sector. With Bashar al-Asad's accession to the presidency, the licensing system became somewhat more flexible at the same time that the authorities began to normalize previously existing informal associations. The combination of these two policies partially unblocked access to the associative sector. If official statistics are to be believed, in just a decade almost nine hundred organizations were registered.

In the framework of this normalization process, MoSAL encouraged informal networks to institutionalize their activities and register their projects as legal associations. This strategy arguably resulted from the regime's desire to eliminate uncontrolled spaces. As Wiktorowitz argues, referring to the Jordanian case, "social groups that operate in the shadows of society outside the panopticon-like gaze of the bureaucracy are unpredictable and thus potentially threatening to state power."[50] Once registered, these associations become visible and find themselves "embedded in a web of bureaucratic practices and legal codes which allows those in power to monitor and regulate collective activities."[51] Numerous previously informal Sunni-based charities were thus registered while dozens (and maybe more) of Christian social and charitable associations remained outside the legal and national institutional framework.

Nonregistered Christian associations were nevertheless also "invited" by the state to formalize their legal status by the mid-2000s. The al-Safina association, for example, received a letter from MoSAL in which it was asked to register with the ministry.[52] Several Christian religious leaders were similarly contacted to discuss the same issue regarding other associations. Many of these associations nevertheless chose to remain under the patronage of Christian religious institutions instead of accepting the authority of the ministry. This decision was sometimes motivated by the conviction that remaining under the sponsorship of religious institutions would preserve an association's autonomy. In other cases, this decision was the consequence of internal conflicts: while the secular administrators of these associations wanted to "legalize" them, the religious "patrons"—who desired to preserve their centrality and their authority over them—refused.

In other words, while Muslim associations were forced to follow the legal path to survive, Christian associations were allowed to make the choice between the two statuses. Furthermore, while Sunni religious men were dismissed from their positions as the heads of Muslim charities in 2008, Christian associations were still allowed to remain under church patronage; some were even led by Christian religious leaders.

The two points analyzed in this section (i.e., Christian charities' strong interaction with foreign actors and their privileged legal status) prove that, during 2000–2010, the Syrian regime did not perceive Christian associations as a real danger to the preservation of its political power. As a result, the state eased its numerous restrictions on civil society actors for Christian agencies.

A Positive-Sum Relationship

Unlike Muslim charities, Christian associations were not viewed as posing a threat to regime stability, and they were not considered to possess either significant social or political power. This is partly due to the fact that they were fewer in number than their Muslim counterparts and, as I previously mentioned, suffered from the same fragmentation and lack of coordination which afflict the Christian communities and the Eastern Churches themselves. Notably, while some Sunni-based initiatives managed to collect several millions of Syrian pounds every year and provide services for thousands of beneficiaries,[53] Christian associations had to content themselves with more modest budgets.[54] Therefore, their capacity to challenge the regime was far less significant. Finally, the Christian communities had—and still have—an institutionalized religious hierarchy that acted as the official representative of the members of the communities and as intermediary between the latter and the state. Furthermore, as previously discussed, many Christian associations active during the 2000s were either effectively under the direct patronage of the church or, when registered with MoSAL, backed by a religious leader. Consequently, the state could control the Christian associations much more easily than the Muslim ones.

Christian associations were thus allowed to go about their business without significant interference, and also benefited from state patronage and autonomy. The First Lady publicly showed her support by visiting many of them. Photographs of these visits were often proudly displayed in the headquarters of these associations, the members of which usually admired and appreciated Asma al-Asad. In exchange, the leaders of these organizations were expected to legitimize the Syrian regime or at least not to challenge government policies.[55] The relationship between the regime and Christian associations must thus be described in positive-sum terms: By promoting the Christian associations, the regime obtained the tacit approval of Christian civil society actors, and in exchange these actors gained relative autonomy and greater freedom of action than their Muslim counterparts.

This tolerant policy toward the Christian associations in Syria during 2000–2010 must be read as a clear example of the wider alliance and the tacit accord existing between the Syrian regime and the Christian communities. Demonstrations of goodwill toward Christians reflect the regime's awareness of its vulnerability regarding minority rule and its concomitant keenness to build alliances with others who share not just a common enemy (Sunni dominance and the threat of militancy) but also similar values.[56] This laissez-faire policy aimed to ensure that Christian civil society organizations, and, more generally, the Christian communities, would not pose a political threat to the regime. In this way, the regime freed itself to focus on fighting against those perceived as internal threats, such as the revival of political Islam or the opposition of human rights activists.

Finally, this implicit accord also contributed to strengthening the official narrative of multicultural tolerance and protection of religious and ethnic minorities—a narrative that had attracted Western governments and international donors for decades—while reproducing old patterns of de facto authoritarian governance (and exemplifying a politics of "divide and rule").

As of March 2015, the Christian communities still represent an important source of support for the Syrian regime or, at least, for the maintenance of the previous political status quo. Prior to 2011, the lack of significant political opposition reinforced the idea that the only alternative to the Ba'thist regime was the Muslim Brotherhood. Yet the specter of Islamist rule under this religious movement has led many Christians, even today under the revolt, to conclude that their way of life might best be guaranteed by the Asad regime.[57] Therefore, as Fiona McCallum has suggested, "security prevails over the democratization argument within the Christian community," especially since a real democratization process in Syria would entail a regime change.[58] In the end, the successful co-optation of the Christian communities and of Christian civil society actors symbolizes more the fear of an Islamist regime rather than the sanction of the Ba'thist regime's policies.

Conclusion

This chapter has provided some keys to understanding the particularities that differentiated the Christian associations during 2000–2010 from their Muslim counterparts, both regarding their structural features (i.e., a cautious attitude toward communitarian and religious issues and gender cohabitation), their activities (with a strongly focused commitment to serving handicapped people), and their access to national and foreign resources.

Christians' political freedoms, like those of all Syrian citizens, were constrained within the authoritarian system of the Ba'thist regime. Yet I have tried to demonstrate that Christian charities—and Christian organizations more generally—have enjoyed a position of de facto privilege in contrast to Muslim associative structures. Their at times exceptional legal status and their strong ties with foreign actors are just two examples of this (partial) freedom of action. In the same vein, the over-representation of Christian organizations in the Syrian associative landscape prior to 2011, and especially in the 1980s and 1990s, symbolizes this position of privilege.

This situation must be understood as a sign of a wider and deeper compromise between a "minority-led" regime aiming to preserve its power and a Christian minority afraid of losing its autonomy in a Muslim-majority country. Finally, this compromise, developed under Hafiz al-Asad and deepened under Bashar al-Asad's rule, is proving to endure during the revolt because—although some Christian voices have strongly criticized the regime's repression—both the clergy and the large majority of the Christian communities either still remain silent or, in some cases, openly back the regime.

7

Performing the Nation

Syrian Christians on the National Stage

ANDREAS BANDAK

Introduction: Snowing Love

"*Thalj, thalj . . .*"—it resounds from several hundred voices on the stage of Dar al-Asad for Culture and Arts, the national opera house in Damascus, planned by former president Hafiz al-Asad, and constructed and inaugurated by his son and successor Bashar al-Asad in 2004. *Snow, snow . . .* —the famous Lebanese singer Fairouz's classic Christmas song goes as Juwqat al-farah, the Choir of Joy, celebrates the upcoming holidays. The choir makes the sound of falling snow by rubbing their hands together, at first gently and then with growing intensity so that thunder and lightning suddenly reverberate. The audience applauds vehemently, and comments on the accuracy of the sound are exchanged: "*al-sawt mazbut!*" two ladies in the front row exclaim. And many more start commenting while giving passionate ovations. Against the prohibitions, people use their cameras and cell phones to capture this vibrant atmosphere.

Such was the opening of the Christmas concert in Damascus on December 17, 2009. The concert was a major attraction and had been for

I would like to thank Anders Hastrup, Christine Asta Crone, and Regnar Kristensen for productive readings. Furthermore, thanks are due to the editors of this volume. For intellectually engaging debates on Syria I want to express my thanks to Sune Haugbølle, Thomas Brønds, and Miriam Younes at SIME, Roskilde University.

several years. Tickets were hard to find, and many Syrians, Christians in particular, could be heard lamenting their scarcity. The concert was held several times in Damascus first before moving on to Aleppo, where it ran for two days. This year the concert was entitled *Snowing Love*. Beyond tapping into the romanticized notion of snow held by many urban Damascenes, the concert was planned to be a staging of brotherly love within the nation-state, a central preoccupation of both the regime and the Christian minorities, albeit one that was articulated differently by both in the time before the uprisings of 2011. The phrase "snowing love" was not expressive of a cooling or even freezing relationship, but rather one of, if not outright cordiality, then at least pragmatic accommodation between the regime and a significant contingent of Syrian Christians.

The role of Christians in Syria's social fabric has not often been given scholarly attention. However, in the study of Syria it is critical to understand the role of the Christian minorities and their position during the time leading up to the Syrian uprisings. Understanding the role of the Syrian Christians may enable us to recognize the ways in which minorities can help to sustain an authoritarian state and suspend work toward more radical forms of change. During the 2000s Christian Syrians grew increasingly wary over what had happened in Iraq post Saddam Hussein. Before 2003, Iraq, like Syria, was approximately 8 percent Christian. After the coalition went into Iraq, instability ensued, and Syria received high numbers of Iraqi refugees, among them a significant number of Christians. Iraqi Christians settled in particular in areas such as Dwaila'a and Jaramana, suburbs to Damascus with high percentages of Syrian Christians. Accordingly, many Syrian Christians heard firsthand stories of the situation in Iraq and became convinced that a fate akin to the one suffered by their Iraqi counterparts would befall them should the Syrian regime lose power. During the same period, international condemnation and pressure mounted upon Syria following the assassination of former Lebanese prime minister Rafiq al-Hariri in February 2005. Although to this day no hard evidence attests to the culpability of the regime in Damascus, little doubt exists that the killing would not have happened without the knowledge thereof within the Syrian leadership. During 2005 many Christians feared that Syria was facing the intervention of an American-led coalition.

In this climate of raised anxiety, Syrian Christians placed their hopes in the stability the regime seemed to guarantee. And, in such a climate, having one of the most renowned Christian choirs participate on the national stage seemed to show how Syria could, or indeed should, look.

In this chapter I will use the event of the Christmas concert and more widely the role of Juwqat al-farah as a prism through which to examine staged atmospheres. In social science Erving Goffman was pivotal in introducing the stage as a central metaphor in his social dramaturgy. Goffman focused not merely on the stage in and of itself but argued for a distinction between social performance on and off stage, or in his terminology, front stage and backstage.[1] He asserted that there exists a rather hard distinction between performance on and off stage, arguing that people on stage deliberately control the impression they make on others, whereas what happens off stage is somehow less coerced. In this chapter the notion of stage is taken up theoretically to shed light on the case of Syrian Christians and their ways of playing their part in Syrian society. However, in contrast to Goffman, I contend that life both on and off stage often may be complicated by the political situation confronting the players. In doing so, I address one of the central discussions on Syria: whether there can be such a thing as popular authoritarianism.[2]

Where much of the scholarly literature on Syria has underscored the complicity of Syrians in upholding the system as resting on a politics of *as if*,[3] I argue here that during the first ten years of Bashar's presidency; that is, between 2000 and 2010, matters often were more complex than this portrayal may purport, as many had hope for a change from within the system. Where Lisa Wedeen's classic analysis presents complicity as a way to kill politics, I think it is important to point to the ways in which the 2000s allowed for different attitudes than merely such complicity. Where the argument of a politics of *as if* asserts that all Syrians were equally aware of the falsity of staged notions of national unity, I draw attention to the ways in which it made sense for certain groups within the nation to participate on this stage. When onstage with or in front of others, one may at times be carried away and start not merely to act *as if*, but to play one's part in staging an atmosphere. My concern here more specifically is the position of Christians within the nation and how their position evolved during

Bashar's first ten years. I will uncover some of the prevalent themes found in Christian attitudes toward the regime in the time leading up to the Syrian version of the Arab uprisings.[4] The question this chapter explores, then, is how Christian perceptions of their position in the time before the current uprisings and Syrian tragedy accommodated the regime's bolstering of a particular ethos of national unity. I argue that Christian participation on the national stage, rather than on its periphery, often removed the sense of staging as mere pretense and instead allowed Christians to see themselves, with varying intensity, as indispensable to the state and its vision of national unity.

Concerted Efforts

As the Christmas concert starts it is instantly possible to see, hear, and feel the immense planning that has taken place to make the event happen. The choreography is lavish. The first song, performed by a single girl in a little shelter on the stage, shows the production's investment in staging. As she sits the sound of falling snow starts to resound and then the curtains are lifted to reveal the entire choir of some 450 singers. They are dressed in glittering white, snow-like costumes, and behind them snow crystals and Christmas balls in red adorn the backdrop and reflect the light onto the stage and toward the audience. *Thalj, thalj . . .* —it resounds from the stage as the audience is carried away, marveling at the perfection of the whole event: the pitch of the voices, the choreography, the sound of snow, and perhaps in some measure their own sense of being present. The choir, accompanied by the large National Orchestra, performs an array of seasonal songs and Christmas carols. Each song has a carefully planned sequence where, for example, a group of children dances with snowmen in red Santa hats, or, during a performance of *Feliz Navidad*, the audience receives wooden castanets and is invited to sing along in English: "We wish you a Merry Christmas!" The concert is replete with Christmas motifs: snowmen, Santas, romantic dances, Christian songs and evocations.

Just before one of the songs, the lead singer for this particular song starts dedicating it to the Palestinian people. A moon drops down from the ceiling while the lights are dimmed in order to emphasize the stark destiny of this neighboring Arab people. The speech has been rehearsed, and the orchestration works to underscore the message. The moon is used as a screen onto which images of the suffering of the world in general and of the Palestinians in particular are projected. This footage and chore-ography conjure up familiar emotions and sentiments of solidarity with the Palestinians. The message echoes what the Syrian regime has propa-gated throughout its reign; namely, that this country shows solidarity with the Palestinian cause and furthermore is a safe haven for the Palestinians residing here, and that social injustice lies not in the Syrian nation per se, but rather in the surrounding world epitomized by Israel as the oppressive state inflicting all sorts of evil on the Palestinians.

Later in the concert Elias Zahlawi, the Christian priest, intellectual, and founder of Juwqat al-farah, steps on the stage with much bravado to deliver a trademark speech. Zahlawi talks of the peaceful relations Syria has maintained throughout many centuries, and of how problems in neighboring countries, such as Yemen, Somalia, Lebanon, Palestine, and Iraq, accumulate with mounting instability and suffering in those states. He also draws attention to the dire situation in Afghanistan. Hav-ing developed this theme of human travail and suffering, Zahlawi then addresses the entire world in the Christian message of peace—a peace, he emphasizes, that abides all, Christians as well as Muslims.

Having described these examples, Zahlawi expresses his thanks to Syrian First Lady Asma al-Asad and to President Bashar al-Asad. Their position in his speech signals that they are paragons of prosperity and stability, and Zahlawi underscores the unity of the Syrian people and makes an appeal for people not to leave the country, but to stay and build it. With this wish, Zahlawi emphasizes what can be achieved when people work together—what the success of the concert itself seems to prove. He then continues to thank the artists, singers, and the conductor for their efforts. He thanks companies supportive of the event and also mentions and thanks the Syrian Television and Addounia Television for filming the concert.

The importance of an event such as the Christmas concert here is that a space for the minority is allowed and used in the center of the nation. Here, the staged image of Syria does not rest merely on a direct appraisal of the regime itself, but also uses more subtle maneuvers. At this concert, central figures of the Christian minority, namely Juwqat al-farah and Elias Zahlawi, are presented to the whole nation. Thus it is the citizens of the state who seem to stage what Syria is or ought be. Beyond the event at the opera house itself, the staging extends to presentations in news features in national newspapers and glossy journals. These written accounts of the concert placed importance on the fact that the presidential couple graced the event with their presence. In various ways, the concert made its way from the stage of the opera house to a general staging of unity sought by the Syrian regime. The image of Syria as a nation with room for all of its citizens, therefore, was orchestrated by the inclusion of one of the central minorities on the national stage. Having the Choir of Joy singing a mix of Christmas and seasonal songs was an apparent sign of Syria's course toward inclusivity. At the same time, the message of the choir was transferred from a particular and direct experience at a concert to a mediated format represented in news. An image was projected of Syria as a country of Arab unity and solidarity in times of instability in the region. However, such news centered here not on a global stage as such, a global stage which—as Jonathan Shannon argues—might be performed for a global audience.[5] Rather, this news shines the spotlight on a national stage where diverse interests are accommodated. For the Syrian regime, ordinary citizens displaying their veneration of if not the Syrian state per se then at least common tropes of Arab unity and solidarity is useful in order to cater to a feeling of popularity and patriotism. For Christians, having one of their most cherished choirs onstage allowed them to picture their own fate as an instrumental part of the Syrian nation. To understand the implications of this dual accommodation, we need to explore the staging a bit more closely.

Collusions of Front and Back Stages

Lisa Wedeen has famously argued that all Syrians in the 1990s were complicit in upholding the regime by participating in various forms of public spectacle with no inner conviction.[6] Likewise, miriam cooke, in her study of artists and authors, has emphasized the falsity and pretense inherent in these public displays of loyalty to the Syrian regime.[7] Where much can be said in favor of this analysis, I want to make a case for a more complex reading. What I draw attention to in this analysis is how particular social situations and political developments made it harder to distinguish the line between *as if*, or staging, and more private sentiments and feelings. In a climate of growing Christian anxiety about the future, what the regime did present to Christian Syrians was the guarantee of stability and security.

In the analysis of the politics of *as if*, Wedeen draws on the famous reading of Vaclav Havel's *The Power of the Powerless*.[8] One of Havel's central examples is how a greengrocer, in order to avoid scrutiny from the secret service and police, places a placard in support of the Communist party in his shop. By doing so, the greengrocer is drawn into the political realm and thereby knows he is culpable for helping to preserve the system. For Havel as well as Wedeen, the very knowledge of one's being implicated in upholding the system is a significant way that politics is killed. As Havel further suggests, a common lack of belief in the political system leads to self-loathing and cynicism. Recently, Paul Anderson likewise has examined how the political system in Syria during the late 2000s led to a particular form of scorn.[9] Syrians knew of the misgivings and frailties in and of the system, and many felt self-contempt for not speaking up against corruption and nepotism. This analysis of scorn draws on and resembles literature of and on former Eastern Bloc states as well as contemporary China, and as such points to the ways in which individuals were alienated from state ideology, or mocked it outright, embracing a cynical positionality.[10]

The understanding of politics as resting on a staging of something one does not subscribe to in many ways echoes Erving Goffman's views on social dramaturgy as elaborated in his classic work *The Presentation of Self in Everyday Life*.[11] In this book Goffman characterizes what happens front stage and what happens backstage as discrete. Goffman thereby presents the actor as controlling what kind of image is being presented for others. Front stage one enacts a role for others, a role where one adjusts to the perceived audience. Backstage, in contrast to this controlled roleplaying, one can act more freely with less focus on an audience. Where the distinction between appearance front stage and backstage has seemed to be consonant with a politics of *as if*, there are some inherent problems in the formulation of a hard distinction. The distinction implies that the actor is always aware of the role he or she is playing, and does not account for how the actor often is played by the situation in which the role is given. In other words, an analysis as proposed by Goffman does only to some extent capture the importance of the social context. If we are to understand reactions such as cynicism or scorn they must be seen as ways to shy away from the game, or only reluctantly play one's part. However, in situations where Syrian society has experienced pressure from international society, the reluctance and cynicism may not remain the dominant responses, particularly for Syria's Christian minority. What happens in such circumstances of pressure may rather be a collusion of front and back stage, a collusion where acting is not merely a matter of *as if*, but just *as is*. For this to happen, the minority as much as the regime seems to invest in the idea and trope of national unity, and it is the notion of national unity we shall now address.

Visions of Unity

After the concert I walk down to the stage to thank Abuna Elias Zahlawi. I am not the only one doing so. Several want his autograph, some exchange kisses with him, and others exchange other forms of courtesies. Zahlawi is a well-known figure in many Christian circles, as he has been an ardent promoter of the contemporary Damascene stigmatic and visionary Myrna Akhras, who since late 1982 has claimed to have received messages from Christ and the Virgin. The devotion to the apparition of the Virgin Mary has been named after the quarter of Damascus where she appeared to Myrna, namely Our Lady of Soufanieh.[12] Having spent nearly two years of anthropological fieldwork studying Syrian Christians since 2004 I have also studied the followers of this particular devotion for several years. During this work I have had the chance to get to know Elias Zahlawi personally and have heard him give sermons and talks on many occasions; I have also interviewed him several times.[13] It was due to this relationship that I got a chance to see the Christmas concert, as Zahlawi gave me the tickets to the performance, which was otherwise already sold out (several of my Syrian interlocutors admitted to being envious of this gift).

Zahlawi serves as priest in the Greek Catholic Church of Our Lady of Damascus, Kanisat al-sayyida Dimashq. The church has an elaborate program for children and youth participating in the Legion of Mary and its voluntary work in the parish and among the poor and elderly of Damascus. Zahlawi is widely known for his learning and has often been featured on television shows on themes including Christian heritage, and one of his favorite themes: unity and interreligious dialogue. At services Zahlawi can be heard voicing many of the same themes as those he accentuated on stage in the opera: that Syria is a country of unity; that Damascus has a particular role in fostering peace in the region and beyond; that Christians and Muslims need to work for unity; and that Christians need to pray for neighboring countries, especially Iraq and to some extent Egypt. Furthermore, Zahlawi's work on unity is manifest in his books and on various electronic outlets such as his Facebook page where he continues to articulate what he sees as a critical message of faith, love, and unity stemming from Damascus, with relevance for the entire region.

The focus on unity is not particular to Christians in Syria. Rather, one of the central ideas promulgated by the Ba'th Party since its inception has been pan-Arab unity. Upon seizing power in 1963, the party incorporated Ba'th ideology into the social fabric via public schools and public spectacles.[14] One was not allowed to voice publicly what characteristics, such as sectarian or tribal identities, differentiated Syrians from each other; rather, one should emphasize the unity of the Socialist Syrian Republic. Crossing the "red lines" would lead to serious consequences.[15] Where such broad ideas of unity may seem contentious, the regime's blatant attempt to co-opt citizens with a glossy version of unity always has come with hard repression as the underlying logic. This said, the notion of unity actually has achieved purchase among many of Syria's minorities. The Druze community has embraced the rhetoric of unity, according to Kastrinou-Theodoropoulou.[16] However, the state also used religion to gain partial legitimacy, though such usage cannot be seen as a token of outright popularity.[17] Likewise, attempts at fostering interfaith dialogue have been promoted, even if these often have not focused on mutual understanding per se but rather on national unity.[18] Furthermore, among Christians in Damascus it was not only in schools that children rehearsed the national anthem or shouted classic slogans of unity, liberty, and socialism of the Syrian nation. Before 2011, on several occasions I experienced children of Christian families shouting the same songs and slogans at home that they had been taught in school. That the children did so did not cause laughter or embarrassment on part of their parents. Rather, on these occasions it seemed to be accepted that children should rehearse these slogans within the space of a private home.

It may very well be that there is no general pattern of children of Christian Syrian families rehearsing slogans of national unity at home. However, it is correct that the Syrian regime has played an active role in allowing Christian communities to rebuild important sites of worship from the 1970s and onwards. In her important work on Greek Orthodox monasteries in Syria, Anna Poujeau has shown the role of the state in renovation of these sites.[19] As a wider consequence of the state support, the Greek Orthodox Church on both a popular and official level has been in favor of the regime and an ideology of pan-Arabism, and has assisted the regime in spreading a message of Arab nationalism.[20] The historical roots of this phenomenon can be traced back to the late period of the Ottomans, in particular from the mid-1850s and onward, when the Christian elites realized the importance of a focus on their Arab rather than their religious identity.[21] In this period Christians were targeted in various parts of the Levant, where Christians most notably were attacked and killed in significant numbers in the Christian quarters of Damascus in 1860. These incidents have been explained by the economic decline of the Ottoman Empire and by discontent with the favoritism of Christians by English and French merchants.[22] Another factor in the same period was the Catholic Church's emphasis on the learning of the colloquial as important as part of a wider education; hereby an elite was fashioned with Arabic language as a primary tool. The theme of a common Arabic identity was later augmented in the Ba'th ideology where Michel Aflaq, himself Greek Orthodox, was instrumental in formulating such a position.[23] Also the contemporary Greek Catholic Church has been in favor of the regime, as the writings and sermons of Archbishop Gregorious III Laham show. Although historically the relationships among Syrian Christian churches—and most notably between the Orthodox and Catholic churches—have been characterized by strife,[24] a stronger sense of unity has been growing for the last two decades. One of the prime examples of this rapprochement is the coordinated march that different Catholic churches organize on the occasion of Easter. The so-called march of the Seven Churches has taken place in several of Syria's larger cities, and with great intensity in Damascus and Aleppo. These events have been intended to emphasize intra-Christian unity. Easter in particular illustrates the challenge of fostering unity among these groups, as the Orthodox churches follow the Julian calendar, whereas the Catholic churches follow the Gregorian calendar and therefore do not celebrate on the same dates on an annual basis. This lack of common footing—such that the most important Christian Feast cannot be unified—is invariably felt as a major disgrace by Christian lay people, even if positions among clergy vary considerably. Concomitantly, the discussion of unity continues to be of great importance to Christian leaders, but also among Christians more widely, even if the stakes and meaning of unity may be slippery, ranging from national unity in the broadest sense to Christian unity in a more restricted sense.

Unity as propagated by the Syrian state and regime may therefore offer more than just a false or inauthentic exteriority, one to which none would ever subscribe; rather, this ideology of unity may be a significant way in which minorities, and in particular those of the urban centers such as Damascus and Aleppo, can be made to feel part of the national fabric. Precisely such complex ways of feeling part of the national fabric while also knowing of the inherent flaws of the system have been captured in Michael Herzfeld's work on cultural intimacy. For Herzfeld, cultural intimacy references the various ideas and ideologies that states, bureaucracies, and citizens are party to and continue to maintain. Cultural intimacy therefore covers tacit and overt common knowledge, including secrets and embarrassing legacies. All these forms of knowledge work in and through a social poetics where ideas of the nation and the state are endowed with life even among those skeptical of the state, because by their very skepticism and ways of assailing the system they still solidify the existence of what is. The idea and idiom of national unity are critical to cultural intimacy: "The nation must always be one and indivisible."[25] Cultural intimacy, as I use and extend the notion, rests on malleable and porous affects, where regional and political climates play an important role in what is staged and felt. And one way to do this has been to make space for a choir such as Juwqat al-farah on the stage of the national opera.

Fakhr baladi—Campaigning for National Pride

Let us here extend our consideration of the social poetics that are at play in the wider use of Juwqat al-farah. Juwqat al-farah and its founder Abuna Elias Zahlawi are well known in Syrian Christian circles, particularly in Damascus, but also outside the capital. The choir has toured and given concerts at famous venues worldwide, and in this way has been used by *both* the regime *and* Christian leaders to present a particular vision of Syria also outside the national stage. Syria has been presented as a country with a strong Christian legacy with viable forms of coexistence in a troubled region. Such concerted efforts in presenting a version of what Syria is shows how the regime and Christian leaders make use of each other to fashion a particular poetics. Herzfeld himself in his deliberation on social poetics presents the following definition: "Social poetics is about the play through which people try to turn transient advantage into a permanent condition in this socially comprehensive sense. It links the little poetics of everyday interaction with the grand dramas of official pomp and historiography to break down illusions of scale."[26] The social poetics in this sense work across domains that otherwise are regarded as private and public, and furthermore the social poetics entail a familiarity with the state in both its functioning and disfunctioning nature; what works well and what works to the detriment of the citizens. In the Syrian context exactly the disfunctioning character is what further makes fearful minorities feel that they need to reinforce the state and thereby bring about transient advantages. In the case of Juwqat al-farah, the primary role of the choir has been to promote a message of unity and peace in Syria, epitomized by the Christmas concerts; although, as Edith Ali-Dib argues, participation in Muslim feasts also has been part of the choir's standard program.[27] But the choir is also incorporated as a part of the Syrian national poetics in an even more overt form than what the campaign for national pride, *fakhr baladi*, attested to in the summer of 2009. In an honorary ceremony at the presidential palace under the auspices of the First Lady, the significance of the choir and its founder in the Syrian nation was staged exactly in a grand drama of official pomp.

The ceremony was edited for popular consumption as a ten-minute video on YouTube.[28] The video as well as the event itself invite reflection on the question of which kind of exchange occurs between figures of the Christian minority and the regime. The video is made very professionally by any standards, and nothing is left to the imagination when Juwqat al-farah is driven up to the presidential palace in four luxurious Mercedes Benz busses. Classical music plays in the background to emphasize the elevated moment. The video stages the event in dramatic, albeit elegant terms and builds up to the address of First Lady. She meets the choir and Elias Zahlawi with a "Good evening!" and is instantly met with the same response from the choir. The First Lady then praises the choir and emphasizes that ever since the first time she heard the choir she understood what it was doing as being important for the nation itself (*'ala mustawa al-watan*). Her key line is then presented, namely of the importance of "Our birth, our youngsters, and the Syrian citizens" ("*Wiladna, shababna, wa al-muwatiyyin Suri!*"). Warm applause follows. She resumes and addresses all of the members of the choir: "Each one of you is capable to participate and partake in the building of the nation and its development" ("*bi al-bina' al-watan wa bi-tatwiru*"). In such an address we see a significant incorporation of the choir and each individual. Here it is not a matter of the individuals shouting stale slogans, but rather of the First Lady praising model citizens. The staging hereby is markedly different from a classic authoritarian style, as what is here staged is mutual dependence.

After having addressed the choir in general, the First Lady addresses Abuna Elias Zahlawi directly. Zahlawi, she exhorts, planted the first seed of what today can be seen as a rose. The First Lady then gives Zahlawi the national award in the form of a pin, which she places on the chest of his jacket. With seeming pride, Zahlawi looks at the First Lady as she attaches the pin. In the staging of the event on the video, music is used to elevate the moment even further. Ovation resounds from the choir as he receives a diploma in a wooden box. The moment has led to a significant transition as the floor now is left to Elias Zahlawi. Zahlawi returns the courtesies in a short speech during which he emphasizes this pride in being here with the choir and in what can be achieved in Syria. The speech again focuses on the core values of being Syrian, of belief and of being part of the nation. The significance of the staged event is again that it here is the model citizen that exemplifies how Syria is supposed to be. Zahlawi is presented as a guardian of a particular Syrian tradition that is embodied both by himself and by the choir and is endorsed by the Syrian First Lady. It is therefore a perfect set up for the next scene, in which Juwqat al-farah sings the national anthem. The anthem entitled *Humat al-diyar*, or in English *Guardians of the Homeland*, with lyrics by Khalil Mardam Bey and music by Mohammad Flayfal, is performed flawlessly and in a less militaristic manner than is often heard. While the choir sings, the camera follows the First Lady as she presents awards to the individual members of the choir.

By singing of the guardians of the nation, the choir members themselves also are used to present, embody even, what form the very nation is to take, what the very words of the First Lady also seem to stage. The choir itself seems to preserve a special Syrian tradition of unity here. In contrast to other classic spectacles of the regime where Hafiz al-Asad was presented as the leader of history itself, no such outrageous claims are presented.[29] Rather, this is a different kind of spectacle where the regime, using the First Lady as a paragon of progress and civil society engagement, allows some of its citizens to participate in a performed representation of what Syria ought to be. Here, the staged image of Syria does not rest on a direct appraisal of the regime itself, but uses more subtle maneuvers; in this case, the Syrian nation seems to be guarded by its citizens, by Juwqat al-farah and Abuna Elias Zahlawi, and their apparent pride at being included in the ceremony and their veneration of the Syrian First Lady evokes a different view of Syria than the stale image associated with coerced public demonstrations.[30] In this form of staged event, various senses of pride and participation allow Christian minorities a sense of position in the national picture. Extending Herzfeld's idea of cultural intimacy, it is possible to argue that this is a deliberate attempt to foster national pride, and that these forms of pride can coexist with or gloss over awareness of corruption and disfunctioning, at least in particular moments. In other words, these social poetics allow the minority to see itself as important and thereby to reflect back a particular version of national unity of which the state is believed to be the guarantor.

Politics of *As If* and Politics of *As Is*

Outside the staged forms of national unity I have described in this chapter, it is important to relate these more public disseminated forms with people's everyday practices. During my fieldwork I often ended up in conversations about Syrian Christian attitudes toward the system and the president. Here the most general reaction I was presented with was one of regime support.[31] Such responses often came unsolicited, and were often intensified in times of perceived threat. For instance, one evening as I walked through the Christian neighborhood of Bab Tuma with Nabil, an interlocutor I had known for several years, I commented on a discussion we had at a dinner at his parents' home, where more than twenty relatives were present. Nabil's uncle had praised the Syrian state with no reservations. Nabil laughed as I raised the topic and continued to speak of his uncle: "He is a liar. Nobody believes it all . . ." Nabil continued laughing to himself as we walk on. However, Nabil himself was markedly less outspoken in other situations. Earlier in the evening Nabil's uncle had asked rhetorically about the virtues of the Syrian state, asking, "Am I right or not?" Nabil had answered affirmatively. Here, Nabil attested to the diverse ways one can be implicated in social situations. Another evening when Nabil visited me, he pointed with a laugh to a photo of the president placed on my table. Immediately he explained: "This is not something you normally have in your home . . . You may have it at your work . . ." I explained that the photo had been an ironic gift from a friend, and I inquired about the massive presence of photos to be found on cars and public facades. Nabil continued: "In cars, yes, but not in people's homes. This is to show that you are with the system." He paused before continuing: "Abu Samir has such a photo at his office, too, an old one . . . This is not something you can believe in. But they will leave you in peace."

Where on the first reading this seems to present a perfect case of acting *as if*, what I think can be taken from such episodes is that affects and situations are strongly interconnected. The use of photos of the president and other nationalistic artifacts is highly selective. Nabil's father, Abu Samir, is very well aware of where it is fitting to display a photo of the president and where it is less fitting. However, this does not entail that there always is a strong divide and separation between what is participated in and what is experienced. Rather, it is often when people are outside the situation that distance most easily can be voiced and parts of the system reviled. Here it may be relevant to return to Erving Goffman, not to reiterate the distinction between front stage and back stage, but to employ a later notion of his; namely, the notion of role distance.[32] In certain situations it becomes relevant for Nabil and Abu Samir to participate in upholding the Syrian system and in many ways to subscribe to the very ideas of national unity as guaranteed. Both would vocally support the Syrian system and Bashar in progressing toward something better. Criticizing the system would not necessarily be the equivalent of refusing to play one's part, but rather would involve engaging in a dialogue in which the state is still seen as the primary frame.

On an afternoon not long after this incident, I talked with Abu Samir and his wife, Umm Samir. As we took a sip of hot tea, both of them spoke of the Christian areas of Damascus with pride. Both started to tell of problems they had experienced with more conservative Muslims. Umm Samir then said: "*Al-hamdu li-llah*, there is security here . . ." Abu Samir readily lent his support: "The security is very strong here in Syria!" He continued: "Hafiz al-Asad was very strong. When something was growing amongst the Muslim Brotherhood, he immediately leveled it. It happened in Hama in the 1980s. Now they are all in Egypt. . . ." Abu Samir then used Egypt as the negative contrast: "In Egypt, there it is much more difficult! Christians have a hard time there. . . . Here we have security, and Bashar will also head in the right direction, democracy and all that." Abu Samir placed hope in the progress he believed the system could guarantee. And given the uncertain developments in the region, many Christians cling to what the regime seems to promise; namely, stability and an incorporation of the minority as a central part of the social fabric. Here a particular version of reality is invested in and thereby strategically intensified.[33] It may be too much to express outright affection for the regime in any given situation, but this does not imply that regime does not affect people's dreams of progress and stability, and that these in other situations can be displayed strongly. Significantly, Nabil and I later had a conversation in his home. Nabil recounted how he in the meantime had been to the opera house for a concert for which he was late. Being late, he suddenly met the First Lady in the lobby. To his amazement, instead of just passing by him, she greeted him personally. Nabil was affected by the event and admitted to having genuine admiration for her. After a moment's thought he says: "Before I never used to stand up when the anthem was played, today I find it difficult not to." A person like Nabil and his close family members all had their bad stories about corruption, nepotism, and malfunctioning. However, alongside these negative stories, more positive experiences were often underscored, and even more so in times of perceived threat.

Against this background we can better understand the Christmas concerts and the role the Christians play in them.[34] The concerts allow for a particular kind of participation where the social position that many from the Christian minority dream of is enacted on the national stage. Despite the misgivings toward the Syrian system, or perhaps because of them, a particular dream is here enacted where not merely cynicism and scorn is felt, but forms of pride and importance. Another way to understand the situation this is by way of the anthropology of theater. Anthropologist Kirsten Hastrup has argued that actors do not merely enact something they are not, but that they become one with the role while playing it. In other words, the distance between role and actor disappears.[35] This implies that participation, in theater as well as in life, crystallizes particular logics and emotions for participants tied to specific situations. This complicates a reading of roles in a Syrian context as merely acted *as if*, as matters of pretense. Rather, particular situations allow roles to become salient and nearly impossible *not* to embrace, that in some situations there is no *as if*, but only *as is*. As I hope to have shown in this chapter, roles can be felt as highly meaningful in social context. In this regard, life in general, like life on stage, is marked by conventions and history as well as by the presence of others. In Hastrup's formulation: "The fact that the world created on stage is in some ways illusory does not detract from the reality of the players, their actions, and their motives for acting."[36]

Akin to the dramas of nationhood found in the television serials Syria has produced in recent years,[37] Syria before the uprising and current tragedy witnessed an opening up of the economy to ventures where new forms of consumption and display garnered entrepreneurship, particularly in larger cities.[38] Evidently, this did not mean that the system did not seriously neglect the rural parts of the country, or that it did anything to inhibit the rich and wealthy from seizing advantages that the growing number of poor Syrians never had a chance to attain. However, it was on a sense of, if not progress, then stability that many Christians hung their hopes for inclusion, a sentiment that translated into support for the regime even more during times of perceived threat and vulnerability.

Conclusion

Where most scholarship on Syria has presented cynicism and killed politics as the predominant tropes, this chapter has argued that this is not always the best way to understand ordinary lives in Syria before the current uprisings. Where such a reading may very well have been fitting for much of the 1980s and 1990s, something did seem to happen when Bashar came to power in the summer of 2000. Syrians, particularly minorities, appeared not to maintain their previous emotional distance from the state's public spectacles. For example, for many Syrian Christians, the illusion of the regime and its ideology by attending spectacles was not upheld merely out of sheer necessity: on many such occasions Christians actually did feel part of the nation. The Christmas concert on the stage of the Damascus Opera House was not merely a scripted moment, but a moment where many Christians saw their role in the nation being solidified and played out not only for themselves but for the nation, and therefore it was a moment with a significant emotional purchase both for those on stage as well as those in the audience. As Juwqat al-farah, or the Choir of Joy, entered the stage of Dar al-Asad, many Christians felt their position in the nation grounded not in the periphery but in the center.

Throughout the 2000s, Juwqat al-farah emblematically attested not merely to Christmas festivity but to the possibility for Christians in the

Syrian nation. I have used this case to reflect on some larger themes for Christians in Syria during the reign of Bashar al-Asad. Concerns about the region's changing political climate led many Christians to support the regime with growing intensity. Instability in neighboring countries—including post-Saddam Iraq and Lebanon following the 2006 war waged by Israel—led Syria to receive displaced persons and large numbers of refugees. These and similar situations made the Syrian state's rhetoric of unity bespeak something better, even if the Syrian situation was by no means close to perfect. For many Christians in the years leading up to March 2011, participation on the national stage rather than withdrawal was seen as key both to their own survival and to the Syrian nation. In this sense, the choir could work as a paragon of national unity, as guardians of the homeland, also amidst serious flaws in the Syrian system. This perspective still seems to be widely shared. Most Syrian Christians fear a situation where the regime is no longer protecting them. Being allowed a central role on the national stage felt reassuring to Christian minorities, and they played their part seemingly with little reluctance. Christians may very well have had a role to play, a role which has appeared to be scripted by the regime. However, in moments of threat this role does not seem to be that difficult to embrace, and what appears saddest these days among many Syrian Christians is the loss of stability, which many felt only the regime could guarantee. It is curious also here that the infamously mistimed *Vogue* feature on the Syrian First Lady—published after the regime had started its violent crackdown on the opposition—allows us to see what the regime tried to stage by using Juwqat al-farah.[39] The *Vogue* feature actually ends at the Christmas concert in Damascus in 2010. The author of this feature followed the presidential couple to the concert where people started to shout "*Docteur, docteur!*" as the president and the First Lady arrived. The journalist here presents the president and the First Lady as actually having some kind of popularity. A reading of the event as mere pretense would be a selective reading. At that point, just before the regime cracked down brutally upon its own citizens, the president turned to the journalist while Juwqat al-farah was performing on stage, and said, "All of these styles belong to our culture. This is how to fight extremism—through art! . . . This is the diversity you want to see in the Middle East. . . . This is how you can have peace!" To understand this quote one has to understand the wider Syrian context, and with this chapter I hope to have shown part of the role that Syrian Christians play in a wider staging of what Syria could be. Sadly, the subsequent bloody developments have not yielded any high hopes for peace, either from the regime or from its opposition.

8

Merchant Background, Bourgeois Ethics

The Syrian 'ulama' and Economic Liberalization

THOMAS PIERRET

Introduction

On a warm morning in May 2008, an unusually large and nervous crowd surrounded the state-owned bakery located at the junction between Kafr Suse, a poor village-turned-suburb of Damascus, and Tanzim Kafr Suse, a recently constructed residential area popular among the pious Sunni bourgeoisie of the Syrian capital. The size and nervousness of the crowd was due to the fact that the people in charge of the bakery had decided to slow the oven down because they were running short of fuel. Distribution of the latter had been disrupted by the chaotic implementation of the government's decision to selectively reduce fuel subsidies. For the same reason, the fares of private collective transport vehicles had just doubled. As in the rest of the world, the sharp increase in the prices of basic goods was making life hard for the working class.

The day before, the Prophet's birthday (*mawlid*) had been celebrated in a mosque located a short distance from the bakery. The event was splendid, both in terms of guest list—dozens of prominent clerics showed up during the evening—and in terms of organization. Speakers and religious singers were filmed by several cameras, their images displayed live on plasma televisions inside the mosque as well as on a giant screen in the courtyard. Moreover, a famous singer had been flown from Aleppo especially for the occasion. To be sure, the celebration was intended more for the bourgeoisie of Tanzim Kafr Suse, who made up most of the audience, than for the inhabitants of the surrounding areas who would queue in front of the oven the following morning. Although he was a member of the same Islamic group as the people who had organized the *mawlid*, one second-rank cleric of the neighborhood did not hide his unease: he objected to spending such a huge sum of money for a religious celebration in view of the "growing poverty" the area was witnessing. "The time has come for us," he insisted, "to stop turning a blind eye on the situation of society."[1]

During the decade that preceded the 2011 uprising, social inequalities markedly increased in Syria: while the exhaustion of the socialist model and a combination of factors like high birth rates and drought resulted in rising poverty, liberalization measures and a sudden flow of capital into the country's economy benefitted the upper class. Senior Muslim clerics remained generally silent about this situation.[2]

To understand their attitude, this chapter analyzes the economic ethics of the Syrian *'ulama'* (religious scholars) by looking at their discourse on issues such as self-employment, wealth, poverty, and general economy organization. My analysis is concerned not with the economic ethics of "Islam" as a religious doctrine, but rather with that of a particular category of Muslims in a particular historical context. Therefore, I link the views of the contemporary Syrian *'ulama'* to their social and economic background.

In this chapter, I will show that the leading Syrian *'ulama'* of the pre-2011 era were characterized by a typically bourgeois ethics that values self-employment, praises hard work, success and prosperity, despises idleness and begging, and rejects state interventions in the economy. Such a posture did not result from a recent ideological shift but is rooted in the long-standing alliance of the country's religious elite with merchant networks. Consequently, Muslim scholars were well prepared for Syria's entry into global capitalism, all the more when the latter was assuming an Islamic character through the development of Islamic finance.

Although I consider that the Syrian *'ulama'*'s material living conditions have played a more decisive role than religious doctrines in the definition of their current economic ethics, it is nonetheless useful to start with a short analysis of classical Sunni doctrines on the issue of wealth: first, because the *'ulama'* are the very people whose vocation consists in the preservation and transmission of these doctrines; second, because in contrast to Catholicism, the scholarly Sunni tradition has never viewed wealth as problematic, which means that it is somewhat misleading to interpret the increasingly pro-business posture of certain Muslim populations in terms of a "Calvinist turn," as has particularly been the case in studies of Turkey.[3]

Ash'arism, the dominant school of theology among Syrian clerics, considers wealth and poverty as morally neutral: what makes them positive or negative in the eyes of God is the *use* humans make of them.[4] Even Ibn 'Arabi (1165–1240), who remains a major reference point for Sufi-oriented Syrian *'ulama'*, defined asceticism less as material poverty than as the use of one's property in a "sanctifying" way: that is, spending money "in the path of God."[5]

Modern Syrian *'ulama'* have been all the more in tune with this worldly ethic for having maintained and even reinforced their close ties to the urban bourgeoisie throughout the twentieth century. The founding figures of the country's contemporary religious networks often had roots in the souk, relying heavily on the resources of their merchant relatives and neighbors in order to finance mosques, Islamic schools, and charities. Clerics remained strongly dependent on the private sector and in particular on small and medium-sized entrepreneurs—because, unlike Nasser and al-Azhar, the Ba'thist regime never sufficiently invested in the "nationalization" of the country's religious elite. Ties between the latter and the business community became even closer during the first years of the twenty-first century as a result of the considerable growth of Islamic charities.[6]

The first four sections of this chapter illustrate the Syrian *'ulama'*'s embrace of typically bourgeois values: the first section deals with their praise for self-employment; in the second one, I show how they link faith to success and prosperity; the third section focuses on their opposition to socialism, and advocacy of a charity-based approach to the problem of poverty; the fourth one is devoted to their discourse on the relationship between work and poverty. The fifth section tackles the emergence of "Islamic" faces of capitalism; namely, Islamic finance and Islamized managerial discourse. The last section is devoted to the few Syrian religious figures who tried to voice nonconformist ideas on social and economic problems.

The Virtues of Self-Employment

The Ba'thist regime did not provide the *'ulama'* with remuneration commensurate with their elite social status: those of them who were working for the state's religious bureaucracy received the mediocre wage of functionaries, and mosque staff were paid only nominal salaries. In order to secure a decent living, they had to turn to the private sector and explore other economic opportunities that emerged during the last decades of the twentieth century. Those who opted for an academic career worked at the Faculty of Shari'a of Damascus or in foreign universities. Some of these academics were also popular writers: in 2009, three of them—Sa'id Ramadan al-Buti, Wahba al-Zuhayli, and Ratib al-Nabulsi—were among the five best-selling authors in the Syrian market.[7] Other clerics, like the members of the Kaftaru and al-Farfur families, dedicated themselves to the management of the private Islamic institutes they inherited from their fathers. These institutes played an important role in the political economy of the clergy because they granted senior Muslim scholars wages that were up to fifteen times higher than the salaries paid to teachers of Islamic education in public religious schools.[8]

The Syrian clergy remained closely tied to the private sector, not only because the latter provided most of the funding for private Islamic schools and charities, but also because the category of the merchant-*'ulama'* did not disappear. In the capital, many were members of the Zayd movement, a group that focused on the religious education of laypeople. Zayd was especially concerned with the training of imams and preachers who maintained a secular occupation in parallel with their religious position. Although the four main leaders of the group were full-time clerics, there were at least two wealthy merchants among Zayd's ten most prominent shaykhs.[9]

The most renowned scholars, who did not have time for business, could easily invest in the commercial operations of their merchant supporters. Such investments were common in Syria as an alternative to the stock market, which only opened in Damascus in March 2009. One of the most elaborate examples of this informal system was the investment fund of the Kaftariyya, a Sufi brotherhood headed by the late Grand Mufti Ahmad Kaftaru, which relied on money provided by the adepts and was managed by sympathetic businessmen.[10]

In view of this social reality, self-employment (in Arabic *'amal hurr*, literally "free work") unsurprisingly figured at the top of the values promoted by the Syrian *'ulama'* in the economic realm. This issue has often been tackled by clerics in the hagiographical accounts devoted to their fathers and/or masters. In such writings, self-employment is described as a guarantee of integrity because it allows a man of religion to carry out his sacred duty without expecting any material remuneration from it. For instance, the biography of Ramzi al-Bazam (1917–91), a manufacturer/seller of candy and one of the founders of the al-Fath Islamic institute, said that "he used to divide his time between *da'wa* [call to God] and trade, so that his *da'wa* only aimed to please God, and not to obtain any money or prestige."[11] Self-employment also allows a scholar to earn a religiously licit income (*al-kasb al-halal*): Hisham al-Burhani (1932–2014), one of Damascus's most prominent scholars, explained to his students that "self-employment is the best possible occupation because when you work for the state, you are never sure that your salary does not contain money whose origin is illicit (*haram*), such as taxes on the selling of alcohol."[12]

Illicit income is not the only problem faced by the *'ulama'* who work for the state: for centuries, the Sunni scholarly tradition has warned against the negative effect of government employment on the political independence of clerics.[13] Usama al-Rifa'i (b. 1944), the spiritual leader of the Zayd movement, conveyed this idea by regularly recounting to his followers the life of Shaykh Ali al-Daqr (1877–1943), a famous merchant-scholar of Damascus. Al-Daqr was shocked when the colonial authorities started to pay salaries to clerics because the goal of this decision was, in al-Rifa'i's term, to allow "the government to dictate the *'ulama'*'s acts and words."[14] Under pressure from the authorities, al-Daqr eventually accepted the salary, but he refused to use it for himself and instead chose to give it to the poor: "[W]hen the civil servant was coming to the mosque to give him his monthly salary, Shaykh Ali used to show him a box to put the money; he never touched it: when a person in need was asking for help, he used to say: 'open the box, and take what you need.'"[15] Al-Rifa'i emphasized that this story should serve as an example for contemporary men of religion, whom he encouraged to occupy mosque positions voluntarily (*hisbatan*).[16] However, although that option was legal in Syria, it made some shaykhs vulnerable with respect to the state, so they opted to imitate their illustrious predecessor Ali al-Daqr. As a merchant-scholar explained: "I do not need this salary because my travel agency brings in much more money. However, I must accept it in order to keep my position in this mosque: my relations with the Ministry of Religious Endowments are pretty bad, and if I preach voluntarily, they will oust me from here by saying that my pulpit should rather be given to someone who needs a salary. Consequently, I receive the remuneration of the state, but I systematically pay it into the mosque's funds."[17]

Get Rich . . . for God's Sake!

In 2011 there was only one *darwish* (person displaying outwards signs of poverty) among the senior Syrian *'ulama'*. Shaykh Shukri al-Luhafi (b. 1920), a Grand Reader of the Qur'an and a Damascene master of the Shadhili Sufi order, used to dress in rags and serve coffee to his disciples in the mosque.[18] Although al-Luhafi's humbleness was widely praised among Damascus's religious circles, it was not considered an example to be followed. Even al-Luhafi's assistant, a successful small industrialist, explains that "true asceticism (*zuhd*) lies in the heart: you can be rich, but in your relation with God, it is as if you own nothing."[19] In other Syrian cities, certain representatives of the Shadhili order were very wealthy, a reality that was perfectly in tune with the worldly orientation of this Sufi tradition,[20] and not considered an anomaly by the disciples, given the fact that the same Sufi masters were said to "purify" their money by giving it to the poor.[21]

Of course, poverty was not a source of shame for a Muslim scholar, provided this situation did not lead him to beg. For instance, the asceticism of

Shaykh 'Abd al-Karim al-Rifa'i (1904-73), the founder of the Zayd movement, was praised by his disciples and imitated by leading 'ulama' of the group.[22] However, second-rank clerics and lay supporters were strongly encouraged to grow rich, since "the Umma [community of believers] needs wealthy and generous people."[23]

According to the Syrian 'ulama', piety and wealth are not only compatible; they reinforce each other. That is what the Grand Mufti of Syria Ahmad Hassun meant when he said, during a private reception organized by an industrialist: "When hearts are lightened with faith, then the money is purified in our pockets . . . and heaven gives us prosperity and grace."[24] According to the hagiography of 'Abd al-Karim al-Rifa'i, the first merchants who answered the latter's da'wa, abided by the rules of shari'a, and funded charitable projects saw their revenue increase considerably "because of baraka [blessing]."[25] The opposite is also true, in the sense that the quest for material success elevates the status of the believer in the eyes of the Lord. Shaykh Sariya al-Rifa'i (b. 1949), a son of 'Abd al-Karim who emerged in the 2000s as the "Sheikh of the Merchants" in Damascus and was consequently able to set up successful charitable projects, expressed this idea clearly during a 2007 celebration of the Prophet's birthday organized in a souk in Damascus: "O merchants of this neighborhood! . . . God is the one who plants the love of things in your heart, so that you love money, work, and take care of your family. On the other hand, if you become an ascetic in this world, if you quit working, if you give up the love of money, if you stay in the mosque, do you think you will be rewarded? . . . In no way, my dear brothers! In fact, it is when you work in the souk that you worship God, provided that you abide by the rules of shari'a."[26]

In Aleppo, Shaykh Mahmud Abu al-Huda al-Husseini (b. 1960), a well-off scholar who was appointed as the head of the city's Directorate of Religious Endowments in 2010, also insisted on the distinguished position of merchants in Islam and called on them to support the da'wa efforts: "There must be no gap between preachers and businessmen: the latter have to understand that the promotion of their interests supposes that they invest in religious projects."[27] Al-Husseini used to repeat a formula of the Turkish Islamic thinker Said Nursi: "[W]e want dunya [this world] for the sake of religion."[28] One of his assistants, a small entrepreneur in the building sector, explained that his master taught him that "being the best in one's work and growing rich is a duty."[29]

The glorification of self-employment and prosperity logically goes hand in hand with a liberal conception of the ideal economic order. As I will show in the next section, this conception was prevalent well before the incursion of liberal globalization in the late twentieth century and the subsequent development of "market Islam."[30]

Socialism versus Charity

Between the French withdrawal of 1946 and the military coup of the Ba'th in 1963, "Islamic socialism" was popularized in Syria by the local branch of the Muslim Brothers. In 1949, the movement set up an electoral coalition called the "Islamic Socialist Front," and its founder Mustafa al-Siba'i published his famous *Socialism of Islam* ten years later.[31] The first leaders of the Syrian Muslim Brothers adopted socialism not out of class interest, since they often came from well-off urban families, but because as professional politicians they had to adapt to the demands of the political field of the time, where left-wing ideas were on the rise as a result of the growing strength of the Communists, Ba'thists, and, later, Nasserites.

Al-Siba'i's socialism was far from radical. His advocacy of state intervention in the economy was intended to put an end to the most blatant injustices, in particular in the realm of land ownership. He advocated the nationalization of the public services that were controlled by foreign companies, such as water supply and electricity, but opposed more statist policies such as the wide-scale nationalizations decreed by Nasser in 1961.

Despite its moderate character, the Islamic socialism of the Muslim Brothers was flatly rejected by the leading *'ulama'* of the time, who had neither an electorate to seduce nor the intellectual flexibility of the reform-minded founders of the Islamist movement. Private property, as leading Syrian shaykhs like Hasan Habannaka and Muhammad al-Hamid argued, represented an inviolable principle of Islamic law.[32] This position was not only the result of close ties between the clergy and the merchant community: it was also grounded in the Sunni scholarly tradition, which has historically harbored a deep distrust of the role of the state in the economy, perceiving the state as a rapacious entity that aims to appropriate the property of its subjects. Although such a vision seemed outmoded in the 1950s, it would eventually prove somewhat more relevant under Ba'thist rule and in particular after 1970, when members of the regime started to build colossal fortunes by embezzling public funds.

As far as one can judge from the press of the pre-Ba'thist period, clerics never criticized the liberal foundations of the economic order of that time. In order to fight poverty and the threat of social unrest, they promoted what are known today as "faith-based initiatives"; that is, Islamic charitable associations. Shaykh 'Abd al-Karim al-Rifa'i, who founded several such charities in the 1950s, reportedly preached that benevolent work "turned the poor and the rich into one same hand, one same heart; they became united in love, fraternity, and cooperation."[33] The best illustration of the 'ulama''s conservative approach to social problems is the fact that al-Nahda al-islamiyya, a nation-wide Islamic charity set up by the country's leading clerics in the 1950s, arrested beggars in the street because they were "harming the reputation of the city and the rich, who were doing their best to answer the needs of the poor."[34] Old people were accommodated by the association, young men were "given work," fake beggars were handed over to the police, and foreigners were expelled to their own countries.[35]

Unsurprisingly, the 'ulama' strongly opposed the socialist measures enacted by the Ba'thist regime in the mid-1960s. Friday preachers remained relatively quiet during the first phase of nationalization, which only targeted banks and large capitalist consortiums, but they castigated the government when the latter turned to medium-sized companies; that is, to the very economic infrastructure of the clergy. According to an unverifiable—but plausible—account, one of the scholars arrested at that time for his denunciation of nationalizations, Krayyim Rajih (b. 1926), the Shaykh of the Readers of the Qur'an, explained his position to the radical leftist lieutenant-colonel Ahmad Suwaydan in the following terms: "Socialism forces capital holders and people endowed with a spirit of enterprise to flee. It deprives people of all motivation to work. It enslaves workers because it prevents them from aspiring to become their own employer. And since any authority will now be in the hands of the state, the new system does not leave any refuge for the workers when they are victims of an injustice."[36] Rajih's words underscore the dual rationales for the opposition of the 'ulama' to Ba'thist socialism: the first reflects the typical preference of the private sector for laissez-faire economic policies,[37] but the second is related to the fear that nationalization provides a despotic regime with a powerful instrument of social control.

The latter argument has also been found in the discourse of the Syrian Muslim Brothers over the last decades. After 1963, the Islamist movement quickly abandoned the rhetoric of Islamic socialism, which was absent from the comprehensive political programs it released in 1980 and 2004.[38] Their current advocacy of a liberal economic system characterized by "as much private initiative as possible" and "as little state intervention as possible" is not only justified by the poor performance of the Syrian public sector, but also by their professed desire to put an end to the "totalitarian practices of the state."[39] In other words, when Syrian Islamists ask for the "downsizing" of the state, they are not merely mimicking Western right-wing parties: whereas the latter's goals are purely economic, the former pursue a political strategy since they posit state intervention in the economy as one of the pillars of authoritarianism.

A Solution to Poverty? Work!

Beginning in the early 1990s, Syria slowly moved toward a more liberal economic system. The pace of reforms accelerated during the following decade, and in 2005 the Ba'th Party officially announced that the country was entering the era of the "social market economy."[40] It was good news for the Syrian clergy because measures of liberalization were taken in a context of economic boom that generated a marked increase in private donations for Islamic associations and schools.[41]

Problems of political economy were rarely dealt with in the Syrian 'ulama''s Friday sermons. The case of the aforementioned Shaykh Mahmud Abu al-Huda al-Husseini, who asked for "less pressure and taxes on small entrepreneurs,"[42] was probably exceptional. In any case, when tackling the issue of class relations, senior clerics showed little concern for the growing social inequalities that came with Syria's turn to capitalism.

On May 1, 2008, Shaykh Muhammad al-Ya'qubi (b. 1962), one of the most prominent Damascene scholars of his generation and a preacher in the upscale neighborhood of Abu Rummaneh, took advantage of International Workers' Day (a public holiday in Syria) to assert that Islam does not recognize the existence of a "working class" in the Western sense. Islam, al-Ya'qubi noted, distinguishes only between the self-employed, or "merchant" (*tajir*), and the salaried employee, or "worker" ('*amil*), a category that includes the "street sweeper" as well as the "prince." Therefore, importing a "Workers' Day" from the West was, he said, nonsense from an Islamic viewpoint.[43] Although al-Ya'qubi did not elaborate further, the logical consequence of his denial of the existence of workers as a class is the rejection of the very principle of labor unionism.

Other leading shaykhs expressed ideas on poverty that in Western countries would be voiced only by right-wing hardliners. Sariya al-Rifa'i, the dominant religious actor in the charitable sector of the Syrian capital, claimed that begging and poverty chiefly resulted from reluctance to work. Therefore, as he argued during a Friday sermon, charitable associations should be reformed so as not to help people unless they work:

> One administrator I spoke with told me the following story: A woman stood in front of his car at a traffic light and said: "Give me a little bit of what God has given to you" (she said that because the administrator has a very nice car). He answered: "Isn't it true that you get 5000 pounds [$100 US] a day?" She answered: "No, that's not true, only 1500 pounds a day."[44] . . . 1500 pounds . . . "only" . . . Of course, you know, when someone gives her 50 pounds, then someone else 100 pounds, and so on. . . . Don't you think that this woman and her children should work?! But why would they work? As long as she can get—according to her own words—1500 pounds a day, why would she content herself with 5000 or 10000 pounds a month? She prefers to send her children along the streets in order to beg for money. . . . A civilized Umma should not be based on consumption but rather on production. I have asked the Ministry of Social Affairs [which is in charge of charitable associations] that it sees to it that in the future, charitable help would be given to a family only in exchange for productive work. A disabled woman that cannot move or walk is perfectly able to work with her hands. . . . Let the

woman work, and let the man work instead of pretending they are sick! Indeed, even a sick man can work, from his bed if necessary! . . . There are many people who work in spite of their disability and who do not beg for money. As the Prophet said: "The hand that gives is better than the hand that receives."[45]

The discourse of the "Shaykh of the Merchants" echoed that of many Syrian entrepreneurs who took advantage of the context of economic liberalization to express ideas that seemed inspired by some form of social Darwinism.[46] At the same time, the aforementioned example of the "anti-vagrant squads" of the al-Nahda al-islamiyya association of the 1950s—which in Damascus was headed by al-Rifaʿi's father—shows that the stigmatization of beggars was nothing new among the Syrian ʿulamaʾ.

As for the idea of turning distribution-oriented benevolent associations into "productive" economic entities, it probably resulted from Sariya al-Rifaʿi's desire to reassure his benefactors about the good use of their money, but it also took place in a broader ideological context. In the framework of its partnerships with foreign actors such as the United Nations Development Program and the European Union, the Syrian Ministry of Social Affairs and Labor had encouraged benevolent associations to shift their activities from "charity" to "development," a call that found little response.[47]

Islamic Faces of Global Capitalism

Of course, the Syrian ʿulamaʾ's support for economic liberalism was not tantamount to a formal embrace of capitalism. To counter the "unrestrained materialism" of the latter, Sariya al-Rifaʿi offered the "humanism" of Islam, which allows for the harmonious coexistence of social classes through both legal and ethical devices (zakat, banning of usury, solidarity with the poor).[48] The global financial crisis that started in 2008 reinforced the ʿulamaʾ's conviction of the superiority of the Islamic economy over capitalism, which Saʿid Ramadan al-Buti, Syria's most famous Muslim scholar, described as "comatose."[49]

As a purported alternative to both socialism, which had oriented the economic policies of the Syrian regime for decades, and capitalism, which was an increasingly important component of the new "social market economy," the Islamic economy may at first glance have appeared as subversive. In the second half of the 1990s, however, it was the subject of public lectures given by the Minister of Religious Endowments and the Grand Mufti Ahmad Hassun.[50] The reason for such tolerance on the part of the regime is the fact that the *'ulama'* have in fact embraced the capitalist version of Islamic economics.

In its drive to attract Gulf capital and to expand private saving, the government authorized the creation of three Islamic banks (International Bank of Syria, al-Sham, and al-Baraka), starting in 2005.[51] As Charles Tripp argues, Islamic finance is less an alternative to capitalist globalization than one of its vehicles.[52] Syrian clerics, however, were relaxed about this fact— a predictable outcome, given that this new economic sector had allowed them to reassert their importance in the early twenty-first century.[53]

In their quest for both legal expertise and social prestige, the newly created banks included prominent religious figures on their shari'a boards, nominating individuals such as 'Abd al-Sattar Abu Ghudda (b. 1940), a Kuwait-based scholar from Aleppo who had been working with numerous financial institutions in the Gulf;[54] Wahba al-Zuhayli, Syria's most renowned expert on *fiqh*; Mufti of Damascus 'Abd al-Fattah al-Bazam; and Sa'id Ramadan al-Buti.[55] Al-Zuhayli and al-Buti were also members of Iltizam ("Commitment"), a Dubai-based organization that grants "Islamic ISO (Independent Service Organization)" certificates to companies whose operations are made in accordance with shari'a.[56]

The growing influence of neoliberal ideology in the Arab world has also been illustrated by the extraordinary popular enthusiasm for concepts such as the "science of management" (*'ilm al-idara*) and "personal development" (*al-tanmiyya al-bashariyya*, literally "human development")— that is, for a discourse that focuses on individual performance (succeeding in one's career and making friends) rather than on the transformation of social and political structures.[57] During the 2000s, these themes were hybridized with Islamic discourse by famous preachers such as Egyptian 'Amr Khalid,[58] Kuwaiti Tariq Suwaydan,[59] Saudi 'A'id al-Qarni,[60] and Syrian 'Abd al-Karim Bakkar.[61] The "secular" version of this genre was also extremely popular in Syria, as exemplified by the success of the books and television programs of Ibrahim al-Fiqqi, an Egyptian specialist in neuro-linguistic programming (NLP).[62] The latter's endorsement was sought by young Syrian clerics who tried to make a name for themselves in the realm of personal development as writers or as coaches.[63] Conversely, a Syrian specialist on NLP invited the famous Damascene preacher 'Abd al-Razzaq al-Humsi to write the foreword for one of his books.[64]

Discordant Voices

In the years that preceded the 2011 uprising, the only prominent Syrian cleric who adopted an overtly populist rhetoric was Mahmud Ghul Aghasi, alias Abu al-Qa'qa' (1973–2007), a firebrand preacher of Aleppo.[65] He became famous in the late 1990s for the violently anti-Zionist and anti-American sermons he was giving in the working-class neighborhood of Sakhur. Aghasi's calls to jihad targeted foreign enemies; his excellent relations with the regime fueled widespread rumors that he served as chief informer for the intelligence service among radical Islamist circles. This suspicion was reinforced by the fact that in the middle of the last decade, the jihadi preacher ditched his Afghan *qamis* for an elegant suit, trimmed his beard, and even joined the local religious establishment as the director of Aleppo's shari'a high school.

Surprisingly enough, it was only *after* his apparent toning-down— and a couple of weeks before he was assassinated under mysterious circumstances in September 2007—that Aghasi turned critical, if not of the regime as a whole, then at least of what he called the "mafias" that had developed within it. More importantly for this account, he did so by contrasting the impunity of the rich with the ruthless enforcement of the law against the humble. Among other examples, he evoked the suffering of a subaltern group that was destined to change the face of the Arab world four years later. Indeed, the way he described the treatment of itinerant greengrocers by the police is strikingly reminiscent of the incident that ignited protests in the Tunisian city of Sidi Buzid in December 2010, ultimately leading to the overthrow of President Ben Ali one month later:

There are poor people, modest people who sell some parsley, tomatoes and fruits on their handcart for their livelihood. Then patrols of the municipal police swoop down on them, as if we were in Tel Aviv. They beat [them] and they break [their handcart] on their head. But this is only for the poor, Oh Leader of this Homeland! As for the rich who are involved in drug trafficking, who protects them? And the organized mafias that steal billions, who protects them? . . . Oh Leader of this Homeland! State officials build houses, estates and palaces, and nobody asks them why, and the law that provides for the destruction [of illegal buildings] is not implemented against them. But when a poor man builds a bedroom for his children, he has it broken on his head![66]

Apart from Aghasi, very few well-known Syrian clerics displayed social conscience during that period. One of these was the reformist Ahmad Mu'adh al-Khatib, the former preacher of the Umayyad mosque and president of the cultural-charitable association al-Tamaddun al-islami, who in 2012 was elected as the chair of the Syrian National Coalition. Unlike his colleague Muhammad al-Ya'qubi, al-Khatib has praised Workers' Day as an occasion to "remind people of their rights."[67] He has also written that charity is not the only way to reduce poverty, since the principles of the welfare state are enshrined in the shari'a.[68]

At the same time, al-Khatib held the regime responsible for the country's social woes and did not address the overall economic system. For instance, he saw grand 'ulama"s lack of support for the workers not as a reflection of class interests, but as a result of "the repression exerted by corrupt regimes [which] have deprived workers of their rights while claiming to act in their name."[69] He also described the growth of private welfare in the 2000s as a mere palliative for the "plundering of the public treasury" by a corrupt elite rather than as a trend that is inseparable from economic liberalization.[70]

Islamic MP Muhammad Habash, another reformist, claimed to express the position of the "Islamic left," although without going beyond vague appeals to the "moralization" of global economy.[71] More concretely, however, he also signed, along leftist intellectuals and deputies, a 2007 petition against the slashing of fuel subsidies.[72]

The proximity of the *'ulama'* to the property-owning elite has only been criticized by subaltern religious actors. In a small Sufi *zawiyya* (lodge) of Aleppo that, unlike the brotherhoods headed by members of the scholarly elite, recruited its adepts from uneducated workers, I saw a young speaker railing against "the *'ulama'* of our times, whose only concern is to line their pockets."[73] Similarly, I heard *Salafi*-leaning people (who by definition oppose the predominantly Sufi *'ulama'*) branding the latter as "religious feudal lords" who "constantly talk about asceticism despite the fact that most of them are very rich."[74]

Conclusion

Because the Ba'thist regime refrained from turning the *'ulama'* into a body of civil servants, the country's religious elite remained reliant on the resources of the private sector. With their merchant background, Syrian Muslim scholars maintained a distinctly bourgeois ethics. They encouraged self-employment for both clerics and laypeople because they saw it as a guarantee of disinterest in the practice of *da'wa*, of religiously legal income, and of political independence from the state. Success and prosperity, which allow the believer to spend his money "on the path of God," were highly valued as both causes and consequences of piety.

In terms of economic thought in the strict sense, the Syrian *'ulama'* rejected all forms of socialism, which they considered both a threat to their economic interests and a dangerous means of social control for despotic regimes. From the 1950s to the 2000s, their response to the problem of poverty materialized in a paternalistic conception of charity. More recently, they wholeheartedly welcomed the introduction of Islamic finance in Syria, which helped them to reaffirm their relevance through the presence of Muslim scholars on the shari'a boards of the newly established banks. The "elective affinities" between the Syrian clergy's economic ethics and the spirit of neoliberalism was also illustrated by the hybridization of local religious discourse with managerial literature.

The *'ulama'*'s alliance with the private sector only partially influenced their behavior after March 2011. Whereas from 1963 to 1982, merchant strikes formed part of the protests against the regime, the bourgeoisie of Damascus and Aleppo remained loyal to the regime during the first year of the uprising. Although conservative Sunni businessmen had never ceased complaining about corruption and unfair competition on the part of regime cronies, the recent liberalization had enriched them. As a result, they favored stability over political change; many feared the predominantly peasant and working-class character of the uprising.

From the first demonstrations on, the clergy's loyalties were split between supporters of the regime and critics of its brutal handling of the crisis. This division reflected no differences in personal class background, since representatives of both trends enjoyed excellent relations with the merchant community.[75] Instead, contrasting clerical discourses about the uprising had their respective origins in relationships with the state that had formed differently throughout the previous decades, as some actors had been co-opted by the regime, whereas others had been excluded and had preserved relative independence.

Irrespective of their warm relations with the bourgeoisie, members of the second category decided to speak out because of considerations that had little to do with the economy. First, some of them sincerely believed that as men of religion, they had to denounce injustices committed by the state when they reached such proportions. Second, some prominent clerics were trying to remain politically relevant to an audience that was much wider than the merchant community, and whose majority was presumably hostile to the regime.

9

Muslim Organizations in Bashar's Syria

The Transformation of the Shaykh Ahmad Kuftaro Foundation

LEIF STENBERG

During the presidency of Bashar al-Asad, Syria has witnessed an increase in piety symbols such as headscarves and new mosques, religious schools, and movements: signs of the growing prominence of religion in the public sphere.[1] Under these circumstances the policy of Bashar al-Asad's regime has been to control religion by establishing a relationship with loyal and supportive Sunni *'ulama'*[2] with the broader aim of accommodating and promote pious forms of Islam and to creating a framework that regulates interpretations of Islam.[3] Muslim religious leaders and their organizations have been under the surveillance of the Syrian security services, but they have also experienced a degree of autonomy. They have established movements and organizations in spaces where the state is weak, such as charity, providing work opportunities, day care, religious education, and orphanages.[4] In more open challenges to state power, Muslim religious scholars have also been active in demonstrations and protests in Syria since 2011, and mosques have been centers of protest. However,

My first visit to Syria was in 1990. I received funding from the Swedish Research Council in 1997 to study Ahmad Kuftaro's interpretations of Islam and the context of these interpretations.

147

not all religious leaders support the opposition: religious scholars like Saʿid Ramadan al-Buti (d. 2013) and the Mufti of Syria, Ahmad Badr al-Din Hassun, are loyal to the regime.

In this chapter I take a closer look at one of the largest religious organizations in Syria, the Shaykh Ahmad Kuftaro Foundation.[5] The foundation is an umbrella organization consisting of several branches, and interwoven with a religious movement. Almost all of the foundation's officials, the students at the mosque, and mosque attendants are linked to a branch of the Sufi tradition of Naqshbandiyya[6] that conveys an interpretation of Islam emphasizing piety, education, ethics, and religious dialogue. This foundation has been an ally of the state since its founding as the Abu Nur Foundation in 1971 (the charity al-Ansar was established already in 1952), but during the reign of Bashar al-Asad it developed into a more independent and self-sustaining structure providing education, charity, and an orphanage. The foundation is centered on the Abu Nur mosque in Damascus. Its theology and rituals are founded on practices linked to Naqshbandiyya and interpretations of Islam that emphasize the creation of a pious modern Muslim—an individual who emphasizes the performance of religious rituals and a modern secular education.[7] In 2008 the Syrian government began to instigate a policy of regulating organizations like the Ahmad Kuftaro Foundation. A decree was implemented in 2009 establishing that most, if not all, of these religious movements would remain under the control of the Ministry of Religious Affairs (*awqaf*).[8] The developments at the foundation since Bashar al-Asad took power demonstrate shifting realities for the organization and illustrate how a foundation meets repressive actions, maneuvers in its interpretations of Islam, and makes use of an informal Sufi network.

The chapter will chronologically explore developments and everyday experiences within the Ahmad Kuftaro Foundation before the events of 2011, with a view to illustrating the historical, religious, administrative, and political context of this key institution in the religious life of Syria. I use accounts of everyday politics and ritual life to contextualize and explain measures taken by the organization to cope with the death of Ahmad Kuftaro in 2004. In particular, I detail the strategy of his son Salah Kuftaro, who was incarcerated in early summer 2009 and released in the fall of 2010, to assume responsibility for the spiritual and charismatic legacy of his father, and his ambition to establish himself as a powerful religious scholar.[9] Plainly, state actions to control Sunni movements have changed the conditions for the Ahmad Kuftaro Foundation and for Salah Kuftaro's ambition as a religious leader. Through a closer look at the last ten to fifteen years of organizational and ritual transformations the foundation has undergone, I will trace and assess the effect of state actions to control the activities of the Ahmad Kuftaro Foundation and the responses from the movement to such encroachments. Moreover, I analyze the possibilities and constraints for a religious organization such as the Ahmad Kuftaro Foundation to act under a repressive state.

Understanding Islam as a dynamic social phenomenon and a set of diverse and evolving socially embedded discursive practices is not particularly novel; nor is it unprecedented to observe that historical moments and conceptual spaces are important in scholarly analyses of the meaning of Islam in everyday experience.[10] Yet reflecting on the function of religion and agency[11] within the constraints of an authoritarian regime provides significant insights into the role Muslim and non-Muslim actors play in the production of Islam, as I will illustrate in this case study. My portrait of the foundation shows that the developments at this organization over the last fifteen years cannot simply be understood as an instance of a hierarchical relationship between the state and the foundation in the form of "official Islam." Moreover, the foundation's link to Naqshbandiyya also demonstrated how Sufi orders are transformed to more formal organizations in order to meet changes in society. This article contributes to the field of Islamic studies by exposing how everyday realities structure ritual life and guide the investments made by leaders as well as followers in the very same rituals, rather than regarding rituals as free from political considerations and formed only in reference to a static and abstract theology. Hence, individuals are the active subjects interpreting and practicing Islam, and Muslims'—individual and/or collective—understanding of Islam is therefore the starting point in this perspective. A general aim is to counteract monolithic and essentialist ideas on Islam and to promote a perspective that studies Islam as dynamic and fluid, analytically centered on the production of religion.

The Shaykh Ahmad Kuftaro Foundation—
The Development of a Mosque Complex

Ahmad Kuftaro, recognized as one of the most important Syrian religious scholars of the twentieth century, was born in Damascus between 1911 and 1915 and died in 2004.[12] Kuftaro belonged to a family of Kurdish religious scholars and was trained in Islamic sciences by his father, the Naqshbandi shaykh and scholar Muhammad Amin Kuftaro (d. 1938). He was also educated by other religious scholars from Damascene mosques specializing in various areas of classical Islamic knowledge. After receiving authorization to teach and to hold Friday prayers, he became active in several Damascus-area mosques. After his father's death, Ahmad Kuftaro inherited his position as shaykh of a Naqshbandi *tariqa* (order), and as a preacher of the small Abu Nur mosque located in the Kurdish area of the city, on the slopes of Mount Qassioun.[13] In the 1940s and 1950s he established himself as a religious scholar. In 1951 he was appointed Mufti of Damascus, and in 1964 he became the Mufti of Syria, a position he held until his death in 2004. Until June 2009, this foundation, centered at the Abu Nur mosque in Damascus, was headed by one of Ahmad's sons, Salah Kuftaro. Throughout the years this organization and its leadership have been perceived as supportive of state-sponsored Islam in Syria.

During Bashar's presidency, charity has been a major activity of the Ahmad Kuftaro Foundation, and the foundation has developed its organizational structures and systems for charitable distributions. It also administers a number of smaller foundations. According to *Syria Today*, the operation's entire financial turnover, including that of all foundations at the Abu Nur mosque complex, was $4.8 million (US) in 2008. The largest charitable foundation, al-Ansar, which funds the orphanage and education, accounted for $2.6 million of the total turnover. The remaining $2.2 million consisted of donations, a large proportion of which comes from non-Syrian donors. However, in a conversation with me in October 2008, Salah Kuftaro expressed hesitation concerning this dependence on donations. In his view the organization needed to find other ways of attracting non-Syrian donors.

The mosque's charity work is primarily based on cash grants to registered recipients and the distribution of food and home supplies.[14] One example is how money is distributed to women in the interior of the mosque complex, more precisely outside the small building said to be the original Abu Nur mosque. The small mosque contains the burial place of Ahmad Kuftaro and his immediate family. The organization of charity asserts the significance of connecting monetary to spiritual powers, and the recipient of a donation is meant to understand that it is linked to the grace of Ahmad Kuftaro. The distribution of charity was organized in this way to increase the spiritual bond between Ahmad Kuftaro and his son Salah Kuftaro to strengthen the latter's claim as spiritual heir. Hence, the strengthening of the foundation's institutional structure and the new conditions under which donations were distributed had the purpose of expanding the number of Salah Kuftaro's disciples and increasing the power of Salah and the organization in Syrian society.

The will to enlarge the local organization is strong within the Ahmad Kuftaro Foundation its leadership. The aspiration of one of the sub-branches of the movement, the al-Ansar Foundation, is to open up a new orphanage for boys in the outskirts of Damascus. Al-Ansar and its charity work have received donations from inside Syria as well as from abroad: during the fall of 2007, a Kuwaiti fund sponsored six hundred young orphans.[15] In parallel to local ambitions the foundation manages a transnational network of organizations. Through its Naqshbandi affiliation and the high profile of Ahmad Kuftaro among Muslims worldwide, it has a network of contacts in many Muslim countries. It also runs centers and mosques in the United States. The foundation has aimed to increase its significance in Syria, and correspondingly on an international level among Muslims all over the world. The transnational links of the foundation are extensive: for example, on the wall of one of the mosque's inner courtyards, a plate expresses the gratitude of the foundation and Salah Kuftaro toward Diyab bin Zayid Al Nahyan of the royal family of the United Arab Emirates for financing a renovation of the mosque completed in 2008. During my visits in 2009 and 2010, mosque officials expressed interest in buying more property in the neighborhood in order to further expand the complex.

In sum, the Abu Nur mosque complex that I have followed since the mid-1990s illustrates how charities, educational institutions and mosques are bound together structurally under the umbrella of a common foundation. The Abu Nur mosque is the heart of the foundation, and since the late 1960s the mosque has developed into an extensive complex that includes a large prayer hall, areas for college education, a library, charity organizations, small shops, and a media center. Throughout the last twenty years, the complex has expanded to include dormitories attached to the mosque and an orphanage for 150–200 girls in its neighborhood.[16]

Ritual and Organizational Developments at the Foundation

The change of rituals, improvements of the organization structure, and a refurbishment of the mosque complex not only display a development carried out in reference to theology, but are closely related to power struggles, a positioning among Sunni movements in Syria, and a general transformation and formalization of movements like the Ahmad Kuftaro Foundation. The physical layout of the Abu Nur mosque has been transformed since the death of Kuftaro in 2004. After completion of the main prayer hall renovation, the mosque was inaugurated in the fall of 2008 in the presence of a number of religious dignitaries, diplomats, and politicians. Among the speakers were Salah Kuftaro, the ambassador of the United Arab Emirates, and the minister of religious affairs in Syria, Muhammad 'Abd al-Sattar al-Sayyid. On large television screens placed on the wall directed toward Mecca, Salah showed historical images and film clips of the Abu Nur mosque and the lives of Amin and Ahmad Kuftaro.[17] This was an important event since it gave Salah Kuftaro an opportunity to demonstrate his connection and strengthen his position within the Ahmad Kuftaro Foundation as well as among the Sunni community in Syria.

In early 2005, on my first visit to Abu Nur after Ahmad Kuftaro's death, the general structure of the Friday ritual had been changed. It started, as usual in this branch of the Naqshbandi order, with a period of *dhikr*— a silent, meditative ritual. After a while the *silsila* (chain of shaykhs) of the order was recited over the mosque's loudspeakers, with Ahmad Kuftaro's name newly added to the list. The reading of the chain of shaykhs, a practice that underscores belief in transmission of spiritual powers from one shaykh to another, is a core feature of this Sufi order. After recitations and songs sung in the honor of Allah and Muhammad, the *dars*[18] began. Those who were closest to Ahmad Kuftaro in the hierarchy of this Naqsh-bandi branch replaced him in performing the *dars*. Among them were shaykhs and *khalifas* (deputies) such as Bashir al-Bani (d. 2008) and Rajab Dib. The shaykhs replacing Kuftaro held a noticeably shorter lesson than he had held. After the *dars*, an edited version of an earlier lesson by Ahmad Kuftaro was projected onto the *qibla* wall (the wall facing Mecca).[19] This lasted for about twenty-five minutes and was followed by the Friday prayer and a longer *khutba* (sermon) delivered by Salah Kuftaro. Two visits to the mosque during April and October 2008 revealed that the ritual had been altered again, and the edited version of Ahmad Kuftaro's lessons projected on the walls and screens of the mosque now lasted for about forty min-utes. The ambition of the foundation in making these changes was to pro-duce a Friday schedule that would appeal to disciples who still regarded themselves as followers of Ahmad Kuftaro, and to encourage them to con-tinue coming to the mosque and remain loyal to the foundation. This was an important contribution to maintaining the spiritual influence of the foundation. These transformations were also intended to promote the new head of the foundation, Salah Kuftaro, and his efforts to monopolize the spiritual inheritance of his father, outmaneuver competition, and become an important religious scholar.

In addition, the modification of the Friday ritual schedule placed less importance on the *dars*, and the focus was no longer exclusively on a lec-ture delivered by a single scholar. Consequently, time was allocated more evenly to the various parts of the Friday ritual, with the abovementioned shortening of the *dars* and a prolonging of the time devoted to the *khutba* sermon.[20] The innovative idea to show edited versions of older Qur'anic lessons of Ahmad Kuftaro is today a prominent and established part of the Friday ritual. Since 2005, a committee headed by one of the shaykhs at the foundation, Ahmad Rajih, has selected and edited the clips. My infor-mants claim that he was chosen because he is regarded as a long-standing disciple of Ahmad Kuftaro and also possessed the necessary technological skills. I am presuming that the editing process carefully conformed to the

ideas of Salah Kuftaro, and that one objective was to strengthen the connection between the disciples and an ambitious new leader, Salah Kuftaro,
with the deceased shaykh as an intermediary. The changes to the Friday
rituals show that the organization of these rituals is certainly not static,
and that they are subject to radical alteration due to power ambitions
within the mosque environment. In addition, these changes serve a desire
among mosque visitors to hear the voice of their dead shaykh—Ahmad
Kuftaro. Hence, the outline of a Friday ritual can clearly be a balancing
act between interests concerning power struggles and the appeal of the
ordinary mosque attendants.

To become an established religious leader and to succeed Ahmad
Kufaro was difficult. The way in which Salah Kuftaro outlined strategies
and tried establish himself as a distinguished religious scholar and successor to his father reveals general dilemmas and tensions regarding whom
to consider a religious scholar. Until his imprisonment in June 2009, Salah
Kuftaro usually performed the *khutba*. It gave him an opportunity to lead
the more oral part of the ritual and to demonstrate his rhetorical skills and
competence in interpreting Islam in a modern context. One can view the
changes to the ritual as an attempt to establish continuity between Amin,
Ahmad, and Salah Kuftaro and to establish Salah Kuftaro as an important
and innovative scholar of Islam—a person who, from his platform at the
Ahmad Kuftaro Foundation, was actively working for the betterment of
society. The transformation of the various rituals accommodated interests within the foundation as well as visitors; and today the *dars* does not
dominate the time as it once did. One possible interpretation of this shift
is that Salah Kuftaro's lack of a thorough and formal theological training
has limited his ability to lead the *dars*. He has stated that his education
was private, and that it mainly involved following in the footsteps of his
father.[21] In this context it becomes clear how religious rituals are adapted
to new realities, such as the competence of the leader of the foundation,
but also how rituals are transformed to express a historic link and endurance. In addition, changes of rituals are not justified by reference to theology. Instead they are motivated by a quest for power. The ambition of
Salah Kuftaro to establish himself as a prominent religious scholar relates
to a more general discussion among Muslim religious scholars concerning

authority and the righteous qualification of a religious scholar—specifically, whether the status of a religious scholar can be attained only through formal religious training or through secular education as well. In the case of Salah Kuftaro, he has consciously worked to appear as a formal religious scholar, but in this work he constantly refers to an informal relationship to his father claiming to be his spiritual heir.

A problem for Salah Kuftaro after the death of his father was that leadership of the branch has been ambiguous, and many of Ahmad Kuftaro's disciples have been doubtful about whom to consider their shaykh. Legitimacy is a pressing issue because Salah Kuftaro did not obtain confirmation officially recognizing him as the spiritual heir to his father.[22] However, before his death Ahmad Kuftaro wrote a letter proposing that disciples should support Salah Kuftaro in his work as the director of the foundation.[23] The heading of the letter consists of a quotation from the Qur'an. It contains the first words of *sura* 3 verse 103: "And hold fast to the rope all of you, and be not divided among yourselves." These words emphasize the intention of the letter to bring together the adherents of the Sufi branch and encourage them to work within a unified spirit for the foundation. The letter was also signed by all the prominent shaykhs and other leaders of this particular Sufi branch. In addition, most of those who endorsed Salah Kuftaro were board members or active in the Ahmad Kuftaro Foundation. It is not uncommon that Sufi orders split into several branches due to contradictions concerning the legitimate heir after the death of a famous shaykh. However, a split has not appeared officially in this branch of the Naqshbandiyya. One reason is that the foundation and the Sufi order are entwined, and a split would be devastating to the work environment and the ambitions within the foundation.

Until his arrest in June 2009, Salah Kuftaro was able to develop and improve the organizational structure of the various foundations within the mosque complex.[24] The new entrance has a reception area for receiving guests, and parts of the complex suggest a modern business environment.[25] For example, the orphanage for girls, Dar al-Rahma, which has succeeded in marketing the Kuftaro Foundation in general, is modeled after the structure of SOS International children's villages. The foundation focused on charity, al-Ansar, was also organized in a more efficient manner than previously. However, the foundation's board consisted primarily of Salah Kuftaro loyalists, such as Muhannad al-Losh, a government information technology adviser, who described himself to me as Salah Kuftaro's *khalifa* and close associate on matters concerning the foundation.[26] Al-Ansar's charitable work supposedly follows the laws and regulations in Syria. However, embezzlement of charity funds was one of the official reasons for Salah Kuftaro's arrest.[27]

In sum, the changes described above suggest that religious foundations like the Ahmad Kuftaro Foundation and Sufi orders transform and act in response to a general transformation of Syrian society, and illustrate how this foundation and branch of the Naqshbandiyya is an example of religious movements formalizing their organizational structure in response to that transformation. This is a case in which *baraka*,[28] usually intimately related to an individual, can be transferred to an organization, especially if a Sufi branch and a foundation are so closely connected. This shift is also underscored by the change of the name of the foundation from the Abu Nur Foundation to the Ahmad Kuftaro Foundation. The evolution of the Ahmad Kuftaro Foundation reflects an aspiration to develop a modern organizational structure, but such changes are politically challenging for a foundation whose ambition, which is shared by other religious movements in Syria and other Muslim countries, is to build an Islamic educational institution and an NGO focused on welfare that corresponds with "Islamic" values and ideas,[29] in this case drawing on an interpretation of Islam that has its roots in a Sunni tradition and a Naqshbandi *tariqa*.

Implementing a Governmental Decree
Concerning Religious Organizations

Transformations of rituals and the organization were not the only developments at the Ahmad Kuftaro Foundation over the last fifteen years. Leaders as well as lay people debated topics like democracy, human rights, free and open elections, the role of religion in society, and the relationship between Sunni and Shi'a Muslims. Not all disciples of this Sufi branch I talked to during these years were in favor of what they considered

"Western" inventions like democracy, which they understood as alien to an Islamic life and polity. However, Salah Kuftaro, as a leader of the foundation, spoke openly in favor of democracy and human rights and met with foreigners, religious leaders, politicians, academics, and journalists. The meetings I discuss below reveal the character of the dialogue within the Ahmad Kuftaro Foundation before March 2011, but are also an example of conversations taking place in many Muslim organizations, movements, and communities today.[30]

During April 2009 I participated in a meeting at the summer residence of Salah Kuftaro in Yafour along the road to Beirut. He had invited religious leaders, journalists, business people, and friends for a meal and to discuss all kinds of questions—the topics were not decided beforehand, but usually concerned international and national politics, and questions about religion and its role in society. There were several international guests and a fairly even gender balance. Meetings like this are not unusual in Damascus, and friends who trust each other and belong to the same families and power circles sometimes gather over a meal to discuss political developments. Salah often organized meetings on Friday afternoons and invited guests with the aim of maintaining and extending his political network. After sharing a meal, men and women sat together and conversed, a rarity in Muslim religious settings in Syria.

One of the female participants asked our host for his opinion about a recent event: the previous week, Friday prayers in Sayyida Zaynab, a Shi'a-dominated suburb of Damascus holding an important shrine for Shi'as, were read in Persian. She claimed this was the first time this had happened in modern history. If true, this would represent a symbolically and politically a sensitive issue for Sunni Muslim leaders, who would be prone to view a Friday prayer in Persian as part of a general Shi'a-fication of Sunni environments: a trend supported by the Iranian government. Salah's reply was rather evasive, but he told us about his public statements that the Iranian ambassador had been financially supporting the payment of Sunnis for their conversion to Shi'a Islam.[31] Our host also believed that the activities of the Iranian Cultural Centre in Damascus had also been restricted due to protests from Sunni leaders. In the ensuing discussion, a female journalist voiced criticism concerning the activities undertaken by

Iranian official representatives in Syria. Her criticism was directed against Arab Shi'a, and questioned their loyalty to Syria.

The critique of the Arab Shi'a and the activities ascribed to the Iranian embassy in Damascus is a sensitive issue in Syria because it touches upon the relationship between the regime and the religious and ethnic minorities in the country, and also on the relationship between the religious majority—the Sunnis—and religious minorities. The conversation therefore turned to the role that the Mufti of Syria, Ahmad Badr al-Din Hassun, could play in easing the increasingly tense relationship between Sunni and Shi'a, but the interlocutors considered him to be restrained by decisions made higher up in the Syrian political hierarchy. The female journalist's view was that Hassun's role is constrained because he is opposed by other religious scholars belonging to the old and established Damascus families—families that have produced religious scholars for generations. As she suggested, Hassun was from Aleppo and not from the religious families of the capital, and he was weak because he had no following. According to our host, he was not the head of a religious movement that would give him a stronger position. The discussion produced no clear message and ended with comments on the general uncertainty concerning the state of Arab Shi'a Muslims' loyalty to Syria, but the discussion revealed a rift between Sunni leaders and the state. The frictions between the Mufti of Syria and other religious scholars reveals a power struggle over who should represent Sunni Islam in Syria, a situation in which progressive interpretations of Islam were in a strained relationship to more conservative understandings closely related to, and enforced by, the power holders.[32] In addition, old antipathies between shaykhly families add to their differences, and the discussion reveals the fragmentation between different Sunni leaders.

At the Abu Nur mosque complex, the Ahmad Kuftaro Foundation has developed educational institutions as an important aspect of its activities, and Salah's visitors discussed the subject of education in relation to a tension between religious communities, as well as the future role of institutions like the Ahmad Kuftaro Foundation. Since this conversation took place in spring 2009, before Salah Kuftaro's imprisonment, the aim to regulate the privately administrated *madrasa* institutes by the state and the state-run institutes was a hot topic that worried many of the participants at Salah's residence. The discussion of the *madrasas* recalled an article in the January 2009 issue of *Syria Today*, regarding how the regime tried to strengthen its grip on thirty-two private religious educational institutions (twenty Sunni and twelve Shi'a) by issuing a governmental decree. According to the article, the idea of the government was to bring these religious educational institutions and their associated foundations under the control of the Ministry of Religious Affairs.[33] Private religious education had previously worked through a license from the Ministry of Religious Affairs, and the charity foundations that operated as part of larger religious foundations had been licensed through the equivalent of social and labor ministries. Many Syrian religious foundations are primarily concerned with education and charity, and private religious educational institutions have been able to control the content of their textbooks and curricula. According to Obaida Hamad, a Syrian journalist, the Syrian state has criticized the private religious educational institutions for low educational standards and ideological bias. The broad goal of the new initiatives by the Syrian government is to discipline and achieve control over private religious education.[34] Private religious *madrasas* are well funded in comparison to state-run institutions. Funds to private bodies come from donations and fees, primarily from Syria, but some programs rely on donations from the Arab peninsula and Muslims in North America and Europe. Since 2008, all donations must be recorded and monitored by government authorities.[35] The efforts to create educational institutions rest on the idea that correct Islamic and secular education is understood as a key component in creating the good society.

A tension between Sunni and Shi'a was not the only reason for the implementation of a governmental decree concerning Muslim religious organizations. After a series of bombings in Damascus in 2008, the repressive Syrian regime took the opportunity to develop a strategy to curb the influence of the more autonomous religious organizations in the country. In April 2009, officials at the Ahmad Kuftaro Foundation gave me documents that emphasize the Syrian government's intentions in regard to Sunni movements. One of the documents, written in the form of a declaration on how private religious education[36] will be organized in Syria, is a decree signed by Muhammad 'Abd al-Sattar al-Sayyid, Minister of

Religious Affairs, and Diyala al-Hajj 'Arif, Minister of Social Affairs and Labor.[37] The decree was signed in September 2008 and addressed to the local offices of both ministries in the fourteen districts of Syria. After an initial statement that the intention of the decree is in the best interests of the country, the decree addresses three points. The first designates the Ministry of Religious Affairs as responsible for all shari'a institutes and other private religious educational institutions, in accordance with the current Syrian laws concerning private organizations. The second point emphasizes that the Ministry of Religious Affairs should administer all religious education and take over control of the education budget of private organizations from the Ministry of Social Affairs and Labor. The third and final paragraph says it is no longer permissible for charitable foundations to collect donations for shari'a institutes. These institutes' compliance is expected. They will be inspected, and if individuals or organizations violate the law they will be subject to punishment. One point that emerges from this legislation is that as the state takes control of the finances of private religious foundations, it becomes difficult for them to accept donations from abroad. These changes have radically altered the operating conditions for mosques, charities, and mosque-linked education, especially concerning how they have financed their activities in recent decades.

The curriculum of religious education is a political matter linked to ambitions within the state about the role of religion in the Syrian society. Participants in the discussion I attended attributed this reorganization to the fact that the regime is terrified of what it perceives as a threat by representatives of Salafi and Wahhabi practices and interpretations of Islam. My interlocutors also pointed out that it is not the threat from the Muslim Brotherhood that is understood as serious in the government's eyes, but a challenge from more radical movements. Further, they suggested that this decree on reorganization came from bodies above the ministerial level, and that the ultimate goal is to create a broader Ministry of Religious Affairs that will eventually also organize and control Syria's Christians—a development that will certainly complicate relations between state authorities and Christian denominations.

Salah Kuftaro was arrested in June 2009, after the abovementioned decree was promulgated. Muhammad Sharif al-Sawwaf was appointed as the new director of the foundation, and board members were changed. An Ahmad Kuftaro disciple who wrote a book about Sufi methods in the thought of his shaykh, al-Sawwaf was appointed not only due to his status as a loyal follower of Kuftaro, but also as a follower of the regime.[38] In October 2010, teachers at the Kuftaro Foundation told me that al-Sawwaf is able to maintain a positive relationship with the current minister of religious affairs. It is unclear how the change of the foundation's leadership has affected the size of donations received from abroad, but it has given the ministry direct financial control. In Damascus in October 2010, Syrians pointed out to me that the authorities had been warned that the decree would encourage institutions to go underground and/or become radicalized. Hence, the more radical would continue their activities, either in clandestine fashion or abroad. The uncertain situation in Syria since March 2011 makes it difficult to analyze developments within religious organizations, but in discussions among religious scholars I attended in Damascus in October 2010, which included representatives of the Saudi-based Rabita al-ʿalam al-islami (The Muslim World League) and the Algerian Nahda movement (Harakat al-nahda al-islamiyya), Syrian participants openly discussed their connections to the Muslim Brotherhood in Jordan.

Private religious institutes that can be characterized as mainstream Sunni have been incorporated into a new system keeping them in check, and they have been transformed in the sense that their education and charity organizations have come under the control of the regime. Before the implementation of the decree, according to Salah Kuftaro, Syrian security services visited various religious leaders, warning against contact with the Muslim Brotherhood, the United States, and the Syrian opposition in exile. In conversations in April 2009, Salah Kuftaro stated that religious leaders expressed criticism of the Ministry of Information over its attempts to influence and control religious leaders. Some religious figures linked to the Ahmad Kuftaro Foundation were also cautioned by the security services, according to Salah, for their attempt to create a dialogue between Sunni and Shiʿa organizations; perhaps a consensus among religious organizations was perceived by the state as a threat to national security. However, the government initiated a series of meetings to promote a dialogue between the various *madhdhahib* (schools of Islamic thought/jurisprudence) in 2009.

The implementation of the decree by the Syrian state was drastic in its effects, and what is more broadly at stake is control over Islam. However, the long-term outcomes of recent protests, demonstrations and civil war, especially their effect on the status of religious organizations among Syria's pious groups, are difficult to judge. In the short term, the regime has lost support among Syria's many Muslim religious individuals and organizations—a failure that could have serious consequences and further spark sectarian-based and religiously justified and motivated violence.

Rethinking the Function of Islam at the Foundation

The way in which the Ahmad Kuftaro Foundation is administrated and ritually structured and the activities that it emphasizes resemble what Peter Mandaville (2007) characterizes as a "new Islamism."[39] The similarities between recent developments in Islamist movements like the Muslim Brotherhood in Egypt and Sufi movements of the kind described above generally concern the Islamization of social space.[40] The focus on charity is one example of such a commonality and an example of a social space in which movements can exercise agency under constrained circumstances. At the Ahmad Kuftaro Foundation, money linked through charity to the deceased and living shaykhs functions as a tool to stress the spiritual bond from Amin Kuftaro to Salah Kuftaro via Salah's father, Ahmad. Another indication of this trend toward new Islamism is the advancement of an idea of the creation of a modern Muslim through an educational development of the individual. Furthermore, Ahmad Kuftaro Foundation's emphasis on dialogue and environmental issues reflects a similarity between this foundation and various movements that aspire to make Islam a broad social resource shaping the good and just society.[41]

This approach to cooperation in general is pragmatic and inclusive of non-Islamic movements. In a conversation in November 2008 Salah Kuftaro stated that he was willing to cooperate with secular individuals and organizations as long as they worked for similar goals. The term "secular" means, in his understanding, nonreligious. He also stated that he would rather cooperate with righteous secular people than with Muslims of a Salafi or Wahhabi affiliation. However, in discussions I attended in 2010 he also revealed that some religious scholars seek to establish contact with international movements that fall within the mainstream of Sunni Islamism; that is, movements and organizations that are not violent, but which regard "Islam" as a political or civil philosophy and an indigenous tradition that constitutes the foundation for the establishment of the good citizen and the good society. Hence, in Salah Kuftaro's perspective, reform and power can be established from below: through a process of *da'wa* (call to Islam), through the creation of a pious population, and through general elections. This perspective is reminiscent of Asef Bayat's statement that "post-Islamism attempts to undo Islamism as a political project by fusing faith and freedom, a secular democratic state and a religious society."[42] For Salah Kuftaro, violence is not necessarily the appropriate vehicle for social transformation, either ideologically or strategically. Instead, restructured rituals, administrative developments and improvements, the expansion of orphanages, and Salah Kuftaro's effort to lead the organization are the major changes that aim to strengthen the Ahmad Kuftaro Foundation as an institution.

The manner in which the Ahmad Kuftaro Foundation has been reorganized and refurbished can be understood as a strategy to keep charisma, in a Weberian understanding, within the institution. When asked if *baraka* (spiritual power) could be transferred from Ahmad Kuftaro to the organization, Salah Kuftaro responded that this was not a problem. However, my impression is that he also consciously cultivates a connection between himself and his father and grandfather, drawing on his pedigree for legitimacy to advance his ambition to become a recognized Sufi shaykh. Since his release from prison in the fall of 2010, Salah Kuftaro has been in house confinement. Hence, he is under the strict control of Syrian security and is forbidden to travel overseas. He has not been prominently active in the Syrian uprising, perhaps because—apart from the control of the Syrian security services—he awaits the outcome of the unrest. Many of his postings on his Facebook page can be seen as cautiously critical of the regime, but on Facebook he often refers to his father and he frequently publishes photos of his father and himself. In a situation of being under surveillance, Salah uses Facebook as a tool to link himself to the religious legacy of his father and grandfather—or even to claim that legacy. He also participates in online discussions about the civil war in Syria and expresses ideas from an Islamic perspective on the conflict. His active presence on Facebook will presumably influence his position on how to interpret Islam, especially questions regarding democracy, justice, the good society, gender relations, and human rights, but also his views on other interpretations. Under the control of security services, social media becomes a tool for Salah as a religious leader to stay in touch with followers and make statements on Islam and developments in Syria. His aspiration is, of course, dependent on the reception of the disciples of this branch of the Naqsh-bandi order, and on whether they ultimately accept him as a shaykh.

It is interesting to view the increasingly well-organized Abu Nur Foundation (and, later, the Ahmad Kuftaro Foundation) developing an interpretation of Islam that attracts middle- and upper-middle-class adherents while at the same time expanding its charity activities serving the poor.[43] In a sense, this resembles the Protestant ethic of rational organization of everyday life not rejecting worldly affairs, but in this case it is justified by—and calling for—Islamic ideals. The latter reflects a number of virtues that will shape the new and modern Muslim through a practice of spiritual ideals. In the case of the Ahmad Kuftaro Foundation, welfare society is intimately related to religious training in general and practice of Sufism in particular. Hence, one can state that the Shaykh Ahmad Kuftaro Foundation invests in piety and that it seeks to produce a good and morally just society. In his work to implement this vision, Salah Kuftaro personifies a new form of dynamic Muslim entrepreneur who is able to maneuver strategically in a repressive environment. Especially after the death of his father, Kuftaro has developed and included a terminology and practices in his organization in order to create a viable future for himself and for the foundation. He has, for example, integrated terms like "human rights" and "NGO" to describe what he politically supports and how he sees his organization. The way in which he has combined modern technology, an organizational structure resembling that of a business, the approach of nongovernmental humanitarian organizations to charity work, and Naqshbandi traditions fostering Islamic excellence and virtue is innovative, and it parallels developments in many Islamic movements. However, charisma is a key requirement for Salah Kuftaro to fulfill his ambition to be accepted as the spiritual heir of his father. Here, charisma is necessary for him to uphold and expand authority and power, and also to legitimize a modern organization.

The transformations described above and the struggles of Salah Kuftaro to succeed his father are certainly about power, but they also suggest that to describe the Ahmad Kuftaro Foundation during recent years as an obedient instrument in the hands of the government is problematic. After a conflict between Salah and his brother before the death of their father Ahmad Kuftaro, Salah replaced Mahmud as the director of the Abu Nur mosque complex. At the same time, the Ministry of Religious Affairs, responsible for mosques and religious education, is now in reality meant to supervise mosques and appoint imams. The ministry administers religious policies founded on Ba'thist secularism. The aim, from the government's point of view, has been to make Sunni religious scholars accommodate to the center of power.[44] In this way scholars can be utilized in support of the regime: religious leaders are co-opted and controlled, as well as divided. In this context the term "official Islam" expresses a power relationship that has limited connections to various interpretations of Islam made by shaykhs and to different Sunni movements. For state-supported exponents of "official Islam" such as Ahmad and Salah Kuftaro, the possibilities to interpret Islam and to build a religious organization have been fairly abundant as long as they don't cross the red line and provoke political opposition.[45] Hence, the notion of an "official Islam" as a linear and limiting ideology concerning interpretations enforced from the top down is not completely accurate. Interpretations of Islam and the relationship between political and religious leaders in Syria have never been as straightforward as the term "official Islam" suggests. One example is the role of the former minister of religion, Muhammad Ziyad al-Ayoubi, as a disciple of Ahmad Kuftaro.[46] This personal relationship gave, according to my discussions with teachers at Abu Nur during Salah Kuftaro's imprisonment, a certain measure of protection for Salah's outspoken expression of opinions on various issues, including democracy and human rights, until a shift of ministers rendered him more vulnerable. Such informal relationships, sometimes founded on an attachment to Sufi orders, parallel the exercise of power through more formal channels, such as ministries. Apparently, interpretations and practices of Islam can be expressed as long as they do not threaten formal power or become exposed to conflicts within the network and, hence, recent developments challenge the view of a straightforward alliance between the state and the organization. The incarceration of Salah Kuftaro in June 2009 suggests that the relationship between the foundation and the state after the elder Kuftaro's death was neither static nor trouble-free.

The evidence I have provided above confirms that individuals and religious leaders in Syria continuously negotiate their understanding of Islam, and also that interpretations are shaped in a dynamic relationship with developments in the wider society. Religious leaders, and to a certain extent Syrian Muslims in general, develop and express interpretations of Islam that may or may not be considered regime-friendly.[47] The accounts above demonstrate that the agency of a religious leader such as Salah Kuftaro is a socially and culturally mediated phenomenon.[48] Consequently, religious, economic, cultural, social, and political environments influence not only leaders' actions, but also how these actions are understood, experienced, and represented. In the case of the Ahmad Kuftaro Foundation, Salah Kuftaro, as a religious actor, had a space to operate within society, and in this space, agency and limited autonomy were permitted, but also restricted by the repressive state. As long as the organization's interpretation and practice of Islam were supported by informal relationships, and were not perceived as oppositional to state policies, the possibility to maneuver was fairly extensive. The many devout adherents participating in the weekly rituals in the Abu Nur mosque do not consider "official Islam" to be an institution in which their leaders are subjected to political manipulation and made into the controlled mouthpieces of a repressive state. Rather, many of the young followers I have come to know over the years appear to perceive their religious leader's prominent role in relation to the state and its leaders as yet another sign of their spiritual power. Hence, a story frequently told to me about how Ahmad Kuftaro once converted Hafiz al-Asad from the ʿAlawi tradition to Sunni Islam indicates how disciples understand their shaykh in more than religious terms. The story strengthens their belief in what is significant for them: the spiritual powers of their religious leader, manifesting in the form of apparent political power.

Conclusions

The period in which Salah Kuftaro was the head of the Ahmad Kuftaro Foundation was an era of dynamic religious entrepreneurship during which its leader's agency was limited by authorities, outlined to adapt to state policies, and linked to informal networks of power that opened possibilities to expand and support the foundation. In the context of state repression in Syria, Salah Kuftaro had to balance the constraints and rules set by the authorities against his ideas of how to develop the foundation and turn it into a viable and modern Islamic institution. Therefore, the portrayal of the Abu Nur mosque and later the Ahmad Kuftaro Foundation as a form of "official Islam" is an outmoded depiction. It is not only theoretically weak, but it is also referring to what the foundation looked like prior to 2000.

Radical modifications of rituals and organization were an adjustment not only to questions of theology and practice, but also to political realities, and were thereby a means to maintain public influence. The refurbishment of the mosque complex from a tall grey and ugly building in a relatively "grey" neighborhood to a white, shining, beautiful building in marble is to be understood as an active modification of the local space in order to signal power and status ascribed with spirituality—conscious architecture of power and sacredness. Moreover, on an individual level the alterations also aimed at strengthening the status of Salah Kuftaro in his roles as leader of both a Sufi movement and a modern religious organization, and as a public figure. Hence, in the context of the interplay between interpretations of Islam and the ritual life at the Abu Nur mosque complex, it is apparent that political realities shaped in specific historical circumstances and conceptual spaces are significant for the organization, understanding, and practice of "Islam." Political, social, and economic realities—regardless of whether they are "Muslim" or "non-Muslim"—are a principal source for reforming the ritual life of the foundation. During Bashar al-Asad's presidency until the imprisonment of Salah Kuftaro, the space for agency transformed the foundation from supporting the state to implicitly or overtly criticizing state actions. However, this development was more apparent in the actions and statements of Salah Kuftaro and his supporters than to many of the followers of his father still declaring themselves disciples of the deceased shaykh. Shifting political realities, the change of a minister of religion, and possibly statements made in public also led to the incarceration of Salah Kuftaro and to the appointment of new leaders of the foundation. Hence, in the case of Salah, the relationship between agency (Salah Kuftaro's and the Ahmad Kuftaro Foundation's possibilities to maneuver in a repressive state) and structure (the regime and its institutions, primarily the Ministry of Religious Affairs) became too tense, leading to a crossing of "red lines" and to imprisonment. The developments since 2000 for Salah Kuftaro and the Ahmad Kuftaro Foundation as well as other Sunni organizations and movements are not only an example of the power in agency, but are also a clear case of a repressive state assuming control. However, it is certainly a possibility that the ambition within the state structure to suppress agency will open up new forms of agency fed by new relationships and interactions in Syria.

Notes

Bibliography

Contributors

Index

Notes

1. Introduction

1. In a 1989 review article, Lila Abu-Lughod identified "prestigious zones" of anthropological research, with Syria decidedly not among them. Syria's unpopularity among anthropologists endures in the present day and extends to other fieldwork-based social sciences and humanities. Until recently, there has also been scant scholarly work on religion in contemporary Syria; see Leif Stenberg, " Muslim Organizations in Bashar's Syria: The Transformation of the Shaykh Ahmad Kuftaro Foundation," chapter 9 in this volume.

2. French academics, and more recently their Danish and Finnish counterparts, have had a stronger presence in Syria as a result of dedicated national research institutions.

3. Nabil Maleh, personal communication with Christa Salamandra, Mar. 30, 2012.

4. Steven Heydemann, "Social Pacts and the Persistence of Authoritarianism in the Middle East," in *Debating Arab Authoritarianism*, ed. Oliver Schlumberger (Stanford, CA: Stanford Univ. Press, 2007) , 21–38; Steven Heydemann, "Upgrading Authoritarianism in the Arab World," *Analysis Paper No. 13* (Washington, DC: Saban Center for Middle East Policy at the Brookings Institution, 2007).

5. Bashar al-Asad trained in London from 1992 until early 1994, then was recalled to Syria upon the death of his brother Basil, heir apparent. Bashar was groomed for the presidency for the remainder of the decade, ascending to power in 2000.

6. In retrospect, it is clear that this language—despite its optimistically modern sound—augured not progressive reform but the sedimentation of power in private yet often regime-linked hands. Haddad understands "social market economy" as a security strategy to control the economy through networks of trust, relationships, and loyalty; Bassam Haddad, *Business Networks in Syria: The Political Economy of Authoritarian Resilience* (Stanford, CA: Stanford Univ. Press, 2012). It is intended to limit control of the economy to the political elite. Salwa Ismail relates this process of consolidation to authoritarianism in crisis; Salwa Ismail, "Changing Social Structure, Shifting Alliances and Authoritarianism in Syria," in *Demystifying Syria*, ed. Fred Lawson (London: Saqi Books and London Middle East Institute SOAS, 2009), 13–28. See also Aurora Sottimano,

"Nationalism and Reform under Bashar al-Asad: Reading the 'Legitimacy' of the Syrian Regime," in *Syria from Reform to Revolt, Volume 1: Political Economy and International Relations*, ed. Raymond Hinnebusch and Tina Zintl (Syracuse: Syracuse Univ. Press), 66–88.

7. *Al-Dumari* was shut down in 2003.

8. The two statements are reprinted in Flynt Leverett, *Inheriting Syria: Bashar's Trial by Fire* (Washington, DC: Brookings Institution Press, 2005) and Alan George, *Syria: Neither Bread nor Freedom* (London & New York: Zed Books, 2003).

9. For a detailed discussion of the Damascus Spring, see Najib Ghadbian, "Contesting Authoritarianism: Opposition Activism under Bashar al-Asad, 2000–2010" *Syria from Reform to Revolt, Volume 1: Political Economy and International Relations*, ed. Raymond Hinnebusch and Tina Zintl (Syracuse: Syracuse Univ. Press), 91–112.

10. According to Leverett (*Inheriting Syria*, 95), Bashar appreciated the need for the gradual development of civil society through the building of NGOs, but most of the "movements" developed have been in the form of GONGOs.

11. See Bassam Haddad, *Business Networks in Syria*.

12. Christa Salamandra, *A New Old Damascus: Authenticity and Distinction in Urban Syria* (Bloomington: Indiana Univ. Press, 2004), 158–64.

13. When the uprising began, the state reintroduced some subsidies and increased salaries for state employees in an effort to contain dissent.

14. Salwa Ismail, "'Authoritarian Civilities' and Syria's Stalled Political Transition" (presentation at the American Political Science Association Annual Meeting, Philadelphia, PA, Aug. 31–Sept. 3, 2006).

15. See John Caughie, *Television Drama: Realism, Modernism and British Culture* (Oxford: Oxford Univ. Press, 2000), 105–8, on the debate over the politics of realism.

16. In general, Sunni Muslims are believed to constitute a little more than 70 percent of the population; the ʿAlawis, Ismaʿilis, and Twelver Shiʿa are about 13 percent; different branches of Christianity 10 percent; and the Druze 3 percent (Line Khatib, *Islamic Revivalism in Syria: The Rise and Fall of Baʿthist Secularism*, Routledge Studies in Political Islam [London: Routledge, 2011], 7). Two studies claim that Christians do not exceed 6 percent of the Syrian population; see Youssef Courbage, "La population de la Syrie," in *La Syrie au present: Reflets d'une société*, ed. Baudouin Dupret, Zouhair Ghazzal, Youssef Courbage, and Muhammad al-Dbiyat (Paris: Sindbad Actes Sud, 2007), 189, and Laura Robson, "Recent Perspectives on Christianity in the Modern Arab World," *History Compass* 9, no. 4 (2011), 313.

17. Jasmine Roman (journalist), personal correspondence with Leif Stenberg, Mar. 2014, after Roman's stay in Damascus early that year. See also "Smell of Fear in Damascus Proves Assad's Illegitimacy," *The National*, Mar. 3, 2014, http://www.thenational .ae/thenationalconversation/comment/smell-of-fear-in-damascus-proves-assads -illegitimacy#page1 for a summary of her observations (retrieved Mar. 13, 2014).

2. What Lies Beneath

1. Mustafa Tlas, ed., *Kadhalika qala al-Asad* (Damascus: Dar Tlas, 2001), 329.

2. Lisa Wedeen, "Acting 'As If': Symbolic Politics and Social Control in Syria," *Comparative Studies in Society and History* 40, no. 3 (1998): 523.

3. Steven Heydemann, *Authoritarianism in Syria: Institutions and Social Conflict, 1946–1970* (Ithaca, NY: Cornell Univ. Press, 1999); and idem, "Social Pacts and the Persistence of Authoritarianism in the Middle East," in *Debating Arab Authoritarianism: Dynamics and Durability in Nondemocratic Regimes*, ed. Oliver Schlumberger (Stanford, CA: Stanford Univ. Press, 2007), 21–38. On the origins of Ba'thism and the early history of the Ba'th Party in Syria, see, inter alia, Kamel Abu Jaber, *The Arab Ba'th Socialist Party: History, Ideology, and Organization* (Syracuse: Syracuse Univ. Press, 1966); John F. Devlin, *The Ba'th Party: A History from Its Origins to 1966* (Stanford, CA: Hoover Institution Press, 1976); David Roberts, *The Ba'th and the Creation of Modern Syria* (London: Croom Helm, 1987); and, Derek Hopwood, *Syria 1945–1986: Politics and Society* (London: Allen & Unwin, 1988).

4. Najib Ghadbian, "The New Asad: Dynamics of Continuity and Change in Syria," *Middle East Journal* 55, no. 4 (Fall 2001): 624–41; Volker Perthes, *Syria under Bashar al-Asad: Modernisation and the Limits of Change* (New York: Oxford Univ. Press for the International Institute for Strategic Studies, 2004); Najib Ghadbian, *Al-Dawla al-asadiyya al-thaniyya: Bashar al-Asad wa al-furas al-da'i'a* (Najib Ghadbian, 2006); Aurora Sottimano and Kjetil Selvik, *Changing Regime Discourse and Reform in Syria* (Fife, Scotland: Univ. of St. Andrews Centre for Syrian Studies, distributed by Lynne Rienner, 2008); Samer Abboud and Ferdinand Arslanian, *Syria's Economy and the Transition Paradigm* (Fife, Scotland: Univ. of St. Andrews Centre for Syrian Studies, distributed by Lynne Rienner, 2009); Annette Büchs, "The Resilience of Authoritarian Rule in Syria Under Hafez and Bashar Al-Asad," *GIGA Research Programme: Institute of Middle East Studies* 97 (2009); Raymond A. Hinnebusch and Søren Schmidt, *The State and the Political Economy of Reform in Syria* (Fife, Scotland: Univ. of St. Andrews Centre for Syrian Studies, distributed by Lynne Rienner, 2009); Fred Lawson, ed., *Demystifying Syria* (London: Saqi in association with The London Middle East Institute, 2009); and Thomas Pierret and Kjetil Selvik, "Limits of 'Authoritarian Upgrading' in Syria: Private Welfare, Islamic Charities, and the Rise of the Zayd Movement," *International Journal of Middle East Studies* 41, no. 4 (2009): 595–614.

5. Wedeen, "Acting 'As If'"; and idem. *Ambiguities of Domination: Politics, Rhetoric, and Symbols in Contemporary Syria* (Chicago: Univ. of Chicago Press, 1999).

6. miriam cooke, *Dissident Syria: Making Oppositional Arts Official* (Durham, NC: Duke Univ. Press, 2007).

7. See, for example, three other contributions to this volume: Donatella Della Ratta, "The 'Whisper Strategy': How Syrian Drama Makers Shape Television Fiction between

Authoritarianism in the Context of Commodification"; Christa Salamandra, "Syria's Drama Outpouring: Between Complicity and Critique"; and Shayna Silverstein, " Cultural Liberalization or Marginalization? The Cultural Politics of Syrian Folk Dance during Social Market Reform." For the case of cinema, see, most recently, Cécile Boëx, *La contestation médiatisée par le monde de l'art en contexte autoritaire: L'expérience cinématographique en syrie au sein de l'organisme général du cinéma 1964–2010* (PhD diss., Univ. Paul Cézanne-Aix Marseille III, 2011).

8. Mohja Kahf, "The Silences of Contemporary Syrian Literature," *World Literature Today* 75, no. 2 (2001): 224–36.

9. Ibid, 229.

10. Claudia Pierpoint Roth, "Found in Translation; The Contemporary Arabic Novel," *New Yorker*, Jan. 18, 2010, http://www.newyorker.com/arts/critics/books/2010/01 /18/100118crbo_books_pierpont (accessed Mar. 19, 2010). But see, too, the thoughtful response by Hilary Plum, "Field Guides to Elsewhere: How We Read Languages We Don't Read," *The Quarterly Conversation*, http://quarterlyconversation.com/field-guides-to-else where-how-we-read-languages-we-dont-read (accessed Mar. 19, 2010).

11. Mustafa Khalifa, *Al-Qawqa'a: Yawmiyyat mutalassis* (Beirut: Dar al-Adab, 2008).

12. Cooke, *Dissident Syria*; Barbara Harlow, *Resistance Literature* (New York: Methuen, 1987).

13. For a fascinating study of the relationship between writing and human rights discourse, see Shareah Taleghani, "The Cocoons of Language, the Betrayals of Silence: Contemporary Syrian Prison Literature, Human Rights Discourse, and Literary Experimentalism," PhD diss., New York University, 2009.

14. See, for example, Samar Yazbak, *Laha maraya: Riwaya* (Beirut: Dar al-Adab li al-Nashr wa al-Tawzi', 2010); and Rosa Yasin Hasan, *Brufa: Riwaya* (Beirut: Riyad el-Rayyes, 2011). I discuss these novels at greater length in a forthcoming publication.

15. In order to respect the wishes of these individuals, I do not cite specific people or the particular conversations upon which these claims are based.

16. Abbas Beydoun, "Riwayat 'al-mukhabarat.'" *Al-Safir*, Aug. 12, 2009.

17. Fawwaz Haddad, *Al-Mutarjim al-kha'in: Riwaya* (Beirut: Riyad el-Rayyes, 2008). References to this novel appear in the text; all translations from the Arabic are my own.

18. Fawwaz Haddad, personal communication with the author, Oct. 26, 2009.

19. Fawwaz Haddad, *'Azf munfarid 'ala al-biyanu: Riwaya* (Beirut: Riyad el-Rayyes, 2009). References to the novel appear in the text; all translations from the Arabic are my own.

20. See, for example, Nihad Sirees, *Riyah al-shamal 1917* (Aleppo: Markaz al-Inma' al-Hadari, 1993).

21. Nihad Sirees, *Al-Samt wa al-sakhab: Riwaya* (Beirut: Dar al-Adab, 2004). References to the novel appear in the text; all translations from the Arabic are my own.

22. Roger Allen, "Arabic Fiction and the Quest for Freedom," *Journal of Arabic Literature* 26, nos. 1/2 (1995): 38.

23. Ibid., 48.

24. Perthes, *Syria Under Bashar al-Asad*, 64.

3. Syria's Drama Outpouring

1. See, for instance, Basma Atassi, "A Colourful Uprising in Damascus," *Aljazeera.net*, Dec. 13, 2011, http://www.aljazeera.com/profile/basma-atassi.html; Mohamed Ali Atassi, "The Puppet Rebellion," *Qantara.de*, Jan. 20, 2012, http://en.qantara.de/content/creative-protest-against-syrias-regime-the-puppet-rebellion; Oliver Holmes, "Syrian Revolt Sparks Art Boom," *Reuters*, Sept. 28, 2011, http://www.reuters.com/article/2011/09/28/us-syria-artists-idUSTRE78R2SW20110928; Salwa Ismail, "Syria's Cultural Revolution," *Guardian*, June 21, 2011, http://www.aljazeera.com/profile/basma-atassi.html; Neil Mac-Farquhar, "In Protests, Syrians Find the Spark of Creativity," *New York Times*, Dec. 19, 2011, http://www.nytimes.com/2011/12/20/world/middleeast/in-uprising-syrians-find-spark-of-creativity.html?pagewanted=2&sq=syrian artists&st=cse&scp=1.

2. Syrians refer to these series as "drama," even when they are comedic.

3. Christa Salamandra, "Spotlight on the Bashar al-Asad Era: The Television Drama Outpouring," *Middle East Critique* 20, no. 2 (2011): 157–67.

4. Laith Hajjo, interview with the author, Oct. 17, 2006.

5. See Marlin Dick, "Syria under the Spotlight: Television Satire that Is Revolutionary in Form, Reformist in Content," *Arab Media and Society* 3 (Fall 2007), for a detailed and engaging analysis of *Spotlight*'s groundbreaking form and content.

6. Christa Salamandra, "Television and the Ethnographic Endeavor: The Case of Syrian Drama," *Transnational Broadcasting Studies* (now *Arab Media and Society*) 14 (2005).

7. Hajjo, interview.

8. One cast member argued that 60 percent of *Spotlight Part Ten*, aired during Ramadan 2014, reflected the regime's position.

9. Hajjo, interview.

10. As pan-Arab television industries operate without reliable ratings systems or audience research, these assessments reflect the views of programming executives and other television industry figures.

11. George Weyman, *Empowering Youth or Reshaping Compliance? Star Magazine, Symbolic Production, and Competing Visions of Shabab in Syria*, MPhil thesis in Modern Middle Eastern Studies, Univ. of Oxford, 2006.

12. The distinction between creative and technical work in media industries is often referred to as "above the line" and "below the line" (Matt Stahl, "Privilege and Distinction in Production Worlds: Copyright, Collective Bargaining and Working Conditions in Media Making," in *Production Studies: Cultural Studies of Media Industries*, ed. Vicki Mayer, Miranda J. Banks, and John. T. Caldwell [New York and London: Routledge, 2009], 58–63).

13. Cécile Boëx, "The End of State Monopoly over Culture: Toward the Commodification of Culture and Artistic Production," *Middle East Critique* 20, no. 2 (2011): 164.

14. Najib Nusair, interview with author, July 19, 2006.

15. See Della Ratta, " The 'Whisper Strategy': How Syrian Drama Makers Shape Television Fiction in the Context of Authoritarianism and Commodification," chapter 4 in this volume.

16. Series are aired throughout the year, but it is airtime during the coveted holy month primetime that makes fortunes and reputations.

17. Christa Salamandra, "Globalisation and Cultural Mediation: The Construction of Arabia in London," *Global Networks* 2, no. 4 (2002): 285–99; and Christa Salamandra, "London's Arab Media and the Construction of Arabness," *Transnational Broadcasting Studies* 10 (2003), http://tbsjournal.arabmediasociety.com/Archives/Spring03/salamandra .html.

18. Both the degree of and the source of this trend are debatable. Countering industry perceptions, Nour Halabi argues that GCC funding has had a liberalizing impact on drama content ("The Impact of Gulf Investment on the Syrian TV Drama Industry: Syrian TV Drama in the Satellite Era," paper presented at International PhD and Research School, "Arab TV Fiction and Entertainment Industries," Danish Institute in Damascus, Syria, Nov. 2010).

19. Mazen Bilal and Najib Nusair, *Syrian Historical Drama: The Dream of the End of an Era* [Al-Drama al-tarikhiyya al-Suriya: Hilm nihayat al-ʿaṣr] (Damascus: Dar al-Sham, 1999), 8.

20. Christa Salamandra, "Creative Compromise: Syrian Television Makers between Secularism and Islamism," *Contemporary Islam* 2, no. 3 (2008): 177–89; Christa Salamandra, "Arab Television Drama Production and the Islamic Public Sphere," in *Rhetoric of the Image: Visual Culture in Muslim Contexts*, ed. Christiane Gruber and Sune Haugbølle, 261–74 (Bloomington: Indiana Univ. Press, 2013).

21. For an analysis of the industry that emphasizes collegiality and compliance with political leadership, and the appeal of neoliberalism among drama creators, see Della Ratta, "The 'Whisper Strategy,'" chapter 4 in this volume.

22. Peter Brooks, *The Melodramatic Imagination: Balzac, Henry James, Melodrama, and the Mode of Excess* (New Haven: Yale Univ. Press, 1995), viii.

23. Lila Abu-Lughod, *Dramas of Nationhood: The Politics of Television in Egypt* (Chicago: Univ. of Chicago Press, 2005).

24. Christine Gledhill, "Speculations on the Relationship between Soap Opera and Melodrama," *Quarterly Review of Film and Video* 14, nos. 1–2 (1992): 107–28.

25. miriam cooke, *Dissident Syria: Making Oppositional Arts Official* (Durham, NC: Duke Univ. Press, 2007).

26. John Caughie, *Television Drama: Realism, Modernism and British Culture* (Oxford: Oxford Univ. Press, 2000), 105–8.

27. On *Behind Bars'* paradoxically uncontroversial reception, see Marlin Dick, "Thin Red Lines: Censorship, Controversy, and the Case of the Syrian Soap Opera *Behind Bars*," *Transnational Broadcasting Studies* 16 (2006), http://www.tbsjournal.com /Dick.html.

28. Examples of realist films set in informal settlements include Jean Renoir's *The Lower Depths* (1936), Pier Paolo Pasolini's *Accattone* (1961), Mira Nair's *Salaam Bombay* (1988), Fernando Meirelles and Kátia Lund's *City of God* (2002).

29. United Nations Environment Programme, *Geo Yearbook 2006*. Nairobi: United Nations Environment Programme, 2006), 32; United Nations Economic and Social Council, "UN ECOSOC Regional Meeting on Sustainable Urbanization Opens in Bahrain" (press release, 2008), http://www.un.org/en/ecosoc/newfunct/amrregpr.shtml.

30. The first was most likely *Happy Days* (*Ayamna al-hilwa*) of 2003, written by the authors of *Waiting*.

31. Lisa Wedeen, *Ambiguities of Domination: Politics, Rhetoric, and Symbols in Contemporary Syria* (Chicago: Univ. of Chicago Press, 1999), 88–92, 100–107). See also, for example, her analysis of Hajjo's comedy *Lost Village* as both "a means to help people cope with their present and an invitation to free them from it" (Wedeen, "Ideology and Humor in Dark Times: Notes from Syria," *Critical Inquiry* 39, no. 4 [2013]: 864).

32. Wedeen, *Ambiguities of Domination*, 90.

33. Rebecca Joubin, *The Politics of Love: Sexuality, Gender, and Marriage in Syrian Television Drama* (Plymouth, UK, and Lanham, MD: Lexington Books, 2013).

34. cooke, *Dissident Syria*, 73–77.

35. Aired in 2008, this episode was directed by Laith Hajjo's friend and collaborator Samer Barqawi.

36. "The Regime Chases 'Spray Can Man' from Homs to Damascus" (Al-nizam yalhathu wara' al-rajul al-bakhakh min Hims ila Dimashq), *Zaman al-Wasl*, July 20, 2011, http://zaman-alwsl.net/readNews.php?id=20481.

37. Rebecca Joubin, "Resistance and Co-optation on the Syrian Television Series, Buq'at Daw', 2001–2012," *Middle East Journal* 68, no. 1 (2014): 23.

38. Matt Stahl, "Syrian Authorities Arrest the Creator of the Spray Can Man in the Series 'Spotlight'" [Al-Sultat al-Suriya ta'atqilu mubtakir al-rajul al-bakhakh fi musalsal "Buq'at daw'], *Al-Sharq*, Mar. 1, 2012, http://www.alsharq.net.sa/2012/03/01/147286. http://www.alsharq.net.sa/2012/03/01/147286; "Arrest of Writer 'Adnan al-Zira'i . . . the Spray Can Man" [I'tiqal al-katib 'Adnan al-Zira'i . . . al-rajul al-bakhakh], *Al-Qabas*, Mar. 2, 2012, http://www.alqabas.com.kw/Articles.aspx?ArticleID=775140&CatID=323.

39. Season two shows the pair in prison, reflecting the fate of many peaceful protestors and activists.

40. Nadine Elali, "The Syrian Revolution in Sketches: Talking to the Horriyeh w Bas team," *Now Lebanon*, July 19, 2011. http://www.nowlebanon.com/NewsArchiveDetails .aspx?ID=292824.

41. In Syria, the term "artist" (*fannan*) generally refers to actors.

42. Nada al-Azhari, "Even the Image Shouts: Freedom and Nothing But!" [Hata al-sura hatifat: Huriya wa bas!], *al-Hayat*, Sept. 23, 2011, http://www.daralhayat.com /internationalarticle/310415.

4. The "Whisper Strategy"

1. I am grateful to Lisa Wedeen for suggesting this phrase.

2. Michel Foucault, "The Confession of the Flesh," in *Power/Knowledge: Selected Interviews and Other Writings, 1972–1977*, ed. Colin Gordon (New York: Pantheon Books, 1980), 202.

3. Ibid., 206.

4. Ibid., 204.

5. Ibid., 195.

6. Volker Perthes, ed., *Arab Elites: Negotiating the Politics of Change* (Colorado: Lynne Rienner Publishers, 2004), 99.

7. This new class of entrepreneurs prospered from the 1991 Investment Law No. 10, which formally opened up various parts of the Syrian economy, including the audiovisual sector. However, informal networks linking state powers with businesses communities had existed in Syria for many years, long before official economic liberalization (Bassam Haddad, *Business Networks in Syria: The Political Economy of Authoritarian Resilience* [Stanford, CA: Stanford Univ. Press, 2012], 1). Moreover, television was not the main business targeted by this law, which "was made for the sake of investments in other sectors," as Riad Nasaan Agha, who was at the time a Member of Parliament and a close advisor to Hafiz al-Asad, has reported (personal interview with the author, Nov. 2010, Damascus). This new class of businessmen took advantage of the opening of the sector and established TV production companies that leveraged their business and family ties toward success on the pan-Arab market.

8. To suggest the extent to which personal relations are relevant to build business ventures in the Arab world, Turki Shabahana, vice president of the Saudi-owned Rotana group, explained how Shaykh Walid al-Ibrahim, chairman of the powerful pan-Arab network MBC, had encouraged the son of Syria's former deputy prime minister, 'Abdul Halim Khaddam, to open a TV production company despite his lack of experience. Shabahana stressed: "Khaddam was the son of the deputy prime minister, he was a man within the *sulta*, and this counts a lot when you want to set up a business in Syria, or in the Arab world in general" (interview with the author, Feb. 2011, Damascus).

9. Most of the drama makers I interviewed between 2009 and 2011 used the word *tanwir* and its adjective *tanwiri* to describe their commitment to "enlighten" society through their TV works.

10. Perthes, *Arab Elites*, 108–9.

11. The words *takhalluf* (backwardness) and *mutakhallif* (backwards) also recurred in the interviews I conducted.

12. The word "discourse" is widely used by Foucault to illustrate how a linguistic device can serve in supporting a given political project. See the example on the creation of the "discourse of philanthropy and moralization," in Foucault, "The Confession of the Flesh," 202–3.

13. Foucault refers to it as "capillarity" ("The Confession of the Flesh," 201).

14. Foucault, "The Confession of the Flesh," 199.

15. For a detailed analysis of Syrian cultural producers, particularly drama makers, see Christa Salamandra, "Creative Compromise: Syrian Television Makers between Secularism and Islamism," *Contemporary Islam* 2, no. 3 (2008): 177–89; and Salamandra, "Dramatizing Damascus: The Cultural Politics of Arab Television Production in the Satellite Era," Copenhagen Univ. Islam Lecture Series, Apr. 14, 2010.

16. Perthes dubs it "era Bashar" (*Arab Elites*, 110).

17. These meetings are usually attended by producers, directors, actors, and representatives of state-owned media and of the Industry Commission for Cinema and Television. During the meetings, many practical issues related to the industrial aspect of television drama production are discussed; such as how to improve productivity, raise exports, and waive taxes. "All these measures shows the interest of the president in—and his personal support for—the growth of Syrian TV drama as a sector of strategic and national interest" (TV director Najdat Anzour, personal interview with the author, Nov. 2010, Damascus).

18. "[The president] said he wanted to learn from us and from Syrian drama on how to move the country forward," TV director Laith Hajjo confirmed in an interview with the author, Dec. 2010, Damascus.

19. Nadia Muhanna, "Behind the Scenes: Political Disagreements and Production Cuts Are Affecting the Creation of Television Series for Ramadan This Year," *Syria Today*, July 2011, http://www.syria-today.com/index.php/july-2011/852-life/16162-behind -the-scenes.

20. According to a report filed in English by Dp-Sana, the 2010 post-Ramadan meeting with the president "focused on the importance of drama and the human and noble goal it could achieve to serve the national and pan-Arab issue." "President al-Asad Is Satisfied with the Syrian Drama," *Dp-Sana*, Sept. 20, 2010, http://dp-news.com/pages/detail .aspx?articleId=54696 (accessed Nov. 20, 2013).

21. It is possible here to draw a parallel with Nicole Khoury's analysis of Egyptian antiterrorism *musalsalat*. According to Khoury, Egyptian TV series are constructed as events (*evénéments*) narrated in a "language code shared by the educated and the politicians" (Nicole Khoury, "La politique antiterroriste de l'État égyptien à la télévision en 1994," *Revue Tiers-Monde* 37, no. 146 [1996]: 266). This offers the opportunity to reiterate positions vis-à-vis a topic of interest and to generate debate through the emotional language of the *musalsalat*.

22. Taysir Khalat, personal interview with the author, Jan. 2011, Damascus.

23. The fight against corruption is a media campaign closely associated with Bashar al-Asad's rise to power, and with his personal commitment to fight the old and corrupted old guard of the Syrian regime. This theme was also reiterated and strongly emphasized in early 2011, at the time when the Syrian uprising broke out. See the president's interview with Syrian TV on Aug. 21, 2011 (http://www.youtube.com/watch?v=9w_Rm_dQbp8).

24. On *Ghizlan fi . . .* , see Salamandra, "Dramatizing Damascus," and Salamandra's chapter in this volume, "Syria's Drama Outpouring: Between Complicity and Critique"; on *Buq'at daw'* see Marlin Dick, "Syria under the Spotlight: Television Satire that Is Revolutionary in Form, Reformist in Content," *Arab Media and Society* 3 (Fall 2007), http://www.arabmediasociety.com/topics/index.php?t_article=173.

25. The eleventh five-year plan, which started in 2011, listed as one of its main objectives "to reduce corruption by introducing performance related pay and decentralizing responsibility." "In the 2010 Corruption Perceptions Index, produced by the anti-corruption organization Transparency International, Syria ranks 127 out of 178 countries." de Blois, M. A. "Syria: Planning Ahead," *Forward Magazine*, 48, Feb. 2011, http://haykal media.com/products/forward.html (accessed Nov. 20, 2013).

26. "The fight against corruption" (*mukafahat al-fasad*) is a slogan regularly repeated by the president, even after March 2011 (see his TV interview with Syrian TV on Aug. 21, 2011 (http://www.youtube.com/watch?v=9w_Rm_dQbp8).

27. "There is something in the way the *musalsalat* are written which does not harm the system: even if a *musalsal* talks about corruption, it never mentions the process which produced corruption. It talks about the people who became corrupt: not about the system which forced them into corruption." Najib Nusair, personal interview with the author, Nov. 2010, Damascus.

28. Imad Fawzi Shoaibi is the chairman of the Syrian think tank Data & Strategic Studies Center, and is a professor of philosophy at Damascus University. See Imad Fawzi Shoaibi, *Min dawla al-ikrah ila al-dimuqratiyya, kan'an li al-dirasat wa al-nashr* (Damascus 2007).

29. See Dick, *Syria under the Spotlight*, 13.

30. After Hafiz al-Asad's death in June 2000, Syria entered a brief period of intense public debate over the political and social reforms commonly known as the "Damascus Spring," which lasted for a few months and ended in 2001. For a further reading, see Alan George, *Syria: Neither Bread nor Freedom* (London and New York: Zed Books, 2003).

31. Mohamed Hamsho, owner of the SAPI production company, is a former Syrian Member of Parliament and influent businessman. He is reportedly very close to Bashar al-Asad's brother Mahir, commander in chief of the Fourth Armoured Division, the core of the country's security forces.

32. Dick, *Syria under the Spotlight*, 8.

33. Najib Nusair, interview.

34. During my fieldwork I was able to observe the oral, informal character of advice. At a formal meeting held by the Industry Commission for Cinema and Television, the body which oversees the industry-related aspects of Syrian drama (Sham Palace Hotel, Damascus, 2 March 2011), head Imad al-Rifae' suggested that companies and channels not do business with broadcasters like Orient TV. Producers could eventually sell the channel their *musalsalat* but not have any programs directly commissioned or co-produced in cooperation with Orient TV. No written or formal directive was ever issued concerning the boycott; the issue stayed as oral, informal advice.

35. Hani al-'Ashi, interview with the author, Damascus, Feb. 2011.

36. See reports on Asma al-Asad sponsoring the first regional conference for Special Olympics back to October 2005 (http://www.caihand.org/syr.htm#asmaa2 [Arabic]).

37. Unicef, Oct. 11, 2010, http://www.unicef.org/infobycountry/syria_56405.html. *DP News*, Sept. 26, 2010, http://www.dp-news.com/en/detail.aspx?articleid=55606.

38. As an example, see the front cover of *Forward Magazine*, Oct. 2010, http://haykal media.com/products/forward.html (accessed Nov. 20, 2013).

39. This virtuous circle proves, as Wedeen notes, that "the regime's power resides in its ability to sustain national fictions" (Wedeen, *Ambiguities of Domination: Politics, Rhetoric, and Symbols in Contemporary Syria* [Chicago: Univ. of Chicago Press, 1999], 519).

40. A good example is provided by a public debate around the *musalsal Zaman al-'ar* (*Time of Disgrace*, 2009), hosted in 2010 at the Social Forum in Damascus *Muntada al-ijtima'i*. Although the *musalsal* dealt with many sensitive topics—such as the corruption of public officials and the poor living conditions in Damascus slums—the debate was entirely focused on the female protagonist's seeking an illegal abortion. During a heated debate that lasted for hours, nobody asked writer Najib Nusair to reflect on other issues, such as corruption or the lack of rule of law in informal neighborhoods. For an analysis of public debates generated by *musalsalat* in Egypt, see Khoury, "La politique antiterroriste."

41. Ibrahim al-Jabin, journalist and former member of the *Lajnat al-qira'a* (reading committee) at Syrian TV, personal interview with the author, May 2010, Damascus.

42. According to Ibrahim al-Jabin, whose job at Syrian state TV was to supervise the scripts and give his opinion regarding final approval, the only *musalsal* that was not approved in 2010 was one related to Shi'ism. It was rejected because of the great sensitivity surrounding religious minorities. All the other proposed *musalsalat* received approval to be produced.

43. Adnan Aouda, personal interview with the author, Dec. 2010, Damascus.

44. Muthanna al Subh, interview with *Forward Magazine*, Oct. 2008, http://www .fw-magazine.com/content/muthana-subh-my-dream-was-become-martyr-or-director.

45. Lina Sinjab, "Honour Crime Fear of Syria Women," *BBC News*, Oct. 12, 2007, http://news.bbc.co.uk/go/pr/fr/-/2/hi/middle_east/7042249.stm.

46. "No Exceptions for 'Honor Killings,'" *Human Rights Watch Syria*, July 28, 2009, http://www.hrw.org/print/news/2009/07/28/syria-no-exceptions-honor-killings.

47. M. Mansour, "Ru'ya ikhrajiyya li al-Muthanna Subh . . . 'Laysa Saraban' . . . drama'an "nahnu wa hum," *Baladna Online*, Sept. 27, 2008, http://www.baladnaonline.net/ar/index.phpoption=com_content&task=view&id=1540.

48. Foucault, "The Confession of the Flesh," 201.

49. "For example, *Wara' al-shams* was not ordered by the First Lady, on the contrary the initiative was taken by its producers. Syrian producers know what the *sulta* likes even if this is not ordered. Sometimes they even anticipate its needs." Taysir Khalat, personal interview with the author, Jan. 2011, Damascus.

50. This is the case of SAPI, the producer of *Laysa saraban*, owned by Mohamed Hamsho, who is also behind Addounia TV, the only existing private channel in Syria.

51. The structure of the Syrian private sector (or new bourgeoisie) is shaped around what Haddad calls "family patterns of business development" (Bassam Haddad, "Enduring Legacies: The Politics of Private Sector Development," in *Demystifying Syria*, ed. Fred Lawson [London: London Middle East Institute, Soas, 2009], 47). Different types of *sultat*—business and political—are also related one to another according to these patterns, which makes for a very restricted distribution of power.

52. The writer clarifies how this mechanism works by giving an example based on a sensitive topic in Syria; that is, Rafik Hariri, a prominent Lebanese politician and former prime minister who died in a terrorist attack in 2005. Syria has been accused of being behind the assassination, although the accusation was never proved. Aouda says: "If I'd like to do something on Rafik Hariri, which is very controversial, I have just to convince the secret services that it is in our interest to do this before others. I can convince them that it is better for Syria to put the message out before other people do: he who tells the story first will win the media battle. And I will win my battle, too, by getting my message out." Adnan Aouda, personal interview with the author, Dec. 2010, Damascus.

53. Sometimes the *mukhabarat* also happens to become a key narrative element of Ramadan drama, such as in the case of *Wilada min al-khasira* (*Birth from the Loins*, 2011–13), a popular series that features Ra'uf (played by Syrian actor 'Abid Fahd), a violent and corrupt secret service officer, as one of its main protagonists. Ra'uf is clearly portrayed as an antihero. However, he is blamed as an individual, a bad apple within a fairly just system; the existence of the *mukhabarat* as an institution is justified to protect citizens from the abuses of power, including those perpetrated by corrupted individuals within the institution itself, like Ra'uf. As some opposition web sources have noticed, the fact that director of the first two seasons of the series, Rasha Shurbatji, was at the time dating Tamam Najim al-Din, a prominent officer in the military intelligence, might have had a direct influence on how the *mukhabarat* was portrayed in the TV series. *All4Syria*, Jan. 17, 2013, http://all4syria.info/Archive/66612 (accessed Nov. 20, 2013).

54. The term "elective affinities" is widely used in Max Weber's sociology "to express the fact that two sets of social facts or mentalities are related to each other or gravitate to each other—even though no direct and simple causality between the two can be established" (Richard Swedberg, *The Max Weber Dictionary: Key Words and Central Concepts* [Stanford, CA: Stanford Univ. Press, 2005], 83).

55. miriam cooke, *Dissident Syria: Making Oppositional Arts Official* (Durham, NC: Duke Univ. Press, 2007).

56. Ibid.

57. It has to be noted that Cooke's intellectuals were mostly coming from literature and filmmaking, whereas the cultural producers described here are mostly engaged in the television business. Starting from the 2000s, especially after the satellite boom and the increasing demand for *musalsalat* by Gulf buyers, TV drama has turned into the most prominent—and profitable—form of cultural production in Syria; at the same time, as Kawakibi emphasizes, drama makers have become the new "intellectuals" (Salam Kawakibi, "Le role de la télévision dans la relecture de l'histoire," *Monde arabe: Maghreb Machrek* 158 [Oct.–Dec. 1997], 49). The current generation of drama makers also includes actors and writers who have worked mostly in the theater and cinema fields. However, even if coming from a confrontational background, many of them have softened their critique, especially after Bashar al-Asad's rise to power and their commitment to a reformist project.

58. *Musalsalat* writer Najib Nusair expressed the distinction in this way: "I would rather speak of an artistic evaluation of the scripts than censorship" (personal interview with the author, Nov. 2010, Damascus). Many other Syrian writers, directors, and producers of *musalsalat* have used the same expression in interviews I conducted from 2009 to 2011 in reference to the parameter used by Syrian censors to judge their works.

59. As pointed out by Abu-Lughod (Lila Abu-Lughod, *Dramas of Nationhood: The Politics of Television in Egypt* [Chicago: Univ. of Chicago Press, 2005]) in her work on Egyptian television drama, also in Egypt the pattern of "development realism" in cultural production "idealized education, progress, and modernity within the nation."

60. In a TV interview with Syrian private channel Addounia (Oct. 19, 2010), writer Najib Nusair stressed that "drama has to criticize society" in order to help it develop and move forward.

61. Writer Najib Nusair strongly believes in what he calls "a *tanwiri* mission. My works don't aim to put a mirror in front of the society. I want them to discuss about issues that are dealt with in my *musalsalat* and progress through this discussion. I don't want to describe, I want to provoke debates and drive social change." Personal interview with the author, Nov. 2010, Damascus.

62. Wedeen used the term "complicit" to describe the relation binding Syrian citizens and Hafiz al-Asad's regime: "to be complicit is to allow oneself to be made an accomplice,

to become bound up in the actions and practices that the regime promotes" (Wedeen, *Ambiguities of Domination*, 74).

63. Wedeen, *Ambiguities of Domination*.

64. See Lisa Wedeen, "Ideology and Humor in Dark Times: Notes from Syria," *Critical Inquiry* 39, no. 4 (2013): 843.

65. For an alternative view on drama makers, see Rebecca Joubin, "Buq'at Dau' (Spotlight) Part 9 (2012): Tanfis (Airing), a Democratic Façade, Delayed Retribution, and Artistic Craftiness," *Syrian Studies Association Bulletin* 17, no. 2 (2012); Joubin, *The Politics of Love: Sexuality, Gender, and Marriage in Syrian Television Drama* (Plymouth, UK, and Lanham, MD: Lexington Books, 2013); and Christa Salamandra, "Syria's Drama Outpouring," chapter 3 in this volume.

66. This paragraph is based on Donatella Della Ratta, "Dramas of the Authoritarian State," *Middle East Report* online, Feb. 2012, http://www.merip.org/mero/interventions/dramas-authoritarian-state.

67. Foucault, "The Confession of the Flesh," 199.

68. Syrian TV producer Adib Kheir, "Where Are Arab TV Serials Heading? The Uprisings and Political Unrest Challenging TV Drama Industries in Syria: An Evaluation after Ramadan 2011," workshop at Copenhagen Univ., Sept. 9, 2011.

69. Contrary to most international media accounts, protests hit the streets of the Syrian capital from the official beginning of the uprising, on March 15, 2011. Even before that, a spontaneous protest against police violence, bringing together around fifteen hundred people, was held in the Hariqa neighborhood, Old Damascus on February 17, 2011. Molly Hennessy-Fiske, "Syria: Activists Protest Police Beating, Call for Investigation," *Los Angeles Times* online, Feb. 17, 2011, http://latimesblogs.latimes.com/babylonbeyond/2011/02/syria-activists-protest-police-beating-call-for-investigation.html.

70. Diana Jabbour, Head of the Radio and TV Production Organization, personal interview with the author, Damascus, May 2010.

71. Wedeen describes the safety valve arguments (*Ambiguities of Domination*, 88) and criticizes them, offering a four-pronged alternative (89–91) to interpret some tolerated criticism in Syrian artistic and TV products.

72. cooke, *Dissident Syria*, 72.

73. Ibid.

74. After Ramadan 2011, I asked many prominent Syrian drama makers about the series, and none had heard of it.

75. Ibrahim al-Jabin, "Where Are Arab TV Serials Heading? The Uprisings and Political Unrest Challenging TV Drama Industries in Syria: An Evaluation after Ramadan 2011," workshop at Copenhagen Univ., Sept. 9, 2011.

76. *Forward Magazine* interrupted the publication in January 2012. All issues are visible online at http://issuu.com/haykalmedia/docs (accessed Nov. 20, 2013).

77. Currently Moubayed lives in Beirut, where he works for Carnegie Middle East Center. He now openly criticizes al-Asad's regime.

78. As an example, see Sami Moubayed, "What Will Post–Arab Spring Intellectuals Write About?" *Huffington Post*, Aug. 12, 2011, http://www.huffingtonpost.com/sami -moubayed/what-will-postarab-spring_b_1136621.html.

79. Ibrahim al-Jabin, Adib Kheir, "Where Are Arab TV Serials Heading? The Uprisings and Political Unrest Challenging TV Drama Industries in Syria: An Evaluation after Ramadan 2011," workshop at Copenhagen Univ., Sept. 9, 2011.

80. Ibid.

81. The roof also symbolizes the platform under which different—and divergent— opinions can come together and be discussed, as suggested by the *musalsal* director Baraqawi in an interview with the online magazine *'Aks al-sir*. When asked about the ambiguity of the series, which seemingly supported both the regime's points of view and the protesters' requests, Baraqawi replied: "We nurtured a form of civilized dialogue. We don't have to present works that feature one side without the other, or entertainment works. My goal is to invite the viewer, whatever his political orientation, to see himself and the other in the series" (A. Halabi, "Al-tilfiziun al-suri yuwaqif 'ard musalsal 'Fawq al-saqf' alladhi yatahaddath 'an 'al-ahdat' fi-Suriya," *'Aks al-sir*, Aug. 26, 2011, http://www.aksalser.com/?page=view_news&id=23de57e4c35b3f297a6061e201d268a2 &ar=99211197#).

82. See, for example, the interview the president gave to Syrian TV on August 21, 2011, in which he used the same metaphor of the roof. The "roof" is a metaphor also used by Syrian artists to emphasize the need for a national platform (*saqf al-watan*) for dialogue; they have repeatedly employed this term, especially in spring 2011, when the beginning of the uprising resulted in splitting of the drama makers' community into different factions supporting the president or the protests. For further discussion, see Donatella Della Ratta, "Dramas of the Authoritarian State," in *The Arab Revolts: Dispatches on Militant Democracy in the Middle East*, ed. David McMurray and Amanda Ufheil-Somers, 188–95 (Bloomington: Indiana Univ. Press, 2013).

83. Joubin ("Buq'at Dau'") reads this metaphor in a more subversive way, quoting the episode "Bila saqf" ("Without a Roof") from *Buq'at daw'* season 9 as a fine satire of the "astounding circumstances of the government commissioning the writing of *Fawq al-saqf* [sic] and the resulting confusion among the screenwriter community."

84. Sami Moubayed and Maher Azzam were appointed as consultants to the project. Each episode was drafted by the group of writers and sent directly to Moubayed and Azzam, bypassing the control of the *Lajnat al-qira'a*, the committee that gives the green light to drama scripts, as well as editing or censoring them. This exception was made because of the Palace's direct involvement in the *musalsal*, as every production is required to submit a written script for prior approval. Only thirty sketches were approved by the

two consultants, Azzam and Moubayed, out of the one hundred presented, and twenty days before Ramadan just eight episodes were ready to be aired.

85. A. Halabi, "Al-tilfiziun al-suri yuwaqif 'ard musalsal 'Fawq al-saqf' alladhi yatahaddath 'an 'al-ahdat' fi-Suriya," 'Aks al-sir, Aug. 26, 2011, http://www.aksalser.com /?page=view_news&id=23de57e4c35b3f297a6061e201d268a2&ar=99211197#).

86. al-Jabin, "Where Are Arab TV Serials Heading?"

87. Ma'an Haider, Director General of Syrian TV, quoted by Halabi ("Al-tilfiziun al-suri yuwaqif 'ard musalal 'Fawg al-saqf' alladhi yatahaddah 'an 'al-ahdat' fi-Suriya") gives the noncompletion of the series as the main reason for stopping it and promises to rebroadcast it once all episodes have been produced and ready to be aired.

88. "The reaction of the Palace was silence, which basically meant agreement to interrupting the broadcast." Maher Azzam, interview with Ibrahim al-Jabin in "Where Are Arab TV Serials Heading?" Sept. 9, 2011.

89. "80% of *Buq'at daw'* was shot this way. Somebody gives his blessing for a project, then it goes into production and the troubles begin." Adib Kheir, "Where Are Arab TV Serials Heading?"

90. In the words of director Laith Hajjo: "*Buq'at daw'* was born in the atmosphere of the Damascus Spring. It is the direct expression of Bashar al-Asad's first phase." Personal interview with the author, Damascus, Dec. 2010.

91. As previously stated, at the time Khaddam's sons owned the production company Sham International, which was a competitor to Hamsho's SAPI, the producer of the series.

92. Dick, *Syria under the Spotlight*, 19.

93. Najdat Anzour is a well-known Syrian director who has authored the "trilogy of terrorism" in TV drama: *Al-Hurr al-'ayn* (*The Beautiful Maidens*), 2005; *Al-Mariqun* (*The Renegades*), 2006; and *Saqf al-'alam* (*The Roof of the World*), 2007.

94. In the words of Sami Moubayed: "After the Muslim Brotherhood allied itself with former vice-president Abdul Halim Khaddam in 2006, the regime found itself in need of flirting with the Islamists to counter-balance the Khaddam-Brotherhood alliance. To do that, the regime needed to court the Islamists, yet also, walk the tightrope and keep them at bay to avoid further Islamification of Syria. To strike this impossible balance, the regime needed to promote secularism simultaneously with the promotion of Islam. But at any cost secularism must prevail. It's either secularism or chaos for Syria." Sami Moubayed, "Islam and Secularism Must Go Hand-in-Hand in Syria," *Gulf News*, June 27, 2006, http://gulfnews.com/opinions/columnists/islam-and -secularism-must-go-hand-in-hand-in-syria-1.242438.

95. The *Sura al-nisa'* reminds that sexual intercourse with married women is forbidden, except with "those whom your right hand possesses," that is, slaves. By using a Qur'anic verse as a title of a TV series, and by implicitly suggesting that some women can be regarded as property of men, the director created the possibility for heated debates, which eventually happened even before the *musalsal* was broadcast.

96. Al-Buti was killed in March 2013 during a bomb attack inside a mosque in Damascus.

97. Asked to comment on the decision not to broadcast the *musalsal*, Anzour stressed that "religious men should not interfere with TV drama." Talking about al-Buti's rejection of *Ma malakat aymanukum*, its director pointed out that the religious scholar "didn't even watch the *musalsal*, but judged it problematic only from its title." Anzour, interview.

98. Ibid.

99. Riad Nasaan Agha, interview with the author, Damascus, Nov. 2010.

100. An informant from Anzour's office states that after the broadcast of the show, Hamsho sent a bouquet of red roses with little keys in each rose, a sign that the director would have interpreted as an invitation to dialogue and reconciliation.

101. Anzour, interview.

102. As of 2015, Anzour resided in Syria and openly supported the president and his politics.

103. Anzour referred to a conversation he had with Bashar al-Asad in 2010 in which he told the Syrian president, "We want the freedom to get these kind of messages out, please do support us in these works" (Anzour, interview).

104. Anzour, interview.

105. In May 2011, a group of four hundred artists, including many drama makers, issued a communiqué known as "the milk statement" (*bayan al-halib*) denouncing a food embargo allegedly imposed on Daraa after the Syrian army had entered the rebel city in response to the ongoing unrest. As a reaction to the "milk statement," which was widely read by regime-supporters as a pro-opposition move, Najdat Anzour, together with twenty-one prominent production companies, issued a notice "announcing they would never again work with anyone who had signed the petition, saying they had 'offended both the Syrian nation and its government.'" Phil Sands, "*Syrian Soap Operas Sidelined by Protests and Censorship*," *The National, July 23, 2011*, http://www.thenational.ae/news /world/middle-east/syrian-soap-operas-sidelined-by-protests-and-censorship.

106. Anzour, interview.

107. Here I strongly disagree with Joubin ("Buq'at Dau'") that the whisper strategy would depict Syrian drama makers as a disempowered subject, deprived of agency and submitted to the *sultat*'s will. Throughout this chapter, I have argued that Syrian cultural producers are active subjects, deeply enmeshed in the dynamics of global markets and engaged in a dialogue with Bashar al-Asad's reformist *sultat* in the joint making of the whisper strategy, which I have described as a multilateral strategy.

108. My doctoral dissertation, "Dramas of the Authoritarian State: The Politics of Syrian TV Serials in the Pan Arab Market" (Univ. of Copenhagen, 2013), is a more comprehensive study of the political economy of contemporary Syrian drama. It takes into account a trilateral dynamic involving Gulf-backed pan-Arab television channels (which are the main buyers of Syrian TV drama); the Syrian *sultat*; and the drama makers. It

focuses on how the Gulf factor can impact the feedback mechanism of the whisper and analyzes whether the pan-Arab market element introduces tensions or induces friction between the local *sultat* and the drama makers. It also reflects on how the domestic dynamic of the whisper can have a regional effect and succeed or fail in mastering media messages for the pan-Arab media sphere.

109. For further discussion of this topic, see Donatella Della Ratta, "Dramas of the Authoritarian State: The Politics of Syrian TV Serials in the Pan Arab Market" (PhD dissertation, Univ. of Copenhagen, 2013).

5. Cultural Liberalization or Marginalization?

1. A popular dance practice set in a duple meter rhythmic groove, *dabke* is typically accompanied by vocals and instruments, including the *mijwiz* reed and the *tabl* drum. It is commonly associated with weddings, and participants often link ties to villages of origin and family lines through stylistic distinctions.

2. James Bennet, "The Enigma of Damascus," *New York Times*, July 10, 2005.

3. Steven Heydemann and Reinoud Leenders, eds., *Middle East Authoritarianisms: Governance, Contestation, and Regime Resilience in Syria and Iran* (Stanford, CA: Stanford Univ. Press, 2013), 13.

4. Caroline Donati, "The Economics of Authoritarian Upgrading in Syria: Liberalization and the Reconfiguration of Economic Networks," in *Middle East Authoritarianisms: Governance, Contestation, and Regime Resilience in Syria and Iran*, ed. Steven Heydemann and Reinoud Leenders, 35–60 (Stanford, CA: Stanford Univ. Press, 2013); and Bassam Haddad, *Business Networks in Syria: The Political Economy of Authoritarian Resilience* (Stanford, CA: Stanford Univ. Press, 2011).

5. Heydemann and Leenders, *Middle East Authoritarianisms*, 2013.

6. Donati, "The Economics of Authoritarian Upgrading," 26.

7. Liberalization also affected popular culture by increasing access to emerging forms of mass media, particularly Arab pop music broadcast on satellite networks and televised music videos. The perceived relevance of nationalistic culture, based on traditionalist attitudes to collective identity, arguably faded with the emergence of new satellite media that provided access to transnational networks of cultural production. Neoliberal expansion in entertainment, fashion, and leisure enabled more individualized strategies of cultural production in the Bashar al-Asad era. Shifting patterns of cultural production and consumption also reproduced distinctions between political and business elites and non-elite groups, compounding the social and economic marginalization of urban poor and rural populations.

8. Christa Salamandra, *A New Old Damascus: Authenticity and Distinction in Urban Syria* (Bloomington: Indiana Univ. Press, 2004); and Christa Salamandra, "Dramatizing

Damascus: The Cultural Politics of Arab Television Production in the Satellite Era," Copenhagen Univ. Islam Lecture Series, Apr. 14, 2010.

9. Max Weiss, "Who Laughs Last: Literary Transformations of Syrian Authoritarianism," in *Middle East Authoritarianisms: Governance, Contestation, and Regime Resilience in Syria and Iran*, ed. Steven Heydemann and Reinoud Leenders, 143–68 (Stanford, CA: Stanford Univ. Press, 2012).

10. See the festival website: http://damascus.org.sy/.

11. Donati, "The Economics of Authoritarian Upgrading."

12. Shayna Silverstein, "Mobilizing Bodies in Syria: Dabke, Popular Culture, and the Politics of Belonging" (PhD diss., Univ. of Chicago, 2012).

13. Cécile Boëx, "The End of State Monopoly over Culture: Toward the Commodification of Culture and Artistic Production," *Middle East Critique* 20, no. 2 (2011): 140.

14. Ibid.

15. These two sectors were not highly segregated but rather, as Cécile Boëx explains in relation to Syrian television drama, overlapping in ways consistent with the partial privatization of the culture industry since the 1970s. Boëx, "The End of State Monopoly."

16. Adonis ('Ali Ahmad Sa'id), *An Introduction to Arab Poetics*, trans. Catherine Cobham (Cairo: American Univ. in Cairo Press, 1992 [1985]), 86, quoted in Jonathan Shannon, *Among the Jasmine Trees: Music and Modernity in Contemporary Syria* (Middletown, CT: Wesleyan Univ. Press, 2006), 73.

17. In the context of modern classical Arab music, this position has been critiqued by Jonathan Shannon, who suggests that the concept of double dependency reinforces modernity as "a product of autochthonous European developments." Rather than project forms of alternative modernity that perpetuate postcolonial relations of dependency, Shannon suggests that a search for cultural alternatives might instead lead to multiple visions of cultural modernities that occur "in the absence of sustained progress in public, political, and material spheres," which can be attributed in part to "underdevelopment under Ottoman and French rule." Jonathan Shannon, *Among the Jasmine Trees: Music and Modernity in Contemporary Syria* (Middletown, CT: Wesleyan Univ. Press, 2006), 64–65.

18. Jennifer Sears, "Adonis at Alwan: Always More Beauty to Be Seen," *Arabic Literature* website, Nov. 3, 2010. http://arablit.wordpress.com/2010/11/03/adonis-at-alwan -always-more-beauty-to-be-seen/ (accessed Nov. 8, 2010).

19. Shayna Silverstein, "Syria's Radical Dabke," *Middle East Report* 263 (Summer 2012): 33–37.

20. Hanan Kassab Hassan, personal interview with the author, Aug. 8 2008, Damascus. Though Dr. Kassab Hassan presented folk dance troupes Omaya and Firqa al-Hamami, who perform *dabke*, *sama'* and other dance traditions in the folkloricized style of Moiseyev, these performances accompanied classical Andalusian and Sufi-based music

concerts in ways that constructed national forms of urban cosmopolitanism rather than rural heritage.

21. Motaz Malatialy, interview with the author, June 2007, Damascus.

22. Noura Murad, interview with the author, June 2007, Damascus.

23. Noura Murad, interview with the author, July 12, 2010, Amsterdam, Netherlands.

24. Mirjam van der Linden, "Syrisch huwelijk kent geen liefde" [Syrian marriage has no love: Interview with the Syrian choreographer Noura Murad], *De Volkskrant*, July 12, 2010.

25. Rebecca Joubin, *The Politics of Love: Sexuality, Gender, and Marriage in Syrian Television Drama* (Plymouth, UK, and Lanham, MD: Lexington Books, 2013).

26. Joubin, *The Politics of Love*, 84.

27. *Alf mabruk!* Live performance at Julidans Festival, Amsterdam, Netherlands, July 12 and 13, 2010.

28. Ahmad Bitar, "Nura Murad wa Firqa Leish ta'arid 'Alf mabruk!' fi madrassa al-Shebanni bi Halab: 'Ard mumayaz wa tajriba jadida yushahiduha jumhour Halab" [Noura Murad and Leish Troupe Present "Alf mabruk!" at al-Shebanni School in Aleppo: A compelling and new experience for audiences in Aleppo], *Discover Syria*, July 31, 2010, translation by the author.

29. Inas Ḥouli, "Sarkha mutamarada fi mujtam'iyya qami'iyya" [Cry of a rebel in an oppressed society], *Esyria*, July 31, 2010, translation by the author.

30. Silverstein, "Syria's Radical Dabke"; and Amy Singer, *Charity in Islamic Societies* (Cambridge and New York: Cambridge Univ. Press, 2008).

6. Christian Charities and the Ba'thist Regime in Bashar al-Asad's Syria

1. "Until recently, the topic of charitable organizations seemed to have fallen in disgrace" (Benoît Challand, "A *Nahda* of Charitable Organizations? Health Service Provision and the Politics of Aid in Palestine," *International Journal of Middle East Studies* 40 (2008): 227).

2. Sarah Ben Nefissa, "Associations et ONG dans le monde arabe: Vers la mise en place d'une problématique," in *Pouvoirs et associations dans le monde arabe*, ed. Sarah Ben Nefissa (Paris: CNRS Editions, 2002), 19.

3. For a general overview on charities, see Jonathan Benthall, "Organized Charity in the Arab-Islamic World: A View from the NGOs," in *Interpreting Islam*, ed. H. Donnan (London: Sage Publications, 2002), 150–66. For a historical perspective, see Michael Bonner, Mine Ener, and Amy Singer, eds., *Poverty and Charity in Middle Eastern Contexts* (New York: State Univ. of New York Press, 2003) and Amy Singer, *Charity in Islamic Societies* (Cambridge and New York: Cambridge Univ. Press, 2008). See also the *International Journal of Middle East Studies* 46, special issue no. 2 (May 2014) on the "Politics of Benevolence."

4. Amélie Le Renard, "Pauvreté et charité en Arabie Saoudite: La famille royale, le secteur des affaires et 'l'État-Providence,'" *Critique Internationale* 41 (2008): 137–56.

5. Challand, "A *Nahda* of Charitable Organizations?"

6. Jonathan Benthall, "Islam et charité institutionnelle: Doctrine, réalité et interprétation," in *Dynamiques de la pauvreté en Afrique du Nord et au Moyen-Orient*, ed. B. Destremau, A. Deboulet, F. Ireton (Paris: Karthala-Urbama, 2004), 183.

7. The number of charitable associations surged from less than 350 in 2002 to approximately 700 associations in 2006. Statistical Abstracts of 2003 and 2007, Central Bureau of Statistics, Syrian Arab Republic.

8. Jamal Barout, "Article préliminaire pour construire une carte associative en Syrie" (unpublished manuscript, 2008).

9. According to the Syrian NGO law, NGOs must register with the Ministry of Social Affairs and Labor if they want to work in the country (see the second section of this chapter).

10. Emulating the Chinese model, Syria's "Social Market Economy" entailed the combination of central planning and free-market enterprise. It aimed at introducing economic reforms (expanding the private sector and reforming rather than privatizing the public sector), while rejecting political changes and maintaining previous forms of social protection for the populace.

11. Steven Heydemann, draft paper presented at the workshop "Authoritarian Renewal in Syria," Sciences Po, Paris, June 2009.

12. The Tenth Five Year Plan (2006–10) (State Planning Commission, 2005), http://www.planning.gov.sy/files/file/FypChapter1En.pdf (accessed Nov. 30, 2011).

13. This number rose from 513 in 2000 to 1,485 in 2009. These figures include all kind of organizations: cultural, charitable, developmental, environmental, etc.

14. Before 2011, there were two unions of charities in Syria: one in Aleppo and one in Damascus. Both of them were private initiatives.

15. Annual Report of the Damascus Charities Union, 2007.

16. See Laura Ruiz de Elvira, "State/Charities Relation in Syria: Between Reinforcement, Control and Coercion," in *Civil Society and the State in Syria: The Outsourcing of Social Responsibility*, ed. L. Ruiz de Elvira and T. Zintl (Boulder: Lynne Rienner, 2012), 5–29.

17. This transformation includes economic transition from one model to another, political changes with the arrival of Bashar al-Asad and a new generation of civil servants, and social transformations with the partial liberalization of the associative sector.

18. See, for instance, Soukaina Boukhaima, "Le mouvement associatif en Syrie," in *Pouvoirs et associations dans le monde arabe*, ed. Sarah Ben Nefissa (Paris: CNRS Editions, 2002), 77–94; Mathieu Le Saux, "Les dynamiques contradictoires du champ associatif syrien," *Revue du monde musulman et de la Méditerranée* 115–16 (2006): 193–209; and Laura Ruiz de Elvira, "L'Etat syrien de Bachar al-Assad à l'épreuve des ONG," *Maghreb-Machrek* 203 (Spring 2010): 41–57.

19. Thomas Pierret and Kjetil Selvik, "Limits of 'Authoritarian Upgrading' in Syria: Welfare Privatization, Islamic Charities, and the Rise of the Zayd Movement," *International Journal of Middle East Studies* 41, no. 4 (2009): 595–614.

20. Before the 2011 uprising Christians were estimated to represent 8 percent of the Syrian population. As I will show later in this chapter, relations between the different eleven Christian communities and the Ba'thist regime have always been mutually beneficial.

21. By foreign actors I mean international donors, international intergovernmental agencies such as the United Nations, international institutions such as the delegation of the European Commission in Syria, foreign NGOs such as the IECD (Institut Européen de Coopération et de Développement), the ICMC (International Catholic Migration Commission), or Caritas and, more generally, western civil society networks.

22. For example, at the beginning of July 2011, when more than fourteen hundred Syrian protesters had already been killed by the army, the security forces, and the *shabbiha*, the priest Elias Zahlawi, one of the most beloved and influential religious leaders of the Syrian Catholic community, publicly exhibited his support for the regime by participating in the "consultative meeting for comprehensive national dialogue" launched by Bashar al-Asad and boycotted by larger parts of the opposition. The aim of the meeting, as announced by the government, was to promote a national dialogue between the regime and opposition, academic, and youth activist figures.

23. As we will see later, access to foreign aid was extremely restricted in Syria until 2011. Public aid was limited and unequally distributed.

24. I consider associations "Christian" on the basis of at least one of the following criteria: operating under the patronage of a Christian religious institution (e.g., al-Safina [The Ark], which is under the authority of the Latin Church, Bayt al-salam, which is under the authority of the Syriac Catholic Church, or Mashgal al-manara [Workshop of the Lighthouse], which is under the authority of the Melkite Greek Catholic Church); headquartered in a building belonging to a religious institution (e.g., Jam'iyyat al-mustawsaf al-khayri [Association of the Charitable Clinic]); founded by Christian clergy (e.g., al-Mahabba [Love] or Usrat al-ikha' [Terre des Hommes Syrie]); having a name referring to Christianity (e.g., Saint Vincent de Paul, the Charitable Association of Saint Gregorius, Sainte Teqla, or Saint Elyes); having a board that includes Christian clerics (e.g., Usrat al-ikha' or al-Mahabba); and, more generally, associations that claim to be Christian in their names (e.g., al-Salib Association for the Armenian People, the Orthodox Association of Saint-Bendlayamun, and the Syriac Catholic Charitable Association of Aleppo).

25. Although I point to overrepresentation, the exact percentage of Christian associations in Bashar al-Asad's Syria is unknown. Despite the fact that the Ministry of Social Affairs and Labor generally published the number of associations registered in the country, the list of individual associations was not publicly available. Furthermore, MoSAL did not classify associations in religious or communitarian terms, but according to activities

and goals. Finally, as we will see, many Christian associations were not registered with MoSAL and, consequently, were not included in the statistics.

26. Boukhaima, "Le mouvement associatif en Syrie," 88.

27. Ibid., 89.

28. Geraldine Chatelard observes the same fragmentation and competition existing between the different Christian churches of the city of Madaba (Jordan) since the end of the nineteenth century, especially in the education sector. Geraldine Chatelard, *Briser la mosaïque: Lien social et identités collectives chez les chrétiens de Madaba, Jordanie 1870– 1997* (PhD thesis, EHESS, Paris, 2000).

29. Elizabeth Picard, "Les liens primordiaux, vecteurs de dynamique politique," in *La Politique dans le monde arabe*, ed. Elizabeth Picard (Paris: Armand Colin, 2006), 55–77.

30. Christmas card sent by the Saint Vincent de Paul charitable association, 2008.

31. However, in the modern period, as Bernard Heyberger and Rémy Madinier suggest, the Christian missions in the Arab region have focused their social activities on Christian populations and other minorities, including Alawites, Druzes, and Ismaelis. See Bernard Heyberger and Rémy Madinier, "Introduction," in *L'islam des marges: Mission chrétienne et espaces périphériques du monde musulman (XVI-XX siècles)*, ed. B. Heyberger and R. Madinier (Paris: IISMM-Karthala, 2011).

32. In Jordan, Geraldine Chatelard notes, a 1953 law requires Christian charities to provide their services on a "non-confessional basis." Chatelard, *Briser la mosaïque*, 216.

33. I thank the researcher Natalia Ribas-Mateos for this information, which she obtained in an interview with a staff member of this association, July 2008.

34. In the year 2010 several evangelical churches were closed by the Syrian authorities, mainly in the north of the country. They were accused, unofficially, of proselytizing.

35. Interview with a staff member of this association, October 2009.

36. A partial list of charities with foreign ties includes the following associations and centers: al-Mahabba (founded in 1980), Bayt al-salam (1992), al-Safina (1995) and the Mashgal al-manara (1997) in Damascus; al-Ard center for Disabled People (1991) in Homs; the Kfarseta Center (1991) near Tartous, and the Iman wa nur network spread throughout the country (1980s).

37. Interview with the president of the board, December 2008.

38. During an event honoring "the creativity of handicapped people" celebrated in Damascus in November 2009, a teenager in a wheelchair read a poem dedicated to the First Lady in which he called her "the protector angel for handicapped people." Asma al-Asad's direct involvement in this sector, and more generally in the associative field itself, was positively received by a large portion of the civil society actors as well as by foreign donors and international organizations.

39. However, there were several significant exceptions, such as the al-Mubarra al-nisa'iyya (the Women's Charitable Institution) association, an important and very active

charity "created by and for women" more than sixty years ago. (Interview with the President of the Board, October 2010.)

40. The Jesuit mission arrived in the Middle East in 1830. Chantal Verdeil, "Une 'révolution sociale dans la montagne': La conversion des alaouites par les jésuites dans les années 1930," in *L'islam des marges: Mission chrétienne et espaces périphériques du monde musulman (XVI-XX siècles)*, ed. B. Heyberger and R. Madinier (Paris: IISMM-Karthala, 2011).

41. Chantal Verdeil, "Travailler à la renaissance de l'Orient chrétien: Les missions latines en Syrie (1830–1945)," *Proche-Orient Chrétien* 51, nos. 3–4 (2001): 267–316.

42. Maryanne Loughry and Julianne Duncan, *Iraqi Refugees in Syria: A Report of the ICMC-USCCB Mission to Assess the Protection Needs of Iraqi Refugees in Syria* (International Catholic Migration Commission, Apr. 2008).

43. The charities that benefited from these funds changed every year. The selection of these charities strongly depended on patronage networks.

44. Government-operated nongovernmental organization.

45. Fund for Integrated Rural Development of Syria; and Modernizing and Activating Women's Role in Economic Development.

46. A new NGO law was drafted by MoSAL in the summer of 2011, then discussed in the Parliament in 2012. As far as I know, the new law has not yet been approved.

47. The authorization process could be very long and complicated, with final determinations made not by MoSAL but by the *mukhabarat* (intelligence services), which investigated the founders of organizations requesting legal status.

48. By "informal structures" I mean nonregistered associations working as informal networks at times linked to previously registered "umbrella" associations or to Christian religious institutions.

49. Central Bureau of Statistics, Syrian Arab Republic.

50. Quintan Wiktorowicz, "Civil Society as Social Control: State Power in Jordan," *Comparative Politics* 33, no. 1 (2000): 49.

51. Ibid., 43.

52. Interview with an association member, April 2008.

53. Some Sunni charities were quite wealthy. For instance, the income of *Sunduq al-'afiya* for the year 2007 was around 165 million Syrian pounds, and the 2008 annual budget of the al-Ansar charitable association was 120 million Syrian pounds. During the month of Ramadan 2010, the charity Hifz al-ni'ma distributed more than 22,000 meals per day to destitute families in Damascus.

54. For instance, in 2008 the annual budget of the Christian Association of Saint Vincent de Paul in Damascus, which was one of the richest Christian associations in the country, was 19 million Syrian pounds.

55. Fiona McCallum, "Religious Institutions and Authoritarian States: Church–State Relations in the Middle East," *Third World Quarterly* 33, no. 1 (2012): 112.

56. Ibid.

57. Barah Mikail, "Les chrétiens de syrie: Un statut enviable, ou une sérénité simulée?" *Confluences Méditerannée* 66 (2008): 52.

58. Fiona McCallum, "Silent Minorities: The Co-optation of Christian Communities in Ba'thist Syria," paper presented at the third World Congress for Middle East Studies, Barcelona, July 22, 2010.

7. Performing the Nation

1. Erving Goffman, *The Presentation of Self in Everyday Life* (New York: Anchor Books, 1959).

2. Raymond Hinnebusch, "Authoritarian Persistence, Democratization Theory, and the Middle East: An Overview and Critique," *Democratization* 13, no. 3 (2006): 373–95.

3. Lisa Wedeen, *Ambiguities of Domination: Politics, Rhetoric, and Symbols in Contemporary Syria* (Chicago: Univ. of Chicago Press, 1999); miriam cooke, *Dissident Syria: Making Oppositional Arts Official* (Durham, NC: Duke Univ. Press, 2007).

4. But see Andreas Bandak, "Reckoning with the Inevitable: Death and Dying among Syrian Christians during the Uprisings," in "Death and Afterlife in the Arab Revolutions," Special Issue of *Ethnos: Journal of Anthropology*, ed. Amira Mittermaier (forthcoming).

5. Jonathan Shannon, "Sultans of Spin: Syrian Sacred Music on the World Stage," *American Anthropologist* 105, no. 2 (2003): 266–77.

6. Wedeen, *Ambiguities of Domination*.

7. cooke, *Dissident Syria*.

8. Vaclav Havel, *The Power of the Powerless: Citizens against the State in Central-Eastern Europe* (London: Faber & Faber, 1990). See also Andreas Bandak, "States of Exception: Effects and Affects of Authoritarianism among Christian Arabs in Damascus," in *A Comparative Ethnography of Alternative Spaces*, ed. Jens Dahl and Esther Fihl, 197–218 (New York: Palgrave, 2013).

9. Anderson, Paul, "The Politics of Scorn in Syria and the Agency of Narrated Involvement," in *The Journal of the Royal Anthropological Institute (N.S.)* 19, no. 3 (2013): 463–81.

10. Alexei Yurchak, "The Cynical Reason of Late Socialism: Power, Pretense, and the *Anekdot*," *Public Culture* 9, no. 2 (1997): 161–88; *Everything Was Forever, Until It Was No More* (Princeton: Princeton Univ. Press, 2005); Peter Sloterdijk, *Critique of Cynical Reason* (Minneapolis: Univ. of Minnesota Press, 1988); Hans Steinmuller, *Communities of Complicity: Everyday Ethics in Rural China* (New York: Berghahn, 2013); "Communities of Complicity: Notes on State Formation and Local Sociality in Rural China," *American Ethnologist* 37, no. 3 (2011): 539–49.

11. Goffman, *The Presentation of Self*.

12. Elias Zahlawi, *al-Sufaniyya khilal khamsatin wa 'ashrin 'aman, 1982–2007* [Soufanieh through twenty-five years, 1982–2007] (Damascus: Dar al-Majid li al-taba'a

wal-nushir wal-khadimat al-tabaʻaiyya Muhammad Insaf Tarabulsi, 2008); see also Andreas Bandak, "Our Lady of Soufanieh: On Knowledge, Ignorance and Indifference among the Christians of Damascus," in *Politics of Worship in the Contemporary Middle East: Sainthood in Fragile States*, ed. Andreas Bandak and Mikkel Bille, 129–53 (Leiden and Boston: Brill, 2013).

13. See also Bandak, "Reckoning with the inevitable."

14. Volker Perthes, *The Political Economy of Syria under Asad* (London: I. B. Tauris, 1997 [1995]); Nicholaos Van Dam, *The Struggle for Power in Syria: Politics and Society under Asad and the Baath Party* (London: I. B. Tauris, 1996); Annika Rabo, *A Shop of One's Own: Independence and Reputation among Traders in Aleppo* (London: I.B. Tauris, 2005).

15. Alan George, *Syria: Neither Bread nor Freedom* (London and New York: Zed Books, 2003).

16. Maria Kastrinou-Theodoropoulou, "The Marriage of Cadmus and Harmony and the Burial and the Martyrs: Syrian Dances in the Arab Spring," *Jadaliyya*, June 6, 2011, http://www.jadaliyya.com/pages/index/1759/the-marriage-of-cadmus-and-harmony -and-the-burial.

17. Paul Heck, "Religious Renewal in Syria: The Case of Muhammad al-Habash," *Islam and Muslim-Christian Relations* 15, no. 2 (2004): 185–207.

18. Edith Szantos Ali-Dib, "Inter-Religious Dialogue in Syria: Politics, Ethics and Miscommunication," *Political Theology* 9, no. 1 (2008), 98.

19. Anna Poujeau, "Monasteries, Politics, and Social Memory: The Revival of the Greek Orthodox Church of Antioch in Syria during the Twentieth Century," in *Eastern Christians in Anthropological Perspective*, ed. C. Hann and H. Goltz, 177–92 (Berkeley: University of California Press, 2010); Anna Poujeau, "Sharing the *Baraka* of the Saints: Pluridenominational Visits to Christian Monasteries in Syria," in *Sharing Sacred Spaces in the Mediterranean: Christians, Muslims, and Jews at Shrines and Sanctuaries*, ed. Dionigi Albera and Maria Couroucli, 202–18 (Bloomington: Indiana Univ. Press, 2012).

20. Poujeau, "Monasteries, Politics, and Social Memory," 178; see also Noriko Sato, "On the Horns of the Terrorist Dilemma: Syrian Christians' (response to Israeli 'terrorism')," *History & Anthropology* 14, no. 2 (2003): 141–55; Noriko Sato, "Selective Amnesia: Memory and History of the Urfalli Syrian Orthodox Christians," *Identities: Global Studies in Culture and Power* 12, no. 3 (2003): 315–33.

21. Bruce Masters, *Christians and Jews in the Ottoman Arab World: The Roots of Sectarianism* (Cambridge: Cambridge Univ. Press, 2001), 172–73.

22. Leila Tarazi Fawaz, *An Occasion for War: Civil Conflict in Lebanon and Damascus in 1860* (Berkeley: Univ. of California Press, 1994).

23. Patrick Seale, *Asad of Syria: The Struggle for the Middle East* (Berkeley: Univ. of California Press, 1989), 27ff., 95–103; Van Dam, *The Struggle for Power in Syria*, 15ff.;

Carsten Wieland, *A Decade of Lost Chances: Repression and Revolution from Damascus Spring to Arab Spring* (Seattle: Cune Press, 2012), 230.

24. Bandak, *Politics of Worship*; see also Michael Provence, *The Great Syrian Revolt and the Rise of Arab Nationalism* (Austin: Univ. of Texas Press, 2005).

25. Michael Herzfeld, *Cultural Intimacy: Social Poetics in the Nation-State*, 2d ed. (New York: Routledge, 2005), 22.

26. Ibid., 26.

27. Szantos Ali-Dib, "Inter-Religious Dialogue in Syria," 110–11.

28. See http://youtu.be/rNBRpqAXVFk (accessed Apr. 3, 2014).

29. Cf. Wedeen, *Ambiguities of Domination*.

30. Rabo, *A Shop of One's Own*, 45.

31. Bandak, "States of Exception."

32. Erving Goffman, *Role Distance, Encounters: Two Studies in the Sociology of Interaction* (Hammondsworth: Penguin Books, 1972).

33. Ghassan Hage, "The Differential Intensities of Social Reality: Migration, Participation and Guilt," in *Arab-Australians Today: Citizenship and Belonging*, ed. Ghassan Hage, 192–205 (Melbourne: Melbourne Univ. Press, 2002).

34. Cf. Victor Turner, *From Ritual to Theatre: The Human Seriousness of Play* (New York: PAJ, 1982); Richard Schechner, *Between Theatre and Anthropology* (Philadelphia: Univ. of Pennsylvania Press, 1985); Arjun Appadurai, "Topographies of the Self: Praise and Emotion in Hindu India," in *Language and the Politics of Emotion*, ed. Catherine A. Lutz and Lila Abu-Lughod (Cambridge: Cambridge Univ. Press, 1990), 106–7.

35. Kirsten Hastrup, *Action: Anthropology in the Company of Shakespeare* (Copenhagen: Museum Tusculanum Press, 2004), 235.

36. Hastrup, *Action*, 19.

37. Christa Salamandra, *A New Old Damascus: Authenticity and Distinction in Urban Syria* (Bloomington: Indiana Univ. Press, 2004); Donatella Della Ratta, "Dramas of the Authoritarian State: The Politics of Syrian TV Serials in the Pan Arab Market" (PhD diss., Univ. of Copenhagen, 2013).

38. Bassam Haddad, *Business Networks in Syria: The Political Economy of Authoritarian Resilience* (Stanford, CA: Stanford Univ. Press, 2011). Lisa Wedeen, "Ideology and Humor in Dark Times: Notes from Syria," *Critical Inquiry* 39, no. 4 (2013): 841–73.

39. Joan Juliet Buck, "Asma al-Assad: A Rose in the Desert," *Vogue*, Feb. 2011.

8. Merchant Background, Bourgeois Ethics

1. Observations and discussion with a second-rank cleric, Tanzim Kafr Suse, Apr. 2008.

2. On the Syrian *'ulama'*, see Thomas Pierret, *Religion and State in Syria: The Sunni Ulama from Coup to Revolution* (Cambridge: Cambridge Univ. Press, 2013).

3. European Stability Initiative, *Islamic Calvinists: Change and Conservatism in Central Anatolia*, Berlin and Istanbul, Sept. 2005, http://www.esiweb.org/index.php?lang =en&id=156&document_ID=69.

4. Éric Chaumont, "Pauvreté et richesse dans le Coran et dans les sciences religieuses musulmanes," in *Pauvreté et richesse dans le monde musulman méditerranéen*, ed. Jean-Paul Pascual (Paris: Maisonneuve et Larose, 2003), 17–38.

5. Denis Gril, "De l'usage sanctifiant des biens en islam," *Revue d'histoire des religions* 215 (1998): 59–89.

6. Thomas Pierret and Kjetil Selvik, "Limits of 'Authoritarian Upgrading' in Syria. Welfare Privatization, Islamic Charities and the Rise of the Zayd Movement," *International Journal of Middle East Studies* 41 (2009): 595–614.

7. *All4Syria*, Dec. 30, 2009, http://all4syria.info/content/view/19183/70/.

8. Interview with a Syrian Muslim scholar, Damascus, Apr. 14, 2008.

9. *Sada Zayd*, Mar. 31, 2008, http://www.sadazaid.com/play.php?catsmktba=2370.

10. Interview with a Syrian businessman, Damascus, June 8, 2007.

11. *Al-Fath Online*, n.d., www.alfatihonline.com/genius/rbezm.htm.

12. Observation, Damascus, May 5, 2006.

13. Daphna Ephrat, *A Learned Society in a Period of Transition: The Sunni 'ulama' of Eleventh Century Baghdad* (Albany: State Univ. of New York Press, 2000), 131–35.

14. *Sada Zayd*, Apr. 17, 2008, http://www.sadazaid.com/play.php?catsmktba=3865.

15. Ibid.

16. Ibid.

17. Interview with an anonymous source, Damascus, July 6, 2007.

18. Repeated observations by the author, Damascus, 2006.

19. Interview with assistant to Shaykh Shukri al-Luhafi, Damascus, Apr. 17, 2006.

20. See Éric Geoffroy, ed., *Une voie soufie dans le monde: La Shâdhiliyya* (Paris: Maisonneuve et Larose, 2005).

21. Interviews with followers of Shadhili shaykhs, Aleppo, Nov. 2006, Homs, July 2007.

22. *Sada Zayd*, Apr. 9, 2008, http://www.sadazaid.com/play.php?catsmktba=2989

23. Ibid.

24. Pierret and Selvik, "Limits of 'Authoritarian Upgrading,'" 600.

25. *Sada Zayd*, Apr. 9, 2008, http://www.sadazaid.com/play.php?catsmktba=2992.

26. Quoted by Pierret and Selvik, "Limits of 'Authoritarian Upgrading,'" 607.

27. Friday sermon, Mar. 10, 2006 (observation).

28. Lesson, Oct. 15, 2006 (observation).

29. Interview with assistant to Shaykh Mahmud Abu al-Huda al-Husseini, Aleppo, July 10, 2006.

30. Patrick Haenni, *L'islam de marché: L'autre révolution conservatrice* (Paris: Seuil, 2005).

31. Johannes Reissner, *Ideologie und Politik der Muslimbrüder Syriens: Von den Wahlen 1947 bis zum Verbot unter Adib ash-Shîshaklî* (Fribourg-en-Brisgau: Klaus Shwarz, 1980), 300–315. On the debates over Islamic socialism in the Arab world during the early postcolonial period, see Charles Tripp, *Islam and the Moral Economy: The Challenge of Capitalism* (Cambridge: Cambridge Univ. Press, 2006), 77–102.

32. 'Adnan Zarzur, *Mustafa al-Sibaʻi: Al-daʻiyya al-mujaddid* [Mustafa al-Sibaʻi: The preacher and renovator] (Damas: Dar al-Qalam, 2000), 146–47; Muhamma al-Hamid (1963) "[On the *Socialism of Islam*]," *Hadarat al-Islam* 3 (1963): 1128–31.

33. *Sada Zayd*, Apr. 9, 2008, http://www.sadazaid.com/play.php?catsmktba=2986.

34. Ibid.

35. Ibid.; Haytham al-Malih, interview with author, Damascus, May 13, 2008; *Ahbab al-Kiltawiyya*, Dec. 19, 2007, http://www.alkeltawia.com/port/news.php?action=view&id=21.

36. 'Abd al-Rahman Habannaka, *al-Walid al-daʻiyya al-murabbi al-shaykh Hasan Habannaka al-Midani* [My father the preacher and educator shaykh Hasan Habannaka al-Midani] (Djedda: Dar al-Bashir, 2002), 248.

37. Rajih himself comes from a very modest background, but as a Muslim scholar, he was intimately tied to the merchant networks of the Midan neighborhood.

38. Umar Abdallah, *The Islamic Struggle in Syria* (Berkeley: Mizan Press, 1983), 220–41; Thomas Pierret, "Le *Projet politique pour la Syrie de l'avenir* des Frères Musulmans," in *La Syrie au présent*, ed. Youssef Courbage, Baudouin Dupret, Mohammed Al-Dbiyat, Zouhair Ghazzal (Paris: Actes Sud, 2007), 729–38.

39. Ibid., 735.

40. *Al-Thawra*, June 10, 2005.

41. Pierret and Selvik, "Limits of 'Authoritarian Upgrading,'" 602.

42. Friday sermon, Mar. 10, 2006 (observation).

43. Muhammad al-Yaʻqubi, Friday sermon, May 3, 2008 (*Nasim al-Cham*, http://naseemalsham.com/speeches.php?ID=435).

44. In 2009, basic pay for a graduate functionary was 9645 pounds a month (*Syria Steps*, May 18, 2009, http://www.syriasteps.com/index.php?d=126&id=36042).

45. Observation of Friday sermon, Dec. 1, 2006.

46. See Kjetil Selvik, "It's the Mentality, Stupid! Syria's Turn to the Private Sector," in *Changing Regime Discourse and Reform in Syria*, ed. Aurora Sottimano and Kjetil Selvik (St Andrews: Lynne Rienner, 2009), 41–70.

47. *Akhbar al-Sharq*, Jan. 31, 2005; *al-Watan al-Qatariyya*, Feb. 1, 2005; Laura Ruiz de Elvira, *Charité, développement et politiques publiques dans le domaine du social: Étude de cas d'une association caritative syrienne* (unpublished paper, 2009), 11.

48. *Sada Zayd*, Nov. 4 2008, http://www.sadazaid.com/play.php?catsmktba=5243.

49. Saʻid Ramadan al-Buti, Friday sermon, Oct. 24, 2008 (personal website, http://www.bouti.com/article.php?PHPSESSID=d1d8a3418590129c568dd76a722facd7&id=727

&PHPSESSID=d1d8a3418590129c568dd76a722facd7). See also Muhammad al-Yaʻqubi, Friday sermon, Oct. 10, 2008 (*Nasim al-Sham*, http://naseemalsham.com/speeches.php ?ID=806).

50. *Al-Thawra*, Nov. 30, 2007; Syrian National Television, Aug. 29, 2007.

51. *Al-Sharq al-Awsat*, May 30, 2006; *SANA*, Feb. 5, 2007; *Sham Press*, Aug. 26, 2007.

52. Tripp, *Islam and the Moral Economy*, 133–49.

53. On the role of the *ʻulama* in Islamic finance, see Monzer Kahf, "Islamic Banks: The Rise of a New Power Alliance of Wealth and Shariʻa Scholarship," in *The Politics of Islamic Finance*, ed. C. Henry and R. Wilson (Edinburgh: Edinburgh Univ. Press, 2004), 17–36.

54. *Al-Aswaq al-ʻArabiyya*, Apr. 29, 2009, http://www.alaswaq.net/articles/2009/04 /24/23048.html.

55. Website of the Syrian International Islamic Bank, http://www.siib.sy/new/mod ules.php?op=modload&name=News&file=article&sid=7 (accessed May 2008); website of Cham Bank, http://www.chambank.com/Main/management.php (accessed May 2008).

56. *Al-Thawra*, Dec. 7, 2007.

57. *Al-tanmiyya al-bashariyya* is entirely different from what is known in English as "human development," a concept that in development studies refers to a population's achievements in terms of standards of living (including such sectors as income, health, and education).

58. See Haenni, *L'islam de marché*, 72–86.

59. See for instance Tariq Suwaydan, *Sinaʻat al-qaʼid* [The making of the leader] (Riyadh: ʻUbaykan, 2003).

60. ʻAʼid al-Qarni, *La tahzan* [Don't be sad] (Ryad: ʻUbaykan, 2004).

61. Born in 1951 in Homs, based in Saudi Arabia. See for instance ʻA. Bakkar, *Al-ʻAysh fi zaman al-saʻb* [Living in difficult times] (Damascus: Dar al-Qalam, 2000).

62. Neurolinguistic programming (NLP) is an approach to personal development that posits a connection between the neurological processes, language, and behavioral patterns learned through experience.

63. Yusuf Khattar Muhammad, *Al-Asrar al-khafiyya li al-barmaja al-lughawiyya al-ʻasabiyya* [The hidden secrets of NLP] (Damascus: Dar al-Taqwa, 2008); website of the personal development center of Shaykh Saʻid Shaʻban in Homs, http://www.alsaer.info /index.php?option=com_content&view=article&id=73&Itemid=95&lang=ar (accessed Sept. 2009).

64. Samir Saqqa Amini, *Nahnu wa al-barmaja al-lughawiyya al-ʻasabiyya* [NLP and us] (Damas: Dar al-Bashaʼir, 2005), 7–8.

65. For his biography, see Arnaud Lenfant, "Les transformations du salafisme syrien au XXᵉ siècle," in *Qu'est-ce que le salafisme?* ed. Bernard Rougier (Paris: PUF, 2008), 176; Bernard Rougier, *L'Oumma en fragments: Contrôler le sunnisme au Liban* (Paris: PUF, 2011), 154–60.

66. Friday sermon, Summer 2007, http://www.youtube.com/watch?v=ENhqvpLw048.

67. *Darbuna*, May 2, 2009, http://www.darbuna.net/word/.

68. Ibid.

69. Ibid.

70. *Darbuna*, Feb. 1, 2007, http://www.darbuna.net/archive/text.php?CID=9&start=15&ID=417.

71. *Al-Thawra*, Nov. 21, 2008.

72. *Al-Hayat*, Aug. 27, 2007.

73. Observation, Aleppo, Nov. 24, 2006.

74. Interview with an anonymous source, Damascus, May 2008.

75. On the Syrian *'ulama*"s response to the uprising, see Thomas Pierret, *Religion and State in Syria*, 216–34.

9. Muslim Organizations in Bashar's Syria

1. See Paulo Pinto, "The Limits of the Public: Sufism and the Religious Debate in Syria," in *Public Islam and the Common Good*, ed. Armando Salvatore and Dale F. Eickelman (Leiden: Brill, 2004), 184–85; Line Khatib, *Islamic Revivalism in Syria: The Rise and Fall of Ba'thist Secularism*, Routledge Studies in Political Islam (London: Routledge, 2011), 1ff. and 146ff.; and Thomas Pierret, *Religion and State in Syria: The Sunni Ulama from Coup to Revolution* (Cambridge: Cambridge Univ. Press, 2013). Religion is rarely treated as an important social or political force in the literature on Syria of recent decades: see, for example Alan George, *Syria: Neither Bread nor Freedom* (London and New York: Zed Books, 2003); Flynt Leverett, *Inheriting Syria: Bashar's Trial by Fire* (Washington, DC: Brookings Institution Press, 2005); Moshe Ma'oz, Joseph Ginat, and Onn Winckler, eds., *Modern Syria: From Ottoman Rule to Pivotal Role in the Middle East* (Brighton: Sussex Academic Press, 1999); Lisa Wedeen, *Ambiguities of Domination: Politics, Rhetoric, and Symbols in Contemporary Syria* (Chicago: Univ. of Chicago Press, 1999); and Eyal Zisser, *Commanding Syria: Bashar al-Asad and the First Years in Power* (London: I. B. Tauris, 2007). While these authors have not aimed to analyze the role of religion in Syria, they often default to a portrayal of religion as controlled by the state and as an institution manipulated for the state's benefit.

2. Hanna Batatu describes the hierarchy concerning the appointments of imams; see Batatu, *Syria's Peasantry, the Descendants of Its Lesser Rural Notables, and Their Politics* (Princeton: Princeton Univ. Press, 1999). See also Radwan Ziadeh, "The Muslim Brotherhood in Syria and the Concept of 'Democracy'" (paper presented at the Ninth Annual Conference of the Center for the Study of Islam and Democracy, Washington, DC, 2009); Khatib, *Islamic Revivalism in Syria;* and Pierret, *Religion and State in Syria,* on the politics of religion and the Syrian state.

3. In this context the term "interpretation" signifies the broader discursive tradition of Islam practiced by Muslims at a specific place and in a certain historical context.

4. See, for example, Thomas Pierret, "Sunni Clergy Politics in the Cities of Baʻthi Syria," in *Demystifying Syria*, ed. Fred Lawson (London: Saqi Books and London Middle East Institute SOAS, 2009) and Thomas Pierret and Kjetil Selvik, "Limits of 'Authoritarian Upgrading' in Syria: Welfare Privatization, Islamic Charities, and the Rise of the Zayd Movement," *International Journal of Middle East Studies* 41, no. 4 (2009): 595–614. The development of sectors like charity among religious organizations parallels a more general growth of NGOs and government-sponsored NGOs. Leverett states that al-Asad encouraged the development of NGOs, and that they represented a gradual empowerment of civil society (Leverett, *Inheriting Syria*, 94ff.). The Ahmad Kuftaro Foundation is an example of this development.

5. In regard to interpretations of Islam, the Ahmad Kuftaro Foundation is linked to other current Muslim movements and organizations. These include the organization headed by Muhammad Habash, the women's organization headed by Habash's sister Houda, and the female Qubaysiyyat movement. On Habash, see Paul Heck, "Religious Renewal in Syria: The Case of Muhammad al-Habash," *Islam and Muslim-Christian Relations* 15, no. 2 (2004): 185–207, and Paul L. Heck, "Muhammad al-Habach et le dialogue interreligieux," in *La Syrie au présent: Reflets d'une société*, ed. Baudouin Dupret, Zouhair Ghazzal, Youssef Courbage, and Muhammad al-Dbiyat (Paris: Sindbad Actes Sud, 2007), 413–20; and on the Qubaysiyyat, see Sarah Islam, "The Qubaysiyyat: The Growth of an International Muslim Women's Revivalist Movement from Syria (1960–2008)," in *Women, Leadership and Mosques: Changes in Contemporary Islamic Authority*, ed. Masooda Bano and Hilary Kalmbach (Leiden: Brill, 2012), and Sara Omar, "Al-Qubaysiyyat: Negotiating Female Religious Authority in Damascus," *The Muslim World* 103, no. 3 (July 2013).

6. Naqshbandiyya is one of the major Sunni Sufi orders with a presence among Muslims all over the world. For more on the Naqshbandiyya, see Elisabeth Özdalga, *Naqshbandis in Western and Central Asia: Change and Continuity* (*Transactions*, vol. 9) (Istanbul: Swedish Research Institute in Istanbul, 1999); and on Sufism in general, see Martin van Bruinessen and Julia Day Howell, eds., *Sufism and the "Modern" in Islam* (London: I. B. Tauris, 2007). The Naqshbandiyya Sufi order is divided in branches, and Ahmad Kuftaro and his disciples are followers of the Khalidiyya branch, performing specific rituals that divide them from other Naqshbandis. This branch is named after the Kurdish Sufi Khalid al-Baghdadi (d. 1827).

7. To some extent the current Abu Nur mosque complex is reminiscent of the *madrasa* institution that emerged in the early history of Islam in its ritual, educational, and social aspects. Hence, *madrasa* in this context refers to an Islamic institution containing religious education within the framework of a larger mosque.

8. Syrians I interviewed in March 2010 pointed out that religious leaders' presence in national media was newly restricted, and that the security services were more active at the time of our conversations than in previous periods. Given these concerns about surveillance, persons I interviewed have asked not to be named in this article.

9. I use the term "charismatic" in its Weberian sense (Max Weber, *On Charisma and Institution Building*, Selected Papers, Edited and with an Introduction by S. N. Eisenstadt [Chicago: The Heritage of Sociology, Univ. of Chicago Press, 1968], 48–49).

10. The view of religion as discursive practices is founded primarily on the ideas of Michel Foucault, *The Archeology of Knowledge and the Discourse on Language* (New York: Pantheon Books, 1972), as well as those of Talal Asad, *Genealogies of Religion: Discipline and Reasons of Power in Christianity and Islam* (Baltimore: Johns Hopkins Univ. Press, 1993). For more on this view, see Leif Stenberg, *The Islamization of Science: Four Muslim Positions Developing an Islamic Modernity* (Stockholm: Almqvist and Wiksell International, 1996); Dale Eickelman and James Piscatori, *Muslim Politics* (Princeton: Princeton Univ. Press, 1996); and, more recently, Daniel Varisco, *Islam Obscured: The Rhetoric of Anthropological Representation* (New York: Palgrave Macmillan, 2005); Jean-Pierre Filiu, *The Arab Revolution: Ten Lessons from the Democratic Uprising* (Oxford: Oxford Univ. Press, 2011), 17–30; and Carool Kersten and Susanne Olsson, eds., *Alternative Islamic Discourses and Religious Authority* (London: Ashgate, 2013).

11. Peter Berger and Thomas Luckmann, *The Social Construction of Reality: A Treatise in the Sociology of Knowledge* (New York: Anchor Books, 1966).

12. Sources discussing the life and ideas of Ahmad Kuftaro include Muhammad Habash, *Al-Shaykh Ahmad Kuftaro wa manhaj fi al-tajdid wa islah* (Damascus: Dar Abu Nur, 1996); Muhammad al-Sawwaf, *Al-Manhaj al-sufi fi fikr wa da'wa samahat al-shaykh Ahmad Kaftaru* (Damascus: Bayt al-hikma, 1999); and Mahmud Kuftaro, *Muhadharat fi al-hiwar al-islami al-masihi li-samahat al-shaykh Ahmad Kaftaru* (Damascus: Dar nadwa al-'ulma', 2008); however, these are not critical sources. My brief introduction is founded on these hagiographic sources since they give a portrait of a confessional historiography that is seen as true history within the Ahmad Kuftaro Foundation. I consider these texts as empirical but also tentative sources. The information given in them is difficult to validate in Syria due to the repressiveness of the state and to their hagiographic character, but also to the animosity between religious leaders. However, in this context it is important to see the historical portrait of Ahmad Kuftaro's life as intimately linked to religiopolitical ambitions.

13. On the web page www.kuftaro.org (accessed Jan. 19, 2012), one can find an example of how the foundation constructs its history and suggests a spiritual bond between Amin and Ahmad Kuftaro through a picture of Amin with his young son Ahmad. Until 2009 the image was also displayed among a collection of pictures of Ahmad Kuftaro in the new entrance of the Abu Nur complex, but it was later taken away and was not present in late 2010. This picture is a Photoshop manipulation, according to some of my informants, and its depiction of Amin and Ahmad Kuftaro can be understood as a form of strengthening the legitimacy of the spiritual bond between father and son. See Gisela Fonseca Chagas, "Muslim Women and the Work of da'wa: The Female Branch of the tariqa Naqshbandiyya-Kuftariyya in Damascus, Syria," *Middle East Critique* 20, no. 2

(Summer 2011); Leif Stenberg, "Young, Male and Sufi Muslim in the city of Damascus" in *Youth and Youth Culture in the Contemporary Middle East*, ed. Jørgen Bæck Simonsen (Aarhus: Aarhus Univ. Press, 2005); Leif Stenberg, "Islamisation d'un quartier: L'héritage du cheikh Ahmad Kuftaro," in *La Syrie au présent: Reflets d'une société*, ed. Baudouin Dupret, Zouhair Ghazzal, Youssef Courbage, and Muhammad al-Dbiyat (Paris: Sindbad Actes Sud, 2007); and Leif Stenberg, "Préserver le charisme: Les consequences de la mort d'Ahmad Kaftaro sur la mosquée-complexe Abu al-Nur," i*Maghreb-Mashrek* 198 (Winter 2008–9) for discussion of recent developments concerning rituals, organization, and charity at Abu Nur and the Ahmad Kuftaro Foundation.

14. The al-Ansar Foundation distributed around $650,000 US during 2007 to support children without fathers, and in four days distributed about $56,000 US to mothers; Rikard Engström, *Ge åt de behövande: En etnografisk fallstudie over social arbete bland muslimer i Damaskus* Högskolan Gävle, Institutionen för humaniora och samhällsvetenskap, Religionsvetenskapliga fältstudier D. (2008), 34, http://www.uppsatser.se /uppsats/8c70664bfe/. In the context of Syria, the amount of money the foundation distributes is enormous. The sums show the economic strength of the foundation and how the foundation utilizes money to attract followers.

15. Engström, *Ge åt de behövande*, 35.

16. The total number of orphans supported by al-Ansar Foundation is around two thousand. For a detailed study on the foundation's charity work and orphanage for girls, see Engström, *Ge åt de behövande*. See also Engström's master's thesis, *Ge åt de behövande* (Give to the Ones Who Are in Need) (2008). For more on charity and Muslim organizations in Syria, see Pierret and Selvik, "Limits of 'Authoritarian Upgrading' in Syria" and Khatib, *Islamic Revivalism in Syria*.

17. English-language promotions of the Ahmad Kuftaro Foundation are available on YouTube. The media section of the foundation produces them, and their aim is to promote a message of the foundation to non-Muslims as well as Muslims. A video clip that exemplifies the foundation's representation of the relationship between Amin and Ahmad Kuftaro and Ahmad's continuation of his father's spiritual mission can be found at http://www.youtube.com/watch?v=EepLH6xmo_Q (accessed Dec. 14, 2013).

18. In its Islamic meaning, a *dars* is a lesson explaining the content of the Qur'an. Ahmad Kuftaro followed the order of the Qur'anic text, and usually discussed the meaning of three to six verses in a *dars*. The length of a *dars* in time was determined by Kuftaro himself, and in later years was also related to his health status. However, a *dars* may take up to two and a half hours. I am here following the idea within this environment to describe Kuftaro's talk as a *dars*. Although *tafsir* (Qur'an commentary) and *dars* are sometimes used synonymously, the term *dars* is a more accurate descriptor for this ritual.

19. On the *qibla* wall there is also an inscription of a saying attributed to the Naqshbandiyya: "O God, you are my goal and to satisfy you is my desire." Besides the oral

recitation of the *silsila*, this engraving announces the foundation's connection to this branch of Sufism.

20. In the last years of Ahmad Kuftaro's life, the time devoted for the *khutba* was about fifteen minutes and Salah Kuftaro often performed it. The changes of the Friday ritual gave Salah Kuftaro, still performing the *khutba*, an hour-long opportunity to show his skills as a preacher.

21. In several conversations from 2004 and onward, Salah Kuftaro argued that in his opinion the lack of formal theological training is not a problem for him in relation to mosque visitors and is in keeping with Abu Nur's ethic of civic engagement to create modern Muslims through both religious and secular education. However, others, both inside and outside Abu Nur, who oppose Salah Kuftaro criticize his lack of formal theological training. In order to strengthen his legitimacy as a religious leader, Salah Kuftaro has, in cooperation with co-authors, published books on various religious topics (see bibliography). Salah also states that he studied at Kulliyya al-da'wa al-islamiyya at Abu Nur, and he has been awarded a PhD from Omdurman University, Sudan.

22. Ahmad Kuftaro did not formally appoint a *khalifa* and he did not issue formal *ijazas* (license to preach) to his disciples. See Annabelle Böttcher, "Sunni and Shi'i Networking in the Middle East," in *Shaping the Current Islamic Reformation*, ed. Barbara Allen Roberson (London: Routledge, 2003), 52. The tradition in this branch is that the *ijaza* concerning leadership is given from father to son, and in al-Sawwaf the *ijaza* from Amin to his son and *khalifa* Ahmad Kuftaro is printed—a sign that this appointment may also be questioned by Ahmad Kuftaro's opponents (al-Sawwaf, *Al-Manhaj al-sufi fi fikr wa da'wa samahat al-shaykh Ahmad Kaftaru*, 93).

23. On request, the letter can be obtained from the author.

24. Böttcher states that Ahmad Kuftaro lacked management skills, and that this shortcoming had negative consequences for the organization, see Böttcher, "Sunni and Shi'i Networking," 52.

25. For more about the strategies and ideas within the Ahmad Kuftaro Foundation, see Stenberg, "Young, Male and Sufi Muslim."

26. Muhannad al-Losh was arrested in 2009 under unclear circumstances; to my knowledge, he was accused of corruption, but the emergency laws of Syria and the new policies directed toward religious organizations make the reasons for his arrest uncertain. An older brother of Salah Kuftaro, Mahmud, was also arrested in 2009. He was a director of the Abu Nur Foundation until he was suspended due to charges of corruption, and Salah Kuftaro replaced him on August 10, 1999. Ahmad Kuftaro's daughter Waffa', leader of the female organization, was also suspended on charges of corruption. As Annabelle Böttcher observes, "Barring relatives and close aides from misappropriation of funds obviously is not an easy task" (Böttcher, "Sunni and Shi'i Networking," 52).

27. In conversations after his release in fall of 2010, Salah Kuftaro stated that in the interrogations during his time in prison he was questioned only about the following

things: his relation to the American embassy and other foreigners, and why he refused to make a public statement denying involvement with the Syrian Muslim Brotherhood after he received condolences via a phone call from Ali Bayanuni, the previous head of the Syrian Muslim Brotherhood in London, after the death of Ahmad Kuftaro. Ali Bayanuni confirmed the call in a conversation in London, June 28, 2010. For links between Sufis and the Syrian Muslim Brotherhood, see Khatib, *Islamic Revivalism in Syria*, 38–39.

28. *Baraka*, understood by disciples as a form of a shaykh's spiritual power, is not identical to charisma. Rather, in this context, it appears as part of a setting that can be analytically characterized as charismatic. See Stenberg, "Préserver le charisme," for a discussion of charisma in relation to the death of Ahmad Kuftaro and subsequent developments at the Ahmad Kuftaro Foundation.

29. I am here referring to what is sometimes called a "new Islamism" (Peter Mandaville, *Global Political Islam* [Routledge: London, 2007]). As has been mentioned above, see Khatib, *Islamic Revivalism in Syria*; Pierret and Selvik, "Limits of 'Authoritarian Upgrading' in Syria"; and Leverett, *Inheriting Syria* for discussion of various aspects of NGOs in Syria. Also, for a broader discussion of NGOs in the Middle East, see Asef Bayat, *Life as Politics: How Ordinary People Change the Middle East* (Stanford: Stanford Univ. Press, 2010).

30. On religion and politics in the Middle East, see Robert D. Lee, *Religion and Politics in the Middle East: Identity, Ideology, Institutions and Attitudes*, second edition (Boulder: Westview Press, 2014).

31. Salah Kuftaro has stated his belief that his history of making public statements regarding the allegations of paying of Sunnis to convert to Shi'a and that the payments were supported by the Iranian ambassador and tolerated by the Syrian government were the reason for his imprisonment.

32. The discussion at the meeting tended toward a consensus that religious scholars who interpret Islam in a more progressive and reform-focused manner in today's Syria are likely to face restrictions and to be under surveillance by the security apparatus.

33. See Obaida Hamad, "Religious Schools Under Review," *Syria Today* 45, January 2009. I also interviewed Obaida Hamad in late March 2010.

34. As a result of a governmental decision, foreign students are no longer able to choose between several institutes. The goal of this policy was that they should all be trained at one state-controlled institution in the Old City of Damascus. In an article in *Syria Today*, Obaida Hamad suggested this was for the state a way to monitor foreign students by grouping them in one institution. Hamad also confirmed this in a discussion with me in March 2010. In conversations in April 2010, teachers at the Ahmad Kuftaro Foundation supported an initiative to mainstream the curricula and textbooks, which may well decrease what they perceived as a tension between Sunnis and Shi'as. A legislative decree (no. 48) from April 4, 2011, announces the establishment of al-Cham Higher Institute for Religious Science, Arabic Language and Islamic Studies and Research, see http://www.sana.sy/eng/361/2012/01/01/391574.htm (accessed July 15, 2011).

35. Donations can be made in different ways. On religious holidays and at every Friday service, boxes for donations are placed at all entrances. Some of my informants donate a specified sum every Friday and receive receipts from the office of al-Ansar.

36. The term "private" is somewhat sensitive, since it indicates an autonomous position with respect to the state. I have used this term to stress the relative freedom or limited authority of religious institutions in terms of curriculum design, expenditure, and general activities. Khatib, *Islamic Revivalism in Syria*, details the Islamization of social space in Syria and how the religious movements were granted a limited authority.

37. Muhammad 'Abd al-Sattar assumed office on December 8, 2007, and Diyala al-Hajj 'Arif in 2004, but the latter was replaced by Radwan al-Habib on April 14, 2011.

38. See al-Sawwaf, *Al-Manhaj al-sufi fi fikr wa da'wa samahat al-shaykh Ahmad Kaftaru*.

39. See Mandaville, *Global Political Islam*, 107–20. Also note the earlier reference to Kersten and Olsson, *Alternative Islamic Discourses and Religious Authority*, 1–12, about homogeneity in regard to Muslim reform movements and their critique of authoritative interpretations.

40. Line Khatib, *Islamic Revivalism in Syria*, 150, describes how a process of "Islamization from below" occurred in Syria and how the religious discourse promoted by the Ahmad Kuftaro Foundation, as one of many Islamic groups, must ensure a certain accommodation from state, and favors the separation of state and religion.

41. In relation to the interest in environmental questions and policies that has developed within the Kuftaro Foundation recently, Salah Kuftaro organized and participated in a conference in 2008.

42. Bayat, *Life as Politics*, 7.

43. My observation regarding charity is inspired by an unpublished paper entitled "The Price of Piety: Religious Markets, Competition and Entrepreneurship in Asia" given by Bryan S. Turner at Lund University in 2007. My remark regarding the class background of foundation supporters follows Salamandra's argument (2004) that charity work is an established middle-class mode of distinction (Christa Salamandra, *A New Old Damascus: Authenticity and Distinction in Urban Syria* [Bloomington: Indiana Univ. Press, 2004]).

44. To a certain extent, Bassam Haddad's analysis of business networks in Syria, and the official and informal networks he describes, applies to the religious sphere as well. On the relation between businesspeople and religious leaders, see Thomas Pierret, "Merchant Background, Bourgeois Ethics: The Syrian 'ulama' and Economic Liberalization," chapter 8 in this volume.

45. From a religious studies point of view, the term "official Islam" is problematic and ambivalent. "Official religion" has a connection to state religion—a state-supported official "church" as the primary expression of religion. See Linda Woodhead, *An Introduction to Christianity* (Cambridge: Cambridge Univ. Press, 2004) for an account of the relation between "state" and "church" in Christianity. To conceptualize a certain interpretation

of Islam as "official religion" is problematic and relates, in regard to the balance between majority and minority religions, to how a politics of secularity has developed in the Syrian context. For a thorough discussion on how moderate interpretations of Islam have empowered Islamic movements in Syria via complex, and sometimes informal, relationships, see Khatib, *Islamic Revivalism in Syria.*

46. In December 2007 he was replaced by Muhammad ʿAbd al-Sattar al-Sayyid.

47. Current processes of differentiation and the discussion of authoritarianism in crisis is linked to the negotiations and interpretations among religious leaders; for a discussion on changing social structures, see Salwa Ismail, "Changing Social Structure, Shifting Alliances and Authoritarianism in Syria," in *Demystifying Syria*, ed. Fred Lawson (London: Saqi Books and London Middle East Institute SOAS, 2009). Anthony Giddens is in favor of an approach that emphasizes the relationship between agent and structure but also "agency" as the vehicle of change, and he states, " . . . constant interaction between agency and structure. Changes and effects can be brought about in patterns of relationships, hierarchies and institutions by using the power embodied in agency" (Anthony Giddens, *A Contemporary Critique of Historical Nationalism, Volume 1: Power, Property and the State* [Berkeley and Los Angeles: Univ. of California Press, 1995], 4).

48. Laura Ahearn, "Language and Agency," *Annual Review* 30 (2001): 112.

Bibliography

Abboud, Samer, and Ferdinand Arslanian. *Syria's Economy and the Transition Paradigm.* Fife, Scotland: Univ. of St. Andrews Centre for Syrian Studies distributed by Lynne Rienner, 2009.

Abdallah, Umar. *The Islamic Struggle in Syria.* Berkeley: Mizan Press, 1983.

Abu-Lughod, Lila. *Dramas of Nationhood: The Politics of Television in Egypt.* Chicago: Univ. of Chicago Press, 2005.

———. "Zones of Theory in the Arab World." *Annual Review of Anthropology* 18, no. 189: 267–306.

Ahearn, Laura. "Language and Agency." *Annual Review* 30 (2001).

Allen, Roger. "Arabic Fiction and the Quest for Freedom." *Journal of Arabic Literature* 26, nos. 1–2 (1995): 37–44.

Anderson, Paul. "The Politics of Scorn in Syria and the Agency of Narrated Involvement." *Journal of the Royal Anthropological Institute (N.S.)* 19, no. 3 (2013): 463–81.

Appadurai, Arjun. "Topographies of the Self: Praise and Emotion in Hindu India." In *Language and the Politics of Emotion,* edited by Catherine A. Lutz and Lila Abu-Lughod, 92–112. Cambridge: Cambridge Univ. Press, 1990.

Asad, Talal. *Genealogies of Religion: Discipline and Reasons of Power in Christianity and Islam.* Baltimore: Johns Hopkins Univ. Press, 1993.

Atassi, Basma. "A Colourful Uprising in Damascus." *Aljazeera.net,* Dec. 13, 2011. http://www.aljazeera.com/profile/basma-atassi.html.

Atassi, Mohamed Ali. "The Puppet Rebellion." *Qantara.de,* Jan. 20, 2012. http://en.qantara.de/content/creative-protest-against-syrias-regime-the-puppet-rebellion.

Azhari, Nada al-. "Even the Image Shouts: Freedom and Nothing But!" [Hata al-sura hatifat: Huriya wa bas!]. *Al-Hayat,* Sept. 23, 2011. http://www.daralhayat.com/internationalarticle/310415.

Bakkar, 'Abd al-Karim. *Al-'aysh fi zaman al-sa'b* [Living in difficult times]. Damascus: Dar al-Qalam, 2000.

Bandak, Andreas. "Our Lady of Soufanieh: On Knowledge, Ignorance and Indifference among the Christians of Damascus." In *Politics of Worship in the Contemporary Middle East: Sainthood in Fragile States*, edited by Andreas Bandak and Mikkel Bille, 129–53. Leiden and Boston: Brill, 2013.

———. "Reckoning with the Inevitable: Death and Dying among Syrian Christians during the Uprisings." In "Death and Afterlife in the Arab Revolutions," Special Issue of *Ethnos: Journal of Anthropology*, edited by Amira Mittermaier, forthcoming.

———. "States of Exception: Effects and Affects of Authoritarianism among Christian Arabs in Damascus." In *A Comparative Ethnography of Alternative Spaces*, edited by Jens Dahl and Esther Fihl, 197–218. New York: Palgrave, 2013.

Barout, Jamal. "Article préliminaire pour construire une carte associative en syrie." Unpublished manuscript, 2008.

Batatu, Hanna. *Syria's Peasantry, the Descendants of Its Lesser Rural Notables, and Their Politics*. Princeton: Princeton Univ. Press, 1999.

Bayat, Asef. *Life as Politics: How Ordinary People Change the Middle East*. Stanford, CA: Stanford Univ. Press, 2010.

Ben Nefissa, Sarah. "Associations et ONG dans le monde arabe: Vers la mise en place d'une problématique." In *Pouvoirs et associations dans le monde arabe*, edited by Sarah Ben Nefissa, 77–94. Paris: CNRS Editions, 2002.

Bennet, James. "The Enigma of Damascus." *New York Times*, July 10, 2005.

Benthall, Jonathan. "Islam et charité institutionnelle: Doctrine, réalité et interpretation." In *Dynamiques de la pauvreté en Afrique du Nord et au Moyen-Orient*, edited by B. Destremau, A. Deboulet, and F. Ireton. Paris: Karthala-Urbama, 2004: 181–92.

———. "Organized Charity in the Arab-Islamic World: A View from the NGOs." In *Interpreting Islam*, edited by H. Donnan, 150–66. London: Sage Publications, 2002.

Berger, Peter, and Thomas Luckmann. *The Social Construction of Reality: A Treatise in the Sociology of Knowledge*. New York: Anchor Books, 1966.

Beydoun, Abbas. "Riwayat 'al-mukhabarat'." *Al-Safir*, Aug. 12, 2009.

Bilal, Mazen, and Najib Nusair. *Syrian Historical Drama: The Dream of the End of an Era* [Al-Drama al-tarikhiyya al-Suriya: Hilm nihayat al-'asr]. Damascus: Dar al-Sham, 1999.

Bitar, Ahmad. "Nura Murad wa Firqa Leish ta'arid 'Alf mabruk!' fi madrassa al-Shebanni bi Halab" [Noura Murad and Leish Troupe Present 'Alf mabruk!' at al-Shebanni School in Aleppo: A Compelling and New Experience for Audiences in Aleppo]. *Discover Syria*, July 31, 2010.

Boëx, Cécile. "La contestation médiatisée par le monde de l'art en contexte autoritaire: L'expérience cinématographique en syrie au sein de l'organisme général du cinéma 1964–2010." PhD diss., Univ. Paul Cézanne-Aix Marseille III, 2011.

———. "The End of State Monopoly over Culture: Toward the Commodification of Culture and Artistic Production." *Middle East Critique* 20, no. 2 (2011): 139–55.

Bonner, Michael, Mine Ener, and Amy Singer, eds. *Poverty and Charity in Middle Eastern Contexts*. New York: State Univ. of New York Press, 2003.

Böttcher, Annabelle. "Sunni and Shi'i Networking in the Middle East." In *Shaping the Current Islamic Reformation*, edited by Barbara Allen Roberson, 42–63. London: Routledge, 2003.

Boukhaima, Soukaina. "Le mouvement associatif en syrie." In *Pouvoirs et associations dans le monde arabe*, edited by Sarah Ben Nefissa, 77–94. Paris: CNRS Editions: 2002.

Brooks, Peter. *The Melodramatic Imagination: Balzac, Henry James, Melodrama, and the Mode of Excess*. New Haven: Yale Univ. Press, 1995.

Bruinessen, Martin van, and Julia Day Howell, eds. *Sufism and the "Modern" in Islam*. London: I. B. Tauris, 2007.

Büchs, Annette. "The Resilience of Authoritarian Rule in Syria Under Hafez and Bashar Al-Asad." *GIGA Research Programme: Institute of Middle East Studies* 97 (2009).

Buck, Joan Juliet. "Asma al-Assad: A Rose in the Desert." *Vogue*, Feb. 2011.

Caugie, John. *Television Drama: Realism, Modernism and British Culture*. Oxford: Oxford Univ. Press, 2000.

Chagas, Gisela Fonseca. "Muslim Women and the Work of da'wa: The Female Branch of the tariqa Naqshbandiyya-Kuftariyya in Damascus, Syria." *Middle East Critique* 20, no. 2 (Summer 2011): 207–18.

Challand, Benoît. "A Nahda of Charitable Organizations? Health Service Provision and the Politics of Aid in Palestine." *International Journal of Middle East Studies* 40 (2008): 227.

Chatelard, Geraldine. *Briser la mosaïque: Lien social et identités collectives chez les chrétiens de Madaba, Jordanie 1870–1997*. PhD diss., EHESS, Paris, 2000.

Chaumont, Éric. "Pauvreté et richesse dans le Coran et dans les sciences religieuses musulmanes." In *Pauvreté et richesse dans le monde musulman méditerranéen*, edited by Jean-Paul Pascual, 17-38. Paris: Maisonneuve et Larose, 2003.

cooke, miriam. *Dissident Syria: Making Oppositional Arts Official*. Durham, NC: Duke Univ. Press, 2007.

Courbage, Youssef. "La population de la syrie." In *La Syrie au présent: Reflets d'une société*, edited by Baudouin Dupret, Zouhair Ghazzal, Youssef Courbage, and Muhammad al-Dbiyat, 173–213. Paris: Sindbad Actes Sud, 2007.

de Blois, M. A. "Syria: Planning Ahead." *Forward Magazine* 48, Feb. 2011. Accessed Nov. 20, 2013. http://haykalmedia.com/products/forward.html.

Della Ratta, Donatella. "Dramas of the Authoritarian State." In *The Arab Revolts: Dispatches on Militant Democracy in the Middle East*, edited by David McMurray and Amanda Ufheil-Somers, 188–95. Bloomington: Indiana Univ. Press, 2013a.

——. "Dramas of the Authoritarian State: The Politics of Syrian TV Serials in the Pan Arab Market." PhD diss., Univ. of Copenhagen, 2013.

——. "Dramas of the Authoritarian State," *Middle East Report* online, Feb. 2012. http://www.merip.org/mero/interventions/dramas-authoritarian-state.

Devlin, John F. *The Ba'th Party: A History from Its Origins to 1966*. Stanford, CA: Hoover Institution Press, 1976.

Dick, Marlin. "Syria under the Spotlight: Television Satire that Is Revolutionary in Form, Reformist in Content." *Arab Media and Society* 3 (Fall 2007). http://www.arabmediasociety.com/topics/index.php?t_article=173.

——. "Thin Red Lines: Censorship, Controversy, and the Case of the Syrian Soap Opera *Behind Bars*." *Transnational Broadcasting Studies* 16 (2006). http://www.tbsjournal.com/Dick.html.

Donati, Caroline. "The Economics of Authoritarian Upgrading in Syria: Liberalization and the Reconfiguration of Economic Networks." In *Middle East Authoritarianisms: Governance, Contestation, and Regime Resilience in Syria and Iran*, edited by Steven Heydemann and Reinoud Leenders, 35–60. Stanford, CA: Stanford Univ. Press, 2013.

Eickelman, Dale, and James Piscatori. *Muslim Politics*. Princeton: Princeton Univ. Press, 1996.

Elali, Nadine. "The Syrian Revolution in Sketches: Talking to the Horriyeh w Bas team." *Now Lebanon*, July 19, 2011. http://www.nowlebanon.com/News ArchiveDetails.aspx?ID=292824.

Engström, Rikard. *Ge åt de behövande: En etnografisk fallstudie over social arbete bland muslimer i Damaskus*. Högskolan Gävle. Institutionen för humaniora och samhällsvetenskap. Religionsvetenskapliga fältstudier D. 2008. http://www.uppsatser.se/uppsats/8c70664bfe/.

Ephrat, Daphna. *A Learned Society in a Period of Transition: The Sunni 'ulama' of Eleventh Century Baghdad*. Albany: State Univ. of New York Press, 2000.

European Stability Initiative. *Islamic Calvinists: Change and Conservatism in Central Anatolia*. Berlin and Istanbul, Sept. 2005. http://www.esiweb.org/index.php?lang=en&id=156&document_ID=69.

Fawaz, Leila Tarazi. *An Occasion for War: Civil Conflict in Lebanon and Damascus in 1860*. Berkeley: Univ. of California Press, 1994.

Filiu, Jean-Pierre. *The Arab Revolution: Ten Lessons from the Democratic Uprising*. Oxford: Oxford Univ. Press, 2011.

Foucault, Michel. *The Archeology of Knowledge and the Discourse on Language*. New York: Pantheon Books, 1972.

———. "The Confession of the Flesh," in *Power/Knowledge Selected Interviews and Other Writings, 1972–1977*, by Michel Foucault, edited by Colin Gordon, 194–228. New York: Pantheon Books, 1980.

Geoffroy, Éric, ed. *Une voie soufie dans le monde: La Shâdhiliyya*. Paris: Maisonneuve et Larose, 2005.

George, Alan. *Syria: Neither Bread nor Freedom*. London and New York: Zed Books, 2003.

Ghadbian, Najib. *Al-Dawla al-asadiyya al-thaniyya: Bashar al-Asad wa al-furas al-da'i'a*. Najib Ghadbian, 2006.

———. "Contesting Authoritarianism: Opposition Activism under Bashar al-Asad, 2000–2010." In *Syria from Reform to Revolt, Volume 1: Political Economy and International Relations*, edited by Raymond Hinnebusch and Tina Zintl, 91–112. Syracuse: Syracuse Univ. Press.

———. "The New Asad: Dynamics of Continuity and Change in Syria." *Middle East Journal* 55, no. 4 (Fall 2001): 624–41.

Giddens, Anthony. *A Contemporary Critique of Historical Nationalism. Volume 1: Power, Property and the State*. Univ. of California Press: Berkeley and Los Angeles, 1995.

Gledhill, Christine. "Speculations on the Relationship between Soap Opera and Melodrama." *Quarterly Review of Film and Video* 14, nos. 1–2 (1992): 107–28.

Goffman, Erving. *The Presentation of Self in Everyday Life*. New York: Anchor Books, 1959.

————. *Role Distance, Encounters: Two Studies in the Sociology of Interaction.* Hammondsworth: Penguin Books, 1972.

Gril, Denis. "De l'usage sanctifiant des biens en islam," in *Revue d'histoire des religions* 215 (1998), 59-89.

Habannaka, 'Abd al-Rahman. *Al-Walid al-da'iyya al-murabbi al-shaykh Hasan Habannaka al-Midani* [My father the preacher and educator Sheikh Hasan Habannaka al-Midani]. Djedda: Dar al-Bashir, 2002.

Habash, Muhammad. *Al-Shaykh Ahmad Kuftaro wa manhaj fi al-tajdid wa islah.* Damascus: Dar Abu Nur, 1996.

Haddad, Bassam. *Business Networks in Syria: The Political Economy of Authoritarian Resilience.* Stanford, CA: Stanford Univ. Press, 2011.

————. "Enduring Legacies: The Politics of Private Sector Development." In *Demystifying Syria,* edited by Fred Lawson, 29–55. London: London Middle East Institute, Soas, 2009.

Haddad, Fawwaz. *Al-Mutarjim al-kha'in: Riwaya.* Beirut: Riyad el-Rayyes, 2008.

————. *'Azf munfarid 'ala al-biyanu: Riwaya.* Beirut: Riyad el-Rayyes, 2009.

Haenni, Patrick. *L'islam de marché: L'autre révolution conservatrice.* Paris: Seuil, 2005.

Hage, Ghassan. "The Differential Intensities of Social Reality: Migration, Participation and Guilt". In *Arab-Australians Today: Citizenship and Belonging,* edited by Ghassan Hage, 192–205. Melbourne: Melbourne Univ. Press, 2002.

Halabi, Nour. "The Impact of Gulf Investment on the Syrian TV Drama Industry: Syrian TV Drama in the Satellite Era." Paper presented at International PhD and Research School, "Arab TV Fiction and Entertainment Industries," Danish Institute in Damascus, Syria, Nov. 2010.

Hamad, Obaida. "Religious Schools under Review," *Syria Today* 45 (Jan. 2009).

Hamid, Muhammad al-. "[On the *Socialism of Islam*]." *Hadarat al-Islam* 3 (1963): 1128-31.

Harlow, Barbara. *Resistance Literature.* New York: Methuen, 1987.

Hastrup, Kirsten. *Action: Anthropology in the Company of Shakespeare.* Copenhagen: Museum Tusculanum Press, 2004.

Havel, Vaclav. *The Power of the Powerless: Citizens against the State in Central-Eastern Europe.* London: Faber & Faber, 1990.

Heck, Paul L. "Muhammad al-Habach et le dialogue interreligieux." In *La Syrie au présent: Reflets d'une société,* edited by Baudouin Dupret, Zouhair Ghazzal, Youssef Courbage, and Muhammad al-Dbiyat, 413–20. Paris: Actes Sud Sindbad, 2007.

————. "Religious Renewal in Syria: The Case of Muhammad al-Habash." *Islam and Muslim-Christian Relations* 15, no. 2 (2004): 185–207.

Herzfeld, Michael. *Cultural Intimacy: Social Poetics in the Nation-State*, 2d ed. New York: Routledge, 2005.

Heyberger, Bernard, and Rémy Madinier. "Introduction." In *L'islam des marges: Mission chrétienne et espaces périphériques du monde musulman (XVI–XX siècles)*, edited by Bernard Heyberger and Rémy Madinier, 5–16. Paris: IISMM-Karthala, 2011.

Heydemann, Steven. *Authoritarianism in Syria: Institutions and Social Conflict, 1946–1970*. Ithaca, NY: Cornell Univ. Press, 1999.

————. Draft paper presented at the workshop "Authoritarian Renewal in Syria," Sciences Po, Paris, June 2009.

————. "Social Pacts and the Persistence of Authoritarianism in the Middle East." In *Debating Arab Authoritarianism: Dynamics and Durability in Nondemocratic Regimes*, edited by Oliver Schlumberger, 21–38. Stanford, CA: Stanford Univ. Press, 2007.

————. "Upgrading Authoritarianism in the Arab World." *Analysis Paper No. 13*. Washington, DC: The Saban Center for Middle East Policy at the Brookings Institution, 2007.

Heydemann, Steven, and Reinoud Leenders, eds. *Middle East Authoritarianisms: Governance, Contestation, and Regime Resilience in Syria and Iran*. Stanford, CA: Stanford Univ. Press, 2013.

Hinnebusch, Raymond. "Authoritarian Persistence, Democratization Theory, and the Middle East: An Overview and Critique." *Democratization* 13, no. 3 (2006): 373–95.

Hinnebusch, Raymond A., and Søren Schmidt, *The State and the Political Economy of Reform in Syria*. Fife, Scotland: Univ. of St. Andrews Centre for Syrian Studies distributed by Lynne Rienner, 2009.

Holmes, Oliver. "Syrian Revolt Sparks Art Boom." *Reuters*, Sept. 28, 2011. http://www.reuters.com/article/2011/09/28/us-syria-artists-idUSTRE78R2SW20110928.

Hopwood, Derek. *Syria 1945–1986: Politics and Society*. London: Allen & Unwin, 1988.

Houli, Inas. "*Sarkha mutamarada fi mujtamʿiyya qamiʿiyya*" [Cry of a rebel in an oppressed society]. *Esyria*, July 31, 2010.

Islam, Sarah. "The Qubaysiyyat: The Growth of an International Muslim Women's Revivalist Movement from Syria (1960–2008)." In *Women, Leadership and*

Mosques: Changes in Contemporary Islamic Authority, edited by Masooda Bano and Hilary Kalmbach. Leiden: Brill, 2012.

Ismail, Salwa. "'Authoritarian Civilities' and Syria's Stalled Political Transition." Presentation at the American Political Science Association Annual Meeting, Philadelphia, PA, Aug. 31–Sept. 3, 2006.

———. "Changing Social Structure, Shifting Alliances and Authoritarianism in Syria." In *Demystifying Syria,* edited by Fred Lawson, 13–28. London: Saqi Books and London Middle East Institute SOAS, 2009.

———. "Syria's Cultural Revolution." *Guardian,* June 21, 2011. http://www.aljazeera.com/profile/basma-atassi.html.

Jaber, Kamel Abu. *The Arab Ba'th Socialist Party: History, Ideology, and Organization.* Syracuse: Syracuse Univ. Press, 1966.

Joubin, Rebecca. "Buq'at Dau' (Spotlight) Part 9 (2012): Tanfis (Airing), a Democratic Façade, Delayed Retribution, and Artistic Craftiness." *Syrian Studies Association Bulletin* 17, no. 2 (2012).

———. *The Politics of Love: Sexuality, Gender, and Marriage in Syrian Television Drama.* Plymouth, UK, and Lanham, MD: Lexington Books, 2013.

———. "Resistance and Co-optation on the Syrian Television Series, Buq'at Daw', 2001–2012." *Middle East Journal* 68, no. 1 (2014): 9–32.

Kahf, Mohja. "The Silences of Contemporary Syrian Literature." *World Literature Today* 75, no. 2 (2001): 224–36.

Kahf, Monzer. "Islamic Banks: The Rise of a New Power Alliance of Wealth and Shari'a Scholarship." In *The Politics of Islamic Finance,* edited by C. Henry and R. Wilson, 17-36. Edinburgh: Edinburgh Univ. Press, 2004.

Kastrinou-Theodoropoulou, Maria. "The Marriage of Cadmus and Harmony and the Burial and the Martyrs: Syrian Dances in the Arab Spring," *Jadaliyya,* June 6, 2011. http://www.jadaliyya.com/pages/index/1759/the-marriage-of-cadmus-and-harmony-and-the-burial.

Kawakibi, Salam. "Le role de la télévision dans la relecture de l'histoire." *Monde arabe Maghreb Machrek* 158 (Oct.–Dec. 1997): 47–55.

Kersten, Carool, and Susanne Olsson, eds. *Alternative Islamic Discourses and Religious Authority.* Ashgate, London, 2013.

Khalifa, Mustafa. *Al-Qawqa'a: Yawmiyyat mutalassis.* Beirut: Dar al-Adab, 2008.

Khatib, Line. *Islamic Revivalism in Syria: The Rise and Fall of Ba'thist Secularism.* Routledge Studies in Political Islam. London: Routledge, 2011.

Khoury, Nicole. "La politique antiterroriste de l'État égyptien à la télévision en 1994." *Revue Tiers-Monde* 37, no. 146 (1996).

Kuftaro, Mahmud. *Muhadharat fi al-hiwar al-islami al-masihi li-samahat al-shaykh Ahmad Kaftaru.* Damascus: Dar nadwa al-ʻulmaʼ, 2008.

Kuftaro, Salah, and ʻAlaʼ al-Din Al Rashi. *Fi muwajaha al-mafiya al-fikriyya fi naqd al-samat wa al-qahr wa al-tarajuʻ.* No publishing company, not dated.

Lawson, Fred, ed. *Demystifying Syria.* London: Saqi in association with The London Middle East Institute, 2009.

Lee, Robert D. *Religion and Politics in the Middle East: Identity, Ideology, Institutions and Attitudes,* 2nd edition. Boulder: Westview Press, 2014.

Lenfant, Arnaud. "Les transformations du salafisme syrien au XXe siècle." In *Quʼest-ce que le salafisme?,* edited by Bernard Rougier, 161-76. Paris: PUF, 2008.

Le Renard, Amélie. "Pauvreté et charité en Arabie Saoudite: La famille royale, le secteur des affaires et ʻlʼÉtat-Providence.'" *Critique Internationale* 41 (2008): 137–56.

Le Saux, Mathieu. "Les dynamiques contradictoires du champ associatif syrien." *Revue du monde musulman et de la Méditerranée,* 115–16 (2006): 193–209.

Leverett, Flynt. *Inheriting Syria: Basharʼs Trial by Fire.* Washington, DC: Brookings Institution Press, 2005.

Loughry, Maryanne, and Julianne Duncan. *Iraqi Refugees in Syria: A Report of the ICMC-USCCB Mission to Assess the Protection Needs of Iraqi Refugees in Syria.* International Catholic Migration Commission, Apr. 2008.

MacFarquhar, Neil. "In Protests, Syrians Find the Spark of Creativity." *New York Times,* Dec. 19, 2011. http://www.nytimes.com/2011/12/20/world/middleeast/in-uprising-syrians-find-spark-of-creativity.html?pagewanted=2&sq=syrian artists&st=cse&scp=1.

Mandaville, Peter. *Global Political Islam.* Routledge: London, 2007.

Maʻoz, Moshe, Joseph Ginat, and Onn Winckler, eds. *Modern Syria: From Ottoman Rule to Pivotal Role in the Middle East.* Brighton: Sussex Academic Press, 1999.

Masters, Bruce. *Christians and Jews in the Ottoman Arab World: The Roots of Sectarianism.* Cambridge: Cambridge Univ. Press, 2001.

McCallum, Fiona. "Religious Institutions and Authoritarian States: Church–State Relations in the Middle East." *Third World Quarterly* 33, no. 1 (2012): 112.

———. "Silent Minorities: The Co-optation of Christian Communities in Baʻthist Syria." Paper presented at the third World Congress for Middle East Studies, Barcelona, July 22, 2010.

Mikail, Barah. "Les Chrétiens de syrie: Un statut enviable, ou une sérénité simulée?" *Confluences Méditerannée* 66 (2008).

Muhammad, Yusuf Khattar. *Al-Asrar al-khafiyya li al-barmaja al-lughawiyya al-'asabiyya* [The hidden secrets of NLP]. Damascus: Dar al-Taqwa, 2008.

Omar, Sara. "Al-Qubaysiyyat: Negotiating Female Religious Authority in Damascus." *The Muslim World* 103, no. 3 (July 2013): 347–62.

Özdalga, Elisabeth. *Naqshbandis in Western and Central Asia: Change and Continuity. (Transactions*, vol. 9). Istanbul: Swedish Research Institute in Istanbul, 1999.

Perthes, Volker, ed. *Arab Elites: Negotiating the Politics of Change*, Colorado: Lynne Rienner Publishers, 2004.

———. *The Political Economy of Syria under Asad*. London: I. B. Tauris, 1997 (1995).

———. *Syria under Bashar al-Asad: Modernisation and the Limits of Change*. New York: Oxford Univ. Press for the International Institute for Strategic Studies, 2004.

Picard, Elizabeth. "Les liens primordiaux, vecteurs de dynamique politique." In *La Politique dans le monde arabe*, edited by Elizabeth Picard, 55–77. Paris: Armand Colin, 2006.

Pierpoint Roth, Claudia. "Found in Translation: The Contemporary Arabic Novel," *New Yorker*, Jan. 18, 2010. Accessed Mar. 19, 2010. http://www.new yorker.com/arts/critics/books/2010/01/18/100118crbo_books_pierpont.

Pierret, Thomas. "Le *Projet politique pour la syrie de l'avenir* des Frères Musulmans." In *La Syrie au présent: Reflets d'une société*, edited by Youssef Courbage, Baudouin Dupret, Mohammed Al-Dbiyat, and Zouhair Ghazzal, 729–38. Paris: Sindbad Actes Sud, 2007.

———. *Religion and State in Syria: The Sunni Ulama from Coup to Revolution*. Cambridge: Cambridge Univ. Press, 2013.

———. "Sunni Clergy Politics in the Cities of Ba'thi Syria." In *Demystifying Syria*, edited by Fred Lawson. London: Saqi Books and London Middle East Institute SOAS, 2009.

Pierret, Thomas, and Kjetil Selvik. "Limits of 'Authoritarian Upgrading' in Syria: Welfare Privatization, Islamic Charities and the Rise of the Zayd Movement." *International Journal of Middle East Studies* 41, no. 4 (2009): 595–614.

Pinto, Paulo. "The Limits of the Public: Sufism and the Religious Debate in Syria." In *Public Islam and the Common Good*, edited by Armando Salvatore and Dale F. Eickelman, 181–204. Leiden: Brill, 2004.

Plum, Hilary. "Field Guides to Elsewhere: How We Read Languages We Don't Read," *The Quarterly Conversation*. Accessed Mar. 19, 2010. http://quarterly conversation.com/field-guides-to-elsewhere-how-we-read-languages-we -dont-read.

Poujeau, Anna. "Monasteries, Politics, and Social Memory: The Revival of the Greek Orthodox Church of Antioch in Syria during the Twentieth Century." In *Eastern Christians in Anthropological Perspective*, edited by C. Hann and H. Goltz, 177–92. Berkeley: Univ. of California Press, 2010.

———. "Sharing the *Baraka* of the Saints: Pluridenominational Visits to Christian Monasteries in Syria." In *Sharing Sacred Spaces in the Mediterranean: Christians, Muslims, and Jews at Shrines and Sanctuaries*, edited by Dionigi Albera and Maria Couroucli, 202–18. Bloomington: Indiana Univ. Press, 2012.

Provence, Michael. *The Great Syrian Revolt and the Rise of Arab Nationalism*. Austin: Univ. of Texas Press, 2005.

Qarni, 'A'id al-. *La tahzan* [Don't be sad]. Riyadh: 'Ubaykan, 2004.

Rabo, Annika. *A Shop of One's Own: Independence and Reputation among Traders in Aleppo*. London: I. B. Tauris, 2005.

Reissner, Johannes. *Ideologie und Politik der Muslimbrüder Syriens: Von den Wahlen 1947 bis zum Verbot unter Adîb ash-Shîshaklî*. Fribourg-en-Brisgau: Klaus Shwarz, 1980.

Roberts, David. *The Ba'th and the Creation of Modern Syria*. London: Croom Helm, 1987.

Robson, Laura. "Recent Perspectives on Christianity in the Modern Arab World." *History Compass* 9, no. 4 (2011): 312–25.

Rougier, Bernard. *L'Oumma en fragments: Contrôler le sunnisme au Liban*. Paris: PUF, 2011.

Ruiz de Elvira, Laura. *Charité, développement et politiques publiques dans le domaine du social: Étude de cas d'une association caritative syrienne*. Unpublished paper, 2009.

———. "L'Etat syrien de Bachar al-Assad à l'épreuve des ONG." *Maghreb-Machrek* 203 (Spring 2010): 41–57.

———. "State/Charities Relation in Syria: Between Reinforcement, Control and Coercion." In *Civil Society and the State in Syria: The Outsourcing of Social Responsibility*, edited by Laura Ruiz de Elvira and Tina Zintl, 5–29. Boulder: Lynne Rienner, 2012.

Salamandra, Christa. "Arab Television Drama Production and the Islamic Public Sphere." In *Rhetoric of the Image: Visual Culture in Muslim Contexts*, edited by Christiane Gruber and Sune Haugbølle, 261–74. Bloomington: Indiana Univ. Press, 2013.

———. "Creative Compromise: Syrian Television Makers between Secularism and Islamism." *Contemporary Islam* 2, no. 3 (2008): 177–89. http://www.springerlink.com/index/e2445574714428g8.pdf.

———. "Dramatizing Damascus: The Cultural Politics of Arab Television Production in the Satellite Era," Copenhagen Univ. Islam Lecture Series, Apr. 14, 2010.

———. "Globalisation and Cultural Mediation: The Construction of Arabia in London." *Global Networks* 2, no. 4 (2002): 285–99.

———. "London's Arab Media and the Construction of Arabness." *Transnational Broadcasting Studies* 10 (2003). http://tbsjournal.arabmediasociety.com/Archives/Spring03/salamandra.html.

———. *A New Old Damascus: Authenticity and Distinction in Urban Syria*. Bloomington: Indiana Univ. Press, 2004.

———. "Spotlight on the Bashar al-Asad Era: The Television Drama Outpouring." *Middle East Critique* 20, no. 2 (2011): 157–67.

Saqqa Amini, Samir. *Nahnu wa al-barmaja al-lughawiyya al-'asabiyya* [NLP and us]. Dama: Dar al-Basha'ir, 2005.

Sato, Noriko. "On the Horns of the Terrorist Dilemma: Syrian Christians' (response to Israeli 'Terrorism')." *History and Anthropology* 14, no. 2 (2003): 141–55.

———. "Selective Amnesia: Memory and History of the Urfalli Syrian Orthodox Christians." *Identities: Global Studies in Culture and Power* 12, no. 3 (2003): 315–33.

Sawwaf, Muhammad Al-. *Al-Manhaj al-sufi fi fikr wa da'wa samahat al-shaykh Ahmad Kaftaru*. Damascus: Bayt al-hikma, 1999.

Schechner, Richard. *Between Theatre and Anthropology*. Philadelphia: Univ. of Pennsylvania Press, 1985.

Seale, Patrick. *Asad of Syria: The Struggle for the Middle East*. Berkeley: Univ. of California Press, 1989.

Sears, Jennifer. "Adonis at Alwan: Always More Beauty to Be Seen," *Arabic Literature*, Nov. 3, 2010. Accessed Nov. 8, 2010. http://arablit.wordpress.com/2010/11/03/adonis-at-alwan-always-more-beauty-to-be-seen/.

Selvik, Kjetil. "It's the Mentality, Stupid! Syria's Turn to the Private Sector." In *Changing Regime Discourse and Reform in Syria*, edited by Aurora Sottimano and Kjetil Selvik, 41–70. St Andrews: Lynne Rienner, 2009.

Shannon, Jonathan. *Among the Jasmine Trees: Music and Modernity in Contemporary Syria*. Middletown, CT: Wesleyan Univ. Press, 2006.

———. "Sultans of Spin: Syrian Sacred Music on the World Stage." *American Anthropologist* 105, no. 2 (2003): 266–77.

Shoaibi, Imad Fawzi. *Min dawla al-ikrah ila al-dimuqratiyya, kan'an li al-dirasat wa al-nashr*. Damascus, 2007.

Silverstein, Shayna. 2012. "Mobilizing Bodies in Syria: Dabke, Popular Culture, and the Politics of Belonging." PhD diss., Univ. of Chicago.

———. "Syria's Radical Dabke." *Middle East Report* 263 (Summer 2012): 33–37.

Singer, Amy. *Charity in Islamic Societies*. Cambridge, UK, and New York: Cambridge Univ. Press, 2008.

Sirees, Nihad. *Riyah al-shamal 1917*. Aleppo: Markaz al-Inma' al-Hadari, 1993.

———. *Al-Ṣamt wa al-sakhab: Riwaya*. Beirut: Dar al-Adab, 2004.

Sloterdijk, Peter. *Critique of Cynical Reason*. Minneapolis: Univ. of Minnesota Press, 1988.

Sottimano, Aurora. "Nationalism and Reform under Bashar al-Asad: Reading the 'Legitimacy' of the Syrian Regime." In *Syria from Reform to Revolt, Volume 1: Political Economy and International Relations*, edited by Raymond Hinnebusch and Tina Zintl, 66–88. Syracuse: Syracuse Univ. Press.

Sottimano, Aurora, and Kjetil Selvik, *Changing Regime Discourse and Reform in Syria*. Fife, Scotland: Univ. of St. Andrews Centre for Syrian Studies distributed by Lynne Rienner, 2008.

Stahl, Matt. "Privilege and Distinction in Production Worlds: Copyright, Collective Bargaining and Working Conditions in Media Making." In *Production Studies: Cultural Studies of Media Industries*, edited by Vicki Mayer, Miranda J. Banks, and John. T. Caldwell, 58–63. New York and London: Routledge, 2009.

———. "Syrian Authorities Arrest the Creator of the Spray Can Man in the Series 'Spotlight'" [Al-Sultat al-Suriya ta'atqilu mubtakir al-rajul al-bakhakh fi musalsal "Buq'at daw']. *Al-Sharq*, Mar. 1, 2012. http://www.alsharq.net .sa/2012/03/01/147286.

Steinmuller, Hans. *Communities of Complicity: Everyday Ethics in Rural China*. New York: Berghahn, 2013.

———. "Communities of Complicity: Notes on State Formation and Local Sociality in Rural China." *American Ethnologist* 37, no. 3 (2011): 539–49.

Stenberg, Leif. "Islamisation d'un quartier: L'héritage du cheikh Ahmad Kuftaro," In *La Syrie au present: Reflets d'une société*, edited by Baudouin Dupret,

Zouhair Ghazzal, Youssef Courbage, and Mohammed al-Dbiyat, 365–77. Paris: Sindbad Actes Sud, 2007.

———. "Préserver le charisme: Les consequences de la mort d'Ahmad Kaftaro sur la mosquée-complexe Abu al-Nur," in *Maghreb-Mashrek* 198 (Winter 2008–9): 65–73.

———. *The Islamization of Science: Four Muslim Positions Developing an Islamic Modernity*. Stockholm: Almqvist and Wiksell International, 1996.

———. "Young, Male and Sufi Muslim in the City of Damascus." In *Youth and Youth Culture in the Contemporary Middle East*, edited by Jørgen Bæck Simonsen, 68–91. Aarhus: Aarhus Univ. Press, 2005.

Suwaydan, Tariq. *Sina'at al-qa'id* [The making of the leader]. Riyadh: 'Ubaykan, 2003.

Swedberg, Richard. *The Max Weber Dictionary: Key Words and Central Concepts*. Stanford, CA: Stanford Univ. Press, 2005.

Szantos Ali-Dib, Edith. "Inter-Religious Dialogue in Syria: Politics, Ethics and Miscommunication." *Political Theology* 9, no. 1 (2008): 93–113.

Taleghani, Shareah. "The Cocoons of Language, the Betrayals of Silence: Contemporary Syrian Prison Literature, Human Rights Discourse, and Literary Experimentalism." PhD diss., New York University, 2009.

Tlas, Mustafa, ed. *Kadhalika qala al-Asad*. Damascus: Dar Tlas, 2001.

Tripp, Charles. *Islam and the Moral Economy: The Challenge of Capitalism*. Cambridge: Cambridge Univ. Press, 2006.

Turner, Victor. *From Ritual to Theatre: The Human Seriousness of Play*. New York: PAJ, 1982.

United Nations Economic and Social Council. "UN ECOSOC Regional Meeting on Sustainable Urbanization Opens in Bahrain." Press release, 2008. http://www.un.org/en/ecosoc/newfunct/amrregpr.shtml.

United Nations Environment Programme. *Geo Yearbook 2006*. Nairobi: United Nations Environment Programme, 2006.

Van Dam, Nicholaos. *The Struggle for Power in Syria: Politics and Society under Asad and the Baath Party*. London: I. B. Tauris, 1996.

van der Linden, Mirjam. "Syrisch huwelijk kent geen liefde" [Syrian marriage has no love: Interview with the Syrian choreographer Noura Murad]. In *De Volkskrant*, July 12, 2010.

Varisco, Daniel. *Islam Obscured: The Rhetoric of Anthropological Representation*. New York: Palgrave Macmillan, 2005.

Verdeil, Chantal. "Travailler à la renaissance de l'Orient chrétien. Les missions latines en syrie (1830–1945)." *Proche-Orient chrétien* 51, nos. 3–4 (2001): 267–316.

———. "Une 'révolution sociale dans la montagne': La conversion des alaouites par les jésuites dans les années 1930." In *L'islam des marges: Mission chrétienne et espaces périphériques du monde musulman (XVI–XX siècles)*, edited by B. Heyberger and R. Madinier. Paris: IISMM-Karthala, 2011.

Weber, Max. *On Charisma and Institution Building*. Selected papers, edited and with an introduction by S. N. Eisenstadt. Chicago: Heritage of Sociology, Univ. of Chicago Press, 1968.

Wedeen, Lisa. "Acting 'As If': Symbolic Politics and Social Control in Syria." *Comparative Studies in Society and History* 40, no. 3 (1998): 503–23.

———. *Ambiguities of Domination: Politics, Rhetoric, and Symbols in Contemporary Syria*. Chicago: Univ. of Chicago Press, 1999.

———. "Ideology and Humor in Dark Times: Notes from Syria." *Critical Inquiry* 39, no. 4 (2013): 841–73.

Weiss, Max. "Who Laughs Last: Literary Transformations of Syrian Authoritarianism." In *Middle East Authoritarianisms: Governance, Contestation, and Regime Resilience in Syria and Iran*, edited by Steven Heydemann and Reinoud Leenders, 143–68. Stanford, CA: Stanford Univ. Press, 2012.

Weyman, George. *Empowering Youth or Reshaping Compliance? Star Magazine, Symbolic Production, and Competing Visions of Shabab in Syria*. MPhil thesis in Modern Middle Eastern Studies, Univ. of Oxford, 2006.

Wieland, Carsten. *A Decade of Lost Chances: Repression and Revolution from Damascus Spring to Arab Spring*. Seattle: Cune Press, 2012.

Wiktorowicz, Quintan. "Civil Society as Social Control: State Power in Jordan." *Comparative Politics* 33, no. 1 (Oct. 2000): 43–61.

Woodhead, Linda. *An Introduction to Christianity*. Cambridge: Cambridge Univ. Press, 2004.

Yasin Hasan, Rosa. *Brufa: Riwaya*. Beirut: Riyad al-Rayyis li al-Kutub wa-l-Nashr, 2011.

Yazbak, Samar. *Laha maraya: Riwaya*. Beirut: Dar al-Adab li al-Nashr wa al-Tawziʿ, 2010.

Yurchak, Alexei. "The Cynical Reason of Late Socialism: Power, Pretense, and the Anekdot." *Public Culture* 9, no. 2 (1997): 161–88.

———. *Everything Was Forever, Until It Was No More*. Princeton: Princeton Univ. Press, 2005.

Zahlawi, Elias. *Al-Sufaniyya khilal khamsatin wa 'ashrin 'aman, 1982–2007* [Soufanieh through twenty-five years, 1982–2007]. Damascus: Dar al-Majid li al-taba'a wal-nushir wal-khadimat al-taba'aiyya Muhammad Insaf Tarabulsi, 2008.

Zarzur, 'Adnan. *Mustafa al-Siba'i: Al-da'iyya al-mujaddid* [Mustafa al-Siba'i: The preacher and renovator]. Damas: Dar al-Qalam, 2000.

Ziadeh, Radwan. "The Muslim Brotherhood in Syria and the Concept of 'Democracy.'" Paper presented at the Ninth Annual Conference of the Center for the Study of Islam and Democracy, Washington, DC, 2009.

Zisser, Eyal. *Commanding Syria: Bashar al-Asad and the First Years in Power.* London: I. B. Tauris, 2007.

Contributors

ANDREAS BANDAK is an assistant professor at the Centre for Compara-
tive Cultural Studies, Department of Cross-Cultural and Regional Studies,
University of Copenhagen. He is co-editor of a special issue of *Ethnos* entitled
Foregrounds and Backgrounds: Ventures in the Anthropology of Christianity
(2012), and he co-edited *Politics of Worship in the Contemporary Middle East:
Sainthood in Fragile States* (Brill, 2013) and *Qualitative Analysis in the Making*
(Routledge, 2014).

DONATELLA DELLA RATTA is a postdoctoral fellow at the University of
Copenhagen. She has previously been affiliated with the Annenberg School for
Communication, University of Pennsylvania, and with the Berkman Center for
Internet and Society at Harvard University. She has authored two monographs
on pan-Arab media, and several book chapters on Syrian media and politics.
She is co-editor, with Naomi Sakr and Jakob Skovgaard-Petersen, of *Arab Media
Moguls* (I. B. Tauris, 2015).

LAURA RUIZ DE ELVIRA holds a PhD in political science from the EHESS
and the Universidad Autonoma de Madrid (2013). Currently, she is a postdoctoral
research associate at the Center for Near and Middle Eastern Studies, Philipps-
Universitat Marburg, Germany. Her research interests focus on charities, civil
society, and the politics of welfare in Syria and in Tunisia, as well as on state-
society relations in Arab countries.

THOMAS PIERRET is a lecturer in contemporary Islam at the University of
Edinburgh. He earned his PhD in political science at Sciences Po Paris and the
University of Louvain, and he occupied postdoctoral positions at Princeton University and the Zentrum Moderner Orient, Berlin. He is the author of *Religion
and State in Syria: The Sunni Ulama from Coup to Revolution* (Cambridge Univ.

Press, 2013), and the co-editor of *Ethnographies of Islam. Ritual Performances and Everyday Practices* (Edinburgh Univ. Press, 2013).

CHRISTA SALAMANDRA is an associate professor of anthropology at Lehman College and the Graduate Center, the City University of New York. She is the author of *A New Old Damascus: Authenticity and Distinction in Urban Syria* (Indiana Univ. Press, 2004) and numerous articles on Arab culture and media. Her forthcoming ethnography, *Waiting for Light: Syrian Television Drama Creators in the Satellite Era,* examines the cultural politics of production in a rapidly changing media landscape.

SHAYNA SILVERSTEIN is an assistant professor of performance studies at Northwestern University. She has taught at Dartmouth College, the University of Chicago, and the University of Pennsylvania, where she was a Mellon postdoctoral fellow in the Penn Humanities Forum. Her work explores embodiment, sound, personhood, modernity, and politics with a focus on contemporary Syria.

LEIF STENBERG is a professor of Islamology and is the director of the Center for Middle Eastern Studies at Lund University. He has been a visiting scholar at Harvard University and at the Institut Français d'Études Arabes de Damas (IFEAD). He is the author of *The Islamization of Science: Four Muslim Positions Making an Islamic Modernity* (Almqvist and Wiksell, 1996), and is the editor, co-editor, and author of numerous books and articles on contemporary Islam.

MAX WEISS is an associate professor of history and Near Eastern studies and is the Elias Boudinot Bicentennial Preceptor at Princeton University. He is the author of *In the Shadow of Sectarianism: Law, Shi'ism, and the Making of Modern Lebanon* (Harvard Univ. Press, 2010), and the translator, most recently, of Nihad Sirees, *The Silence and the Roar* (Other Press, 2013).

Index